GLOBAL POLICY STUDIES

SAGE FOCUS EDITIONS

1. **Police and Society**
   David H. Bayley
2. **Why Nations Act**
   Maurice A. East, Stephen A. Salmore, and Charles F. Hermann
3. **Evaluation Research Methods**
   Leonard Rutman
4. **Social Scientists as Advocates**
   George H. Weber and George J. McCall
5. **Dynamics of Group Decisions**
   Hermann Brandstatter, James H. Davis, and Heinz Schuler
6. **Natural Order**
   Barry Barnes and Steven Shapin
7. **Conflict and Control**
   Arthur J. Vidich and Ronald M. Glassman
8. **Controversy**
   Dorothy Nelkin
9. **Battered Women**
   Donna M. Moore
10. **Criminology**
    Edward Sagarin
11. **To Augur Well**
    J. David Singer and Michael D. Wallace
12. **Improving Evaluations**
    Lois-ellin Datta and Robert Perloff
13. **Images of Information**
    Jon Wagner
14. **Churches and Politics in Latin America**
    Daniel H. Levine
15. **Educational Testing and Evaluation**
    Eva L. Baker and Edys S. Quellmalz
16. **Improving Policy Analysis**
    Stuart S. Nagel
17. **Power Structure Research**
    G. William Domhoff
18. **Aging and Society**
    Edgar F. Borgatta and Neil G. McCluskey
19. **Centre and Periphery**
    Jean Gottmann
20. **The Electorate Reconsidered**
    John C. Pierce and John L. Sullivan
21. **The Black Woman**
    La Frances Rodgers-Rose
22. **Making Bureaucracies Work**
    Carol H. Weiss and Allen H. Barton
23. **Radical Criminology**
    James A. Inciardi
24. **Dual-Career Couples**
    Fran Pepitone-Rockwell
25. **Policy Implementation**
    John Brigham and Don W. Brown
26. **Contemporary Black Thought**
    Molefi Kete Asante and Abdulai S. Vandi
27. **History and Crime**
    James A. Inciardi and Charles E. Faupel
28. **The Future of Education**
    Kathryn Cirincione-Coles
29. **Improving Schools**
    Rolf Lehming and Michael Kane
30. **Knowledge and Power in a Global Society**
    William M. Evan
31. **Black Men**
    Lawrence E. Gary
32. **Major Criminal Justice Systems**
    George F. Cole, Stanislaw J. Frankowski, and Marc G. Gertz
33. **Analyzing Electoral History**
    Jerome M. Clubb, William H. Flanigan, and Nancy H. Zingale
34. **Assessing Marriage**
    Erik E. Filsinger and Robert A. Lewis
35. **The Knowledge Cycle**
    Robert F. Rich
36. **Impacts of Racism on White Americans**
    Benjamin P. Bowser and Raymond G. Hunt
37. **World System Structure**
    W. Ladd Hollist and James N. Rosenau
38. **Women and World Change**
    Naomi Black and Ann Baker Cottrell
39. **Environmental Criminology**
    Paul J. Brantingham and Patricia L. Brantingham
40. **Governing Through Courts**
    Richard A.L. Gambitta, Marlynn L. May, and James C. Foster
41. **Black Families**
    Harriette Pipes McAdoo
42. **Effective School Desegregation**
    Willis D. Hawley
43. **Aging and Retirement**
    Neil G. McCluskey and Edgar F. Borgatta
44. **Modern Industrial Cities**
    Bruce M. Stave
45. **Lives in Stress**
    Deborah Belle
46. **Family Relationships**
    F. Ivan Nye
47. **Mexico's Political Economy**
    Jorge I. Domínguez
48. **Strategies of Political Inquiry**
    Elinor Ostrom
49. **Reforming Social Regulation**
    LeRoy Graymer and Frederick Thompson
50. **Cuba**
    Jorge I. Domínguez
51. **Social Control**
    Jack P. Gibbs
52. **Energy and Transport**
    George H. Daniels, Jr., and Mark H. Rose
53. **Global Policy Studies**
    Gary K. Bertsch
54. **Job Stress and Burnout**
    Whiton Stewart Paine
55. **Missing Elements in Political Inquiry**
    Judith A. Gillespie and Dina A. Zinnes

GLOBAL POLICY STUDIES

edited by

GARY K. BERTSCH

Published in cooperation with the Center for Global Policy Studies, University of Georgia

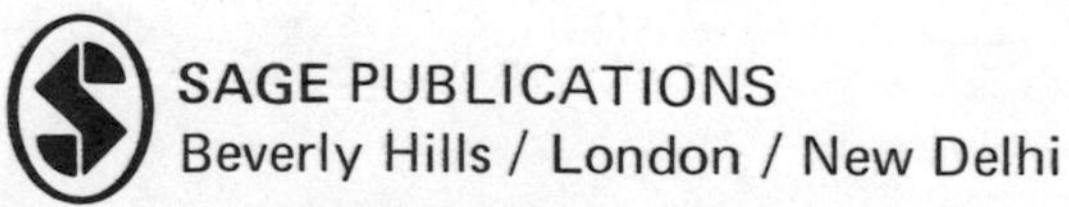

For information address:

SAGE Publications, Inc.
275 South Beverly Drive
Beverly Hills, California 90212

SAGE Publications India Pvt. Ltd.
C-236 Defence Colony
New Delhi 110 024, India

SAGE Publications Ltd
28 Banner Street
London EC1Y 8QE, England

Printed in the United States of America

Library of Congress Cataloging in Publication Data

Main entry under title:

Global policy studies.

(Sage focus editions ; 53)
Includes bibliographical references.
Contents: Introduction / by Gary Bertsch—In search of global political theory / Miriam Steiner—Development and global challenges / Hans S. Park—[etc.]
1. International organization—Addresses, essays, lectures. 2. International relations—Addresses, essays, lectures. 3. International economic relations—Addresses, essays, lectures I. Bertsch, Gary K.
JX1954.G55 341.2 82-5693
ISBN 0-8039-0781-8 AACR2
ISBN 0-8039-0782-6 (pbk.)

FIRST PRINTING

Contents

Foreword

One who has spent a quarter century in or very close to academia and almost the same amount of time as a public official often thinks about the extraordinary difference between the world of opinion and the world of decision insofar as world affairs are concerned. We in academia and in the news media are not required to have an opinion. We can defer it indefinitely; we can have one opinion today and exactly the opposite opinion tomorrow and nothing very much happens; we can make up our minds for good reasons, bad reasons, or no reasons at all; we can determine our views on the basis of one or two elements in a problem that has within it dozens and dozens of secondary and tertiary issues.

Colleges and universities are giving more and more attention to studies of public policy and to the types of questions that present themselves to decision makers who bear official responsibility. It is important for them to do so because the students now in our classrooms must grapple with a series of human issues that are different in kind and scope from those we have faced before. One thinks of the unfinished business of organizing a durable peace in a world in which thousands of megatons are lying around in frail human hands; one thinks of our reckless consumption of finite resources of fossil fuels and inadequate attention to thc alternative sources of energy that soon will be desperately needed. We now are aware that *Homo sapiens* can inflict irreparable damage upon the thin biosphere around the earth's surface in which our species must exist. We must expect that, in the lifetimes of students now in our classes, they shall be dealing with the prospect of 12 to 15 billions of people upon this small planet. One of the oldest causes of war in the long history of the human race—the pressures of peoples upon resources—is being revived in a nuclear world in which there is little likelihood that masses of people will starve peacefully.

It would be reckless for colleges and universities not to give intensive thought to these and related matters. At the same time, it would be prudent to be aware of the gulf that separates the world of opinion from the world of decision. There is such a thing as responsible scholarship and the decision maker is responsible for his actions. These responsibilities, however, are not identical because of the far-reaching consequences that flow from the decisions made by top officials around the world.

The Department of State has a group whose task it is to follow the output of academia and to call the attention of policy officers to books and articles that seem to be interesting, relevant, or helpful. As a grateful beneficiary of this process, this writer must observe that the general flow of such material is of limited help with regard to the daily problems facing those carrying official responsibility. The factor of time provides one reason. The preparation and production of books and articles in academia is relatively slow; by the time they become available to the decision maker, the subject matter has usually changed in major respects and the pace of change continues to accelerate. Foreign policy decisions usually deal with the future in an effort to guide the course of events in one direction rather than another; the output of academia tends to be tilted toward the past through emphasis upon the techniques of research.

It is entirely appropriate for scholars to examine a selected aspect of a particular event or problem. The decision maker must try to take into account all of the elements of a problem and its ramifications with respect to a diverse and turbulent world situation which itself is filled with contradictions. It is not easy to examine a question in all of its ramifications and the dozens upon dozens of secondary and tertiary questions that are involved in any significant foreign policy decision.

Borrowing from their colleagues in the natural sciences, there are scholars in the social sciences and the humanities who try to find unifying concepts that might help us to bring order out of chaos and to discover ongoing principles of human behavior. The search is important, but one must deal with the results with some care. Those who call for a "concept" or a "strategy" for U.S. foreign policy must understand that 160 nations will not simply salute and fit themselves into an intellectually constructed concept. The verbal consistency of a concept clashes with the endless contradictions of the real world, in which more than four billion people live.

In a most interesting chapter in this volume, Professor Miriam Steiner discusses the debate among the adherents of three "images" of the world scene: a state of war, a society of states, and a world community of individuals making up the Family of Man. In the real world of official action, all three elements (and more) are present. Since World War II the pendulum of perception has swung back and forth between "cold war" and "detente" to describe relations between the two nuclear superpowers. In fact, both elements are always present: the unceasing search for points of possible agreement and the occasional confrontations where fundamental differences between the two are reflected in actions affecting each other's interest.

There are major and essential roles for some of us in academia to play with respect to world affairs. One is to be ever alert to the discovery of new ideas that are hovering just beyond our fingertips, many of which would appear to be obvious when brought to the surface. Another is to serve as critic if we remember that the word comes from the Greek word for judge—to provide that criticism that attempts to assess the merits and demerits of ideas and actions. It has been said that the principal function of a university is to help young people discover nonsense; policymakers can be caught in situations where they do things which the common sense of any schoolchild would know is on the wrong track.

The central role of a campus is education, and a democracy must be sustained by a people who make a genuine effort to understand the increasing complexities of modern life. No President or Congress can pursue a major policy for any significant period of time without the understanding and support of the American people. Beyond this point, the education of a decision maker is of critical importance. When a problem arises in our relations with other countries, there is usually very little time before a judgment has to be made about the attitude or action of the United States. At that point one cannot call for an extended thesis or monograph. Everything that the decision maker has read, learned, and experienced will come into play. Contrary to the general belief, most policy officers spend an enormous amount of time reading and studying matters that are not connected with the decisions of the day but are a part of the process of trying to be ready for decisions of another time and another day. Here the contributions of academia can play a most important part.

Finally, we in the world of opinion can help to find the questions that ought to be asked. The proper framing of the question may at times be the first step toward wisdom. This writer has seen a considerable number of models, simulations, games theory exercises, and other such devices. My impression is that such exercises are very valuable for those who participate, even though the answers may be severely lacking. Out of such activity, however, may come the discovery of questions that might otherwise be overlooked. The policy officer is haunted by the ghost of the missing factor—the element in a problem that might be overlooked but that will play an unexpected and significant role in the course of events. Scholars can and do help in this search for the right questions.

The Center for Global Policy Studies and its programs recently launched by the University of Georgia represent a fresh start in mobilizing interdisciplinary interest in major issues that affect us all. It is a natural responsibility for a land-grant institution that has a charter commitment to be involved with the world about us. This volume is an early reflection of that interest.

—*Dean Rusk*

Introduction

GARY K. BERTSCH

The contemporary world is interdependent, rapidly changing, and increasingly dangerous. It is interdependent in the sense that developments in one part of the globe have significant consequences in other parts. Decisions by a few elites in the Persian Gulf states have a direct effect on petroleum prices in other areas. Grain harvests and trade between the United States and the Soviet Union affect the price of a loaf of bread around the globe; inflation and monetary instability at home mean inflation and economic problems abroad. Decisions about defense expenditures in Washington and Moscow affect the course of human survival and welfare everywhere. Conversely, the actions of millions of people in the less developed regions of the world can have a significant impact on the superpowers. These links and relationships between domestic and international events and conditions suggest some interesting observations about the global system in which we live.

The world has also witnessed a fundamental reordering of national military capabilities, political and economic power bases, social structures, and value systems. The traditional state-centric environment in which nation-states, particularly the powerful states in Europe and North America, could control the destinies of their citizens and other people has largely disappeared. In its place are many more increasingly outspoken actors—Third World states, regional organizations and cartels such as OPEC, multinational corporations, and others—who have assumed a larger and more direct role in determining the politics and even the evolution of the global system.

The world is also increasingly dangerous and faces the constant threat of nuclear disaster and continuing problems of poverty, hunger, and environmental deterioration. Many states are plagued by economic problems and monetary instability, and the growing threat of ecological crisis hovers menacingly in the background. In view of this threatening environment, observers in all parts of the world express growing concern that existing institutions are ill-equipped and often unsuited to address and resolve these problems.

Although the problems and challenges accompanying this changing global system are widely recognized, methods of viewing, addressing, and attempting to deal with them are matters of considerable controversy. For example, what sort of theory and images must be used to guide thinking, research, and analysis? What are the dynamics of global change? Where is the world headed? What approaches, strategies, and modes of analysis are necessary to address the complex problems on the research agenda? How can ideas and research findings be translated into policy and policy into actions that are most likely to promote the course of human dignity? These difficult questions will perhaps never be fully and satisfactorily resolved.

Nevertheless, a group associated with the Center for Global Policy Studies at the University of Georgia began to address these and related issues in the late 1970s. This group was instrumental in creating the Center, which explores and develops interdisciplinary and interprofessional programs of instruction, research, and service on a range of global issues. The Center administers undergraduate and graduate certificate programs in global policy studies, sponsors instructional and research-oriented symposia, lectures, and publications, and serves as a focal point for those with an interest in foreign languages and international studies, both inside and outside the university.

The scholars associated with the Center share a desire to work toward new and more promising approaches to the study of global politics and policies. The search for new perspectives was the focus of a round-table discussion organized by the group at the Twenty-Second Annual Convention of the International Studies Association in Philadelphia in March 1981. This book is also an outgrowth of that group's endeavors and is intended to stimulate thinking about possible ways of viewing, addressing, and managing global problems.

The contributors to this book are sensitive to the inescapable global dimensions of modern life. They share an appreciation of diverse viewpoints and accept the need to free themselves from the confines of parochial perspectives. They also recognize a pluralism of ideas, attitudes, and values and their important role in the intellectual process of defining and resolving global challenges.

A global outlook does not always mean that the interests of the international community or humankind, for that matter, must be given precedence over national, group, and self-interests. But it does mean giving global concerns legitimate attention. It means recognition of different value systems and religions in order to appreciate more fully their perceptions of justice, equality, welfare, and other basic issues of political life. It means expressing interest in, and concern for, the problems of inhabitants in remote Third World villages, as well as urban dwellers in industrialized Western societies. Such an outlook does not mean that all problems facing the world must be addressed at the same time, but it does mean that more problems should be viewed from a global perspective.

The global outlook puts the authors at odds with many prevailing ideas, approaches, and theories of international relations, comparative politics, and policy studies. The traditional disciplines and fields tend to view power, interests, and policy from regional, national, or group perspectives. The global perspective takes into account the interests of all humankind.

Theoretical issues are also important to the emerging field of global policy studies and to the contributions in this volume. Contrasting and sharply divergent theories and images for viewing global politics provide competitive guides to research and action in the global arena. Miriam Steiner addresses this issue in her chapter, "In Search of Global Political Theory." Steiner examines the way articulate advocates of different images deal with the issue of a just distribution of the world's resources and its relationship to world order. After considering these images and questioning whether they provide an adequate guide to politics in the global context, she calls attention to a number of difficult problems associated with existing images. She concludes that global political theorists should work toward new images (or provide new interpretations of classical images) of real global significance. Since the global system is so immense, complex, and different from traditional nation-state and city-state systems, reconsideration of basic philosophical questions may be the first step in such efforts.

Values, ethical concerns, and normative considerations are also important to the field of global policy studies. In a world beset with various forms of injustice and degradation, policy scientists cannot ignore ethical issues of global concern. What is the good life? What is human dignity? What is the task of individuals, societies, and governments in achieving it? The contributors to this volume are humanists and scientists committed to world peace and international stability, more democratic power structures, social well-being and human rights, and the cause of human dignity. As Philip Meeks notes in Chapter 4, the role of humanist suggests an overriding interest in the human condition. And the scientist seeks to understand the condition. Thus, the contributors to this volume are both scientists and humanists in the sense that they advocate use of the scientific approach to improve the human condition.

Policy analysis is an appropriate tool for combining the analytical, empirical objectives of the scientist with the ethical concerns of the humanist. The humanist focuses on policies and problems of genuine importance to people, and the policy scientist addresses these policies and problems in an objective and systematic manner. What programs pursued by governments and other actors affect human concerns? Why do they sponsor the programs? And with what effects? In raising these questions, global policy scientists bring together the ethical concerns of the humanist, the pragmatism of the policymaker, and the scientific rigor of the scholar.

The dynamics of change and development are also critical to understanding the global community. What does it mean to assert that the global system is undergoing profound change? What is the nature of this change? What forces contributed to the change, and what problems have they created? In his chapter, "Development and Global Challenges," Han Park traces the evolution of various societies and explains the origin and nature of industrialization as a key factor in the developmental process. He draws attention to some major problems of industrialization and suggests that a number of global developments may pose serious threats to the survival of humankind.

Another important objective of our studies is improved understanding of the human condition and forces that affect it. Why does one-fourth of the planet's population live in absolute poverty, a condition of life so limited that it prevents realization of natural potential? Where do these people live? What can be done to upgrade their economic well-being? Chapter 3, "Comparative Analysis: Economic Well-Being and the Global Condition," argues that comparative analysis is a useful tool in addressing such questions. After identifying and operationalizing elements of the human condition, such as economic well-being, one can use the comparative method to assess the human predicament in various parts of the world and analyze differences in living conditions among urban and rural inhabitants and various national, ethnic, religious, and racial groupings. Comparative analysis also provides a framework for systematically examining the impact of global forces, such as wars and depression, and domestic forces, such as ideology and governmental structures, on the quality of life and other elements of the human condition.

We must also try to understand and plan for the future. Robert Clute (Chapter 5) notes that some research into the future examines current global issues as a basis for projecting trends and suggesting alternate scenarios. Although such futures research is extremely difficult, an even greater challenge is to translate the findings and recommendations into policy. Divergent national views, cumbersome structures for international negotiation, and similar obstacles pose enormous problems for the global community in developing plans to meet the challenges of the future. Nevertheless, translating quality futures research into policy is an important function for global policy studies. In the present international environment, it will not be an easy task.

Interdisciplinary efforts are also an important part of global policy studies. In Chapter 4, Philip Meeks points out that the complexity of global problem-solving requires the collective contribution of many disciplines. History, philosophy, the humanities, and the natural and social sciences have much to offer. The contributors to this volume recognize that no single individual or discipline can satisfactorily address the world's problems. The contributors' experiences in working on this joint enterprise have convinced them of the utility of interdisciplinary efforts. As an emerging field, global policy studies can benefit from similar efforts.

Yet, academic studies still give major emphasis to disciplinary approaches and analyses. Some observers contend that synthesis of these approaches and analyses will lead to an understanding of the whole problem. An alternative is to approach an issue or problem as a whole—in human terms. What values are at stake in the issue? How has the issue developed? What similarities and differences among peoples affect human behavior with respect to these values? What should humankind do with regard to this issue?

The last question suggests the potential role of prescriptive analysis in global policy studies. In view of the mounting world challenges, one is tempted to think in terms of some centralized global authority that can deal effectively with them. There may well be a need for such an authority, but, in the final chapter, William Chittick prescribes a different approach. Establishment of a single global authority seems excessively utopian in an age of such profound diversity in culture, ideology, and stages of international development. Chittick argues that global challenges are too imminent to await the emergence of global authority; he suggests that individuals or groups representing various communities should begin now to address more general interests and concerns. His approach acknowledges that the world's problems are too complex for solution by any one authority or even a number of authorities or experts. Since possible solutions to many of these problems involve human development, Chittick places special emphasis on the role of universities in global society. He feels that universities are in a unique position to encourage and develop appropriate behavior at both the individual and local levels.

Most of the urgent problems and challenges facing humankind at this point in the twentieth century are common to men and women around the globe. No one can observe the escalation of the arms race and nuclear proliferation, the possibility of ecological disaster, and threats to human dignity without sensing their global commonality and their urgency. Individuals, groups, and nations will be unlikely to solve these problems alone, and some of the problems may be insoluble. But the authors believe that chances for success are greater in a joint yet pluralistic enterprise characterized, at this point in time, by a number of perspectives and approaches. We hope that *Global Policy Studies* will aid in the definition and direction of that necessary and important endeavor.

1

In Search of Global Political Theory

E. MIRIAM STEINER

At least three images of global politics compete for the loyalties of scholars, diplomats, politicians, and politically aware people in the West today: the global state of war, the international society of states, and the cosmopolitan community of humankind.[1] The state-of-war image depicts an anarchical system in which states are pitted against one another in an unending struggle for power and status that is limited only by the rules of prudence and expediency. The society-of-states image depicts a global social framework in which states regulate conflict and structure cooperation on the basis of common rules and institutions. The cosmopolitan image focuses not on states, but on individuals who are joined by transnational interests and universal values into a community of humankind.

None of these images is new. They represent three traditions of thought that have been in competition throughout the history of the modern states system.[2] The state-of-war image is associated with the Hobbesian tradition, the society-of-states image with the Grotian or natural law tradition, and the cosmopolitan image with the universalist tradition.[3] As Bull notes, "Each of these traditions embodies a great variety of doctrines about international politics, among which there exists only a loose connection."[4] The universalist tradition, for example, contains

Christian, Kantian, and utopian Marxist doctrinal strands.[5] These are strands in the same tradition in the sense that they are structured by a common image. The doctrinal dress in which the three images have appeared in any given historical period is a function of the problems and preoccupations of that period.[6]

From the end of World War II through the early 1960s, debate in the West consisted in the main of exchanges between advocates of the state-of-war image and advocates of the society image, that is, between realists and idealists.[7] The idealists, who had been ascendant in the post-World War I period, were now on the defensive as the realists attacked their "society" image with the memory of Hitler and the specter of new "deviants" like Stalin or even Nassar. The cosmopolitan image was associated with Communist ideology and so did not enter into Western debate as a positive option. By the 1970s, however, growing scholarly interest in interdependence, transnationalism, and international distributive justice opened the way once again for the formulation of non-Marxist versions of cosmopolitanism.[8] Today state-of-war and society proponents are as concerned with defending their respective images against cosmopolitanism as with criticizing one another.[9]

Yet what difference will it make whether one or another of these images gains ascendancy in the years ahead? Does any of them promise to provide an adequate guide to politics in the global era? A good place to begin to look for answers to these questions is in the arguments of articulate advocates of each of the images who are concerned with common contemporary global problems. Robert Tucker's *The Inequality of Nations,* Charles Beitz's *Political Theory and International Relations,* and Hedley Bull's *The Anarchical Society* are all concerned with the problem of global distributive justice and its relationship to world order.[10] Tucker's book is an argument for viewing this problem from the perspective of the state-of-war image; Beitz's, for viewing it from the perspective of the cosmopolitan image; and Bull's, for viewing it from the perspective of the society image. By briefly recounting the arguments presented in each of these books, the first section of this chapter will illustrate how profoundly an analyst's understanding of global problems is shaped by the image he or she adopts. From the perspective of the state-of-war image, the cry for global distributive justice looks like a challenge to the interstate power hierarchy on which global order is believed to depend. From the cosmopolitan perspective, it is a cry for a morally legitimate global order. From the society image perspective, the cry for distributive justice is evaluated in terms of its impact on the prevailing social contract, on which global order is believed to depend. In the final sections of the chapter the question of whether or not any of these images provides an adequate guide to politics in the global era will be taken up.

Three Perspectives on North-South Inequality and Global Order

State-of-War Image: A Power Perspective

In the anarchical system, depicted by the state-of-war image, states confront one another in an unending struggle for power and status that is limited only by the rules of prudence and expediency. The parameters of state action are set by perceived power relationships. International order is believed to depend upon the stability (static or dynamic) of these relationships.

The state-of-war image also embodies a sharp distinction between political theory and international theory. As Martin Wight pointed out some years ago, political theory is the theory of the good life.[11] It seeks to define the intellectual and moral bases for a just distribution of values within societies. Its principle aim is to bring political power within the state under moral control by subjecting it to moral requirements concerning its sources, limits, ends, and purposes. In contrast, international theory is the theory of survival. Its primary concern is with the effective use of power by states, espccially in power balancing, to control and limit the power of other states. International theory tells the state how to protect its borders and further its interests beyond them so that the good life may be pursued behind them.

According to this perspective, justice is a matter of domestic, not international, politics.

Robert Tucker's *Inequality of Nations* provides an excellent example of the distinctive shape the problem of global distributive justice takes when viewed through the lenses of the state-of-war image. In keeping with this image, the fundamental assumption informing Tucker's analysis is that the controversy over global distributive justice is really a ruckus about power, even though on the surface it appears to be a ruckus about justice and welfare. Consequently, Tucker believes that political groups on the world stage today who advocate approaches to the problem of global distributive justice that reflect the cosmopolitan or society images are best understood in terms of their underlying power and status motives, rather than in terms of their moral or social concerns. The two groups he concentrates on in his analysis are the liberal elites of the Western industrial countries, whom he associates with the cosmopolitan image, and Third World elites, whom he associates with the society image. He depicts the Western liberal elites as having adopted the cosmopolitan approach in order to protect as much of their own living standard as possible against Third World efforts to bring about a more equitable distribution of global values. He describes the Third World elites, in turn, as having adopted the society image as a smoke screen behind which to pursue unlimited power ambitions.

As Tucker explains, Western liberal elites argue that equality is the principal moral imperative of our time and insist on the duty of the rich to redress global inequalities.[12] They interpret equality in humanitarian terms as ensuring that the basic needs of all persons are met. They draw a parallel between growing demands for global equality and the growth of equality within domestic societies in the West as national economies developed. They believe that the world community is destined to become a welfare community, just as the nation-state has become a welfare state. This projected welfare community will be first and foremost not a community of sovereign states, but a community of equal individuals. The state will not disappear, but will become "what might be called the 'tamed' state, the state from which the sharp teeth of sovereignty have been drawn, and the state in which the parochial interests of the past have been replaced by the planetary interests that the logic of interdependence presumably necessitates."

In Tucker's view, the cosmopolitanism of the Western liberal elites is the product not primarily of moral motives and convictions, but of faulty power analysis. He sees cosmopolitanism as a liberal effort to give up only as much as is absolutely necessary, given the power position of the Third World. The problem is that Western liberals have overestimated the power of the Third World. Tucker argues that the liberals have erred by taking far too seriously Third World threats to disrupt the system if redistributive demands are not met, that they have mistakenly equated the Third World's rhetorical excess with actual power to disrupt. At the same time, the liberals have underestimated both the degree of redistribution that would be required to satisfy Third World elites and the depth of Third World commitment to the principle of *raison d'état*. As a consequence, Tucker fears that Western elites do not have a clear idea of just how threatening even the minimal level of redistribution they are calling for would be, not only to their own values and interests, but also to the whole global order.

Tucker emphasizes that Third World elites understand equality not primarily in terms of minimal subsistence, but as equality of opportunity, and equality of opportunity for states rather than for individuals.[13] He argues further that the elites of the new states want equality of opportunity not in order to participate on equal footing in an imagined democratic society of states, as they sometimes claim, but in order to compete for power and status. Since competition for power and status is inherently divisive, Tucker warns that redistribution (and development) will not prove on balance a source of consensus, as Western liberal elites assume.[14] Instead, the egalitarianism sought by Third World elites "clearly portends a competitive rather than cooperative future." In Tucker's view, the global aspirations of Third World elites clearly conform to the state-of-war image, rather than to either the cosmopolitan or the society pattern.

Tucker concludes by urging Western elites to safeguard power advantages rather than give them up. In a world dedicated to competition for power and status, order depends on power inequalities, on hierarchy. If Western elites wish to preserve dearly held values against the self-interested and probably unlimited claims of the new states, they have little choice, in his view, but to operate from within the perspective of the state-of-war image, the only image that reflects a proper appreciation of the role of power and power inequalities in global politics. In order to preserve the good life at home, Tucker believes they must operate in terms of competitive, power politics at the international level. In a world of competitive states, the rich and the powerful can have no obligations to the poor in other parts of the world beyond the duty of charity.

The Cosmopolitan Image: A Moral Perspective

The central focus of the cosmopolitan image is not on competitive states but on individuals who are joined by transnational interests and universal values into a community of humankind. It conceives of world order as based on moral consensus rather than power. No distinction is made between international theory and political theory; the problem of defining and realizing the good life is interpreted in global terms. Tucker presents a somewhat jaundiced view of cosmopolitanism by interpreting it in terms of the material self-interest of Western liberal elites. Charles Beitz's *Political Theory and International Relations* provides a more authentic example of cosmopolitanism.

In sharp contrast to Tucker, Beitz approaches the problem from the standpoint of normative political theory. He emphasizes not people's desire for power and status, but their need to understand and live in accordance with their true moral identities. In Bietz's view, the stability of a political order ultimately depends on its moral legitimacy. If the rules, practices, and expectations that shape and order international life are to be widely accepted as legitimate, they must flow from an image of global politics that correctly pictures the moral relations among states, people, and other actors in the international realm. Beitz believes that neither the state-of-war nor the international society image provides a correct picture of these moral relations.

Beitz calls the moral view associated with the state-of-war image "international moral skepticism." This skepticism is reflected in the sharp distinction drawn between political and international theory. Beitz argues that international moral skepticism is an incorrect moral stance in today's world because the state-of-war image itself no longer accurately describes global reality. It pictures states "as purposive and autonomous agents coexisting in an anarchic environment without significant social, political, or economic activity and devoid of stable expectations regarding the agents' behavior with respect to one another."[15] Beitz maintains that this conception

> fails to capture either the increasingly complex pattern of social interaction characteristic of international relations or the variety of expectations, practices, and institutions that order these interactions. Indeed, international relations is coming more and more to resemble domestic society in these respects, which are analogous to those on which the justification of normative principles for domestic society depends.

Beitz concludes that under such circumstances one cannot consistently maintain international moral skepticism without being pushed into a more general skepticism about domestic morality as well, an extreme position that even Tucker appears unwilling to embrace wholeheartedly.

Unlike the state-of-war image, the international society image does involve a positive normative theory, a theory Beitz calls "the morality of states." Although the morality of states might be an improvement over international moral skepticism, Beitz maintains that it nevertheless fails to provide an adequate normative basis for world order. At its heart is the view that "states have some sort of right of autonomy in international relations analogous to the right of autonomy possessed by persons in domestic societies."[16] The flaw in this view, according to Beitz, is a faulty analogy of states to persons. First, states are not sources of ends in the same sense that persons are. Second, the participation of individuals in states is rarely based on their prior and active consent. In Beitz's view, "government inevitably involves the use of coercion without the consent of those against whom it is used." Consequently, violation of a state's autonomy by an external agent cannot be deemed illegitimate simply because it involves the exercise of coercion against persons without their consent, without at the same time rendering most of the domestic governments of the world illegitimate.

Beitz concludes that if national boundaries are not "morally decisive features of the earth's social geography," and if international relations is coming more and more to resemble domestic society in terms of the complex patterns of cooperation and interaction that are developing, then the cosmopolitan image of a world of individuals joined by transnational interests and universal values into a community of humankind becomes more relevant than either of the other two images.[17] Beitz admits that such a community is still nascent. A clear sense of the transnational interests that form its basis has not yet emerged. He sees it as one of the tasks of the empirical study of international relations to identify and clarify these interests. Furthermore, knowledge of the appropriate universal values is also lacking. It is the task of international political theory to identify and clarify these values. This is the task to which Beitz directs his own efforts.

Accordingly, he focuses on the question of the distributive values that would be appropriate in a global community. If, as Beitz believes, the domestic analogy is becoming more and more appropriate to international relations, one way of exploring the distributive question is to consider the potential effects of extending various domestic theories of distributive justice to international relations. Beitz chooses to work with Rawls's theory.[18] He imagines rational persons from around the globe meeting in a Rawlsian "original position" to choose among alternative principles. He expands the Rawlsian "veil of ignorance" that surrounds these cosmopolitan souls to exclude knowledge of their national citizenship or, more to the point, of the natural resource endowments of their respective countries, as well as knowledge of personal identities, interests, and talents. He believes that in this global original position the same principles of justice would be chosen as in the domestic original position. Hence, if Rawls's difference principle ("social and economic inequalities are to be arranged so that they are . . . to the greatest benefit of the least advantaged") would be chosen at the domestic level, it would also be chosen for the world as a whole. Adoption of the difference principle would produce a global distribution principle that would probably require "radical changes in the structure of the world economic order and in the distribution of natural resources, income, and wealth."[19] In addition, because in a global community distributive principles would apply ultimately to persons rather than states, these principles would probably require intrastate, as well as interstate, redistributions.

In contrast to Tucker, for whom inequalities are the basis for global order, Beitz suggests that major efforts to reduce global inequalities will be required not because the disadvantaged have the power to force such changes, but because, he believes, human beings over the long haul will uphold only those rules and practices that are morally legitimate. In his view, the cosmopolitan image provides a better picture of emerging moral relations among contemporary actors than does either the state-of-war or the society image. Despite the existence of separate states and nations, Beitz believes people will increasingly come to see their obligations concerning distributive justice as applying to all humankind.

The Society-of-States Image: A Sociological Perspective

The society-of-states image depicts a global social framework in which states regulate conflict and structure cooperation on the basis of common rules and institutions. Hedley Bull's *Anarchical Society* provides an interesting application of this image to the problem of global order and distributive justice. In accordance with the society image, Bull places his emphasis on people's need for an ordered social life rather than their desire for power or their aspirations to live in accordance with universal moral ideals. He defines order as a pattern of human activity that sustains the elementary and universal goals of social life, that is, those goals without which social life would be impossible. He offers life, truth, and property as basic goals of this sort:

> First, all societies seek to ensure that life will be in some measure secure against violence resulting in death or bodily harm. Second, all societies seek to ensure that promises, once made, will be kept, or that agreements, once undertaken, will be carried out. Third, all societies pursue the goal of ensuring that the possession of things will remain stable to some degree, and will not be subject to challenges that are constant and without limit.[20]

Bull argues that the achievement of values like status, moral integrity, or economic justice presupposes to some degree the realization of the elementary goals. Moreover, there are numerous different patterns in terms of which the elementary goals may be (and have been) sustained in human social life. From the standpoint of Bull's minimalistic conception of order, the important question is not what a given pattern of order is like, but whether or not there is a consensus supporting it. For Bull, consensus on a given pattern of order is itself a primary constituent of order.

From this sociological perspective, the state-of-war, society, and cosmopolitan images appear as alternative global social ordering principles.[21] Theoretically, any one of them could constitute the basis for order. Although the history of the modern international system has been marked by persistent competition among them, Bull maintains that international order has always depended on one or another of them being clearly ascendant, providing a common basis by which state leaders could know what to expect from others, how to interpret one another's actions, and how to structure their own actions. While discord among the images has been a cause of disorder, consensus on one of them has been a primary determinant of order.

Bull argues that the society image prevails in our era. The consensus on which it rests, however, is not deep, so that the global order it supports is precarious and uncertain. Yet Bull doubts that either of the other images could achieve a consensus even of this depth in today's world. Great cultural diversity makes meaningful consensus on a cosmopolitan ordering principle doubtful. The state-of-war image, on the other hand, does not adequately reflect the extensive global economic and commercial interactions that join diverse peoples together into a loose global network. Bull concludes that the best way to maintain that elementary degree of order without which the achievement of secondary values like economic justice would be impossible is to preserve and to strengthen the element of international society in today's world.

According to Bull, states form an international society when, recognizing

> certain common interests and perhaps some common values, they regard themselves as bound by certain rules in their dealings with one another, such as that they should honor agreements into which they enter, and that they should be subject to certain limitations in exercising force against one another. At the same time they cooperate in the working of institutions such as the forms of procedures of international law, the machinery of diplomacy and general international organization, and the customs and conventions of war.[22]

Bull avers that in today's international society, common interests, common rules, and common institutions have a more precarious foothold than in the period before World War I, one of the heydays of international society. Yet, "given the stresses to which international society has been subjected in this century, what is most remarkable is perhaps that it has survived at all."[23] The new states appear to have accepted the basic structure and tenets of the European-derived system of international law, even though they have criticized and sought changes in many of its provisions. The mechanisms of diplomatic relations among states were shaken by the cold war, ideological struggle, and the sudden independence of so many new states, but appear to have survived both. A balance of power, based on the Soviet-American relationship of mutual deterrence and brought about partly by

Soviet-American contrivance, exists in spite of the fact that "there is no general consensus in international society, at least in explicit terms, as to the need for balance of power or how it should be maintained." Finally, the United Nations "has succeeded in surviving as a single, universal international organization, and thus as a symbol of a sense of common interests and values that underlies the discord of the present international system."

Nevertheless, Bull believes that if international society is again to constitute the basis for more than a precarious and uncertain global order, steps must be taken to strengthen the consensus on which it rests. He argues that this will require a major effort on the part of the Western states to address the new states' demands for greater equality. Unlike the advocates of cosmopolitanism, he does not see international society as an obstacle to economic justice, but as a means for achieving it, perhaps the only means available in today's world. In his view, international society is compatible with a much greater degree of economic justice than currently exists, although it is clearly incompatible with the radical individual justice envisaged in the cosmopolitan image. But Bull concludes that since the world is not yet ready to accept the cosmpolitan ordering principle, cosmopolitan justice is not a realistic alternative to the justice of international society.

The Adequacy and Utility of the Three Images

The arguments Tucker, Beitz, and Bull present for and against the three images ostensibly turn on the issue of empirical relevance, both theoretical and practical. Each author argues that the image he favors provides a more accurate description of global reality than either of the other images, and hence a more reliable guide for understanding global problems and for making global policy. The arguments have a circular quality to them, however, since from the outset each author approaches global reality from the perspective of the image he ends up defending. Tucker views the problem of the relationship between inequality and order as a power problem from the very beginning, just as Beitz views it as a moral problem, and Bull, as a sociological problem. Clearly, each prefers his image as much for philosophical as for empirical reasons.

Each image may be seen as a set of loosely related answers to what Tinder has called "the perennial questions of political life," questions like: What is the nature of human beings? Why are there so many divisions and conflicts among them? Can human beings ever live together peacefully? Is there any source of order other than power? How should power be controlled? To the attainment of what affirmative ends should power be directed? Is humankind capable of rationally initiating, and managing, a total revolution? Can serious injustices be corrected without violence?[24] These are the kinds of questions human beings have not succeeded in answering in any definitive, enduring way. In periods of change and instability, answers that just yesterday seemed adequate become problematic and unsatisfactory, and the questions themselves become live and urgent once again.

Even within relatively stable periods, the received answers are never unassailable.[25] Few if any of them can be either proven or refuted conclusively. Yet most can be severely shaken. Every answer, in fact, appears to be attended by counteranswers. This is something Bull seems to be more aware of than either Beitz or Tucker. He notes that the idea of international society has had to "do battle" with the competing principles of the state-of-war and the cosmopolitan communities throughout the history of the modern states system.[26] Moreover, he cautions that,

> because international society is not more than one of the basic elements at work in modern international politics, and is always in competition with the elements of a state of war and of transnational solidarity or conflict, it is always erroneous to interpret international events as if international society were the sole or dominant element. This is the error committed by those who speak or write as if . . . international law were to be assessed only in relation to the function it has of binding states together, and not also in relation to its function as an instrument of state interest

> and as a vehicle of transnational purposes; . . . as if wars were to be construed only as attempts to violate the law or to uphold it, and not also simply as attempts to advance the interests of particular states of transnational groups. The element of international society is real, but the elements of a state of war and of transnational loyalties and divisions are real also, and to reify the first element, or to speak as if it annulled the second and third, is an illusion.[27]

Nevertheless, Bull concludes that the society image provides "a truer guide" to global politics than does either of the other images.[28]

At no point in *The Anarchical Society*, however, do the arguments Bull makes against the other images completely subdue them. These images persist throughout the book as troublesome counteranswers. Tucker makes a more determined and aggressive effort than Bull to slay the counteranswers to his preferred image. The result, however, is an analysis that seems ideological. In contrast to both Bull and Tucker, Beitz combines a strong effort to refute the counteranswers to his preferred image with a defense that he admits is only tentative and hypothetical.

Perhaps the most obvious criticism that can be made of each of the three images is theoretical incompleteness. By focusing on just one facet of contemporary global politics, each clarifies at the cost of oversimplification. Thus, on the issue of distributive justice, for example, the state-of-war approach ignores (denies) the structural (or world-societal) roots of radical inequalities, as well as the fact that "there are enough doubts about the legitimacy of the international distribution of resources—whatever the disagreements on causes and remedies—to have blown away the good conscience of charity" as defining the limits of global obligations of justice.[29] On the other hand, humankind as a whole is still very far from seeing global obligations from Beitz's cosmopolital perspective. Beitz's view does not take seriously enough the fact that an international society of states does exist and that within it moral significance is still attached to borders and to the communities they demarcate. Furthermore, force in the contemporary world is organized around the claims of states. Unfortunately, Bull's international society image does not provide a pragmatic middle ground between the cosmopolitan and state-of-war extremes, for it underplays the depth of the structural transformations that will be needed to mitigate radical inequalities and overplays the sorts of transformations that can be made through the existing society of states. Perhaps what is needed is a broader perspective, a supraimage that would illuminate the interplay of power, society, and morality in contemporary global politics. It is not easy to imagine what such a supraimage would look like.

A less obvious and perhaps more fundamental criticism that needs to be made of all three of the writers surveyed (as well as of many other contemporary global theorists) concerns their method of theorizing. Each takes an image that represented a plausible answer (or perhaps counteranswer) for an earlier historical period and for a less than global arena, and tries to stretch it to global size. They attempt to develop global theory by means of historical analogy and enlargement.

Tucker assumes that the power motive will and, indeed, ought to manifest itself in the global world of today in the same way it manifested itself during the rise of the states system in Europe. But why should the world be "destined to repeat the cycle of nation-state development we have already witnessed in the West," as Tucker assumes?[30] In fact, how could the world possibly repeat that cycle of development, even if it wanted to, since that cycle brought with it social, economic, technical, and other developments that fundamentally altered the parameters of human existence?

Indeed, the earth no longer offers hospitable soil for the expansive, profligate power psychology that impelled the rise of Western civilization and the globalization of its influence. There are no more territorial frontiers. The oceans, outer space, and weather and climate systems, all objects of increasingly intense international controversy, are realms that are global in scope and in general unsuitable for division and appropriation.[31] Politically, few people remain who are ripe for imperial conquest.

Ecologically, the burgeoning world population pushes toward the limits of the earth's carrying capacity.[32] Militarily, ICBMs and other modern weapons delivery systems have created a disjunction between the ability to wage war and the ability to defend national values behind state borders.[33] In addition, global economic interdependence and increased political awareness in the Third World have created a parallel disjunction between the ability to project military power and the ability to defend values and interests beyond national borders. Furthermore, the exponential growth in the destructive capabilities of modern weapons has undermined the efficacy of uninhibited power politics as a means for achieving affirmative ends.

Finally, the new states are clearly not the same sorts of dynamic actors the Western states were. To equate the new states with the aspirations of their current leadership, as Tucker does (assuming even that he has correctly identified these aspirations) downplays the extraordinary horizontal gap between elites and masses in these states, as well as the vertical divisions among ethnic, religious, and linguistic groups. But even to the extent that the elites of the new states (and the elites of the old states too, for that matter) are motivated by the same sorts of power fantasies that impelled Western civilization into the modern era, the context in which these fantasies seek realization is very different from what it was even fifty years ago. While the state-of-war image may illuminate the ways in which the power motive manifested itself throughout the rise and spread of the multistate system, stretching this image to global size will not, in the global era, provide accurate insights into either the direction politically motivated violence is headed and the new forms it will take, or the appropriate means for restraining it.

Paralleling Tucker, Beitz theorizes about the role of the moral motive in the global era by taking the analogy of Western domestic societies during the late nineteenth and the twentieth centuries and trying to stretch it to global size. He does not specifically mention Western societies when he discusses the domestic analogy, but what he says seems to refer to Western domestic experiences during the last century or so, rather than to domestic societies in general. He points out that it was the development of complex and substantial patterns of social cooperation within these domestic societies that provided the justification for domestic principles of distributive justice. He then argues that growing global economic and commercial interdependence is producing analogous schemes of social cooperation at the global level that ought to justify analogous global principles of distributive justice.

But why should the moral relations associated with global cooperation in our era be considered as an essentially expanded version of the moral relations that grew out of Western domestic schemes of cooperation? As schemes of social cooperation expanded during the course of human history from the family, to the tribe, and to the state, the character of the moral relations associated with social cooperation changed. The changing character of moral relations was a function not only of the larger scale and decreasing intimacy of the cooperative patterns, but also of concomitant changes in modes of production and ways of living as well. Domestic society is not in its essence simply the tribe writ large, nor was the tribe essentially the family writ large, even though we sometimes employ "family" or "tribe" as metaphors for limited aspects of tribes and nations respectively. Why should we assume, then, that the moral relations characteristic of a global world will be, or ought to be, simply an expanded version of those that characterized Western societies during the nineteenth and early twentieth centuries?

And even if these cooperation relations do turn out to be structurally analogous, they do not rest on the same sort of community sense. Beitz worries about the possible effects of the absence of a global principle of distributive justice but ignores the more important problems the absence of a global community presents to coming up with an acceptable global principle in the first place.[34] Rawls's theory of distributive justice is controversial even in the domestic societies Beitz uses as analogies. And why should we assume that the justifications and principles of distributive justice that served Western societies during a long period of economic growth and expansion will be appropriate for an era in which population is beginning to push at the limits of the earth's carrying capacity? While moral relations in the global arena of today may be more like those in Western domestic societies of the recent past than they are often thought to be, there is room to question whether the similarities are deep enough to justify theorizing by historical analogy and enlargement.

Likewise, Bull takes European international society of the eighteenth and especially the nineteenth centuries as his analogy. He assumes that the elementary goals of social life can be achieved in today's global world in much the same way they were achieved in that earlier and smaller arena, in spite of the revolutionary changes that have occurred in the social environment since that time. Although Bull's sociological interpretation of global order represents a major contribution to the theoretical literature, his model of nineteenth century international society cannot be expected to illuminate adequately either the challenges to the elementary goals of social life that will confront the inhabitants of emerging global society, or the best means for meeting them.

Toward Global Political Theory

The three images as interpreted by Tucker, Beitz, and Bull derive from the Western experience of the past several hundred years. But that experience produced a fledgling global civilization that has not only set ruthless social revolutions in train in the many cultures of the world it has touched from the inside; it has also outstripped the experience of the European culture that spawned it. Consequently, neither the Western welfare state nor nineteenth-century international society nor traditional power politics provides an adequate image to guide global policymaking today. To call attention to the limited cultural and historical perspectives in which Tucker's, Beitz's, and Bull's interpretations of the three images are rooted, however, is not to downplay the considerable contribution these three authors make to stimulating thought and discussion about global problems and world order.

Nevertheless, instead of trying to salvage patterns that are being outgrown as the theater of life expands and changes, global political theorists should begin to work toward new images (or perhaps new interpretations of the classical images) that are of truly global relevance. This sort of global theorizing calls upon theorists to transcend what Laszlo calls the inner limits of culture.[35] It requires efforts not only to discern, define, and evaluate, and speculate about patterns that are emerging, but also to reformulate the perennial questions from a global perspective and to ask them anew. At the very least, thinking about global politics in terms of the perennial questions, rather than from within the overstretched confines of one traditional image or another, will help to open our minds to the new ideas and insights that are necessary if human civilization is to survive the globalization of human existence.

Participants in the World Order Models Project (WOMP) have been engaged in an effort of this sort for over a decade.[36] They have tried to conjure up positive images, "relevant utopias," for the end of this century and to develop transition strategies for getting humankind from here to there. Their relevant utopias tend to reflect the society-of-states and cosmopolitan images, although not in the conventional Western forms already discussed. For example, Rajni Kothari envisages a world society of around twenty-five equal, culturally autonomous states.[37] He believes that such a world would provide the basis for individual autonomy and self-realization, which to him are the paramount values. Gustavo Lagos's WOMP vision also reflects the society image.[38] He envisages humankind organized into numerous "teaching-learning societies" which would "[train] man for being more rather than for having more."[39] The relationship between these societies would be "ecumenical and solidaristic."[40]

Alternatively, Robert Johansen depicts a cosmopolitan world of planetary citizens who have created a global security system.[41] The paramount value for Johansen is a world free from the threat of nuclear holocaust. Ali Mazrui's preferred world also reflects the cosmopolitan image.[42] He conceives of world order in terms of a World Federation of Cultures that could "engineer" cultural convergence on a global scale.[43] For Mazrui, the development of shared values, tastes, images, political emotions, prejudices, and sensibilities is the necessary prerequisite for a safer, more humane world order. Johan Galtung's vision falls somewhere between the society and cosmopolitan images.[44] He imagines a world of many small, culturally distinctive communities among which people are free to move about as they see fit: "People move, in and out. Some stay at a place for a lifetime, others for a month. They are free to join, free to leave, but to the extent that they stay they are committed."[45] The paramount values for Galtung are diversity and equity.

A number of critics have complained that WOMP's relevant utopias are more utopian than relevant.[46] Another problem with WOMP is suggested by the implicit value disagreements among the WOMP authors themselves. Although at a very general level they all express allegiance to the same broad values—peace, economic well-being, social justice, ecological stability, and positive identity[47]—when it comes to concrete arrangements to realize these values, many of their conceptions are incompatible.[48] Kothari's world of culturally autonomous states, for example, is diametrically opposed to Mazrui's world of cultural convergence. To date, each WOMP author has devoted more energy to fleshing out his own preferred vision and developing strategies which he believes could bring it into being, than to justifying why anyone else ought to prefer his vision over other visions which have, or could be, dreamed up. Perhaps this is one of the reasons some critics have dismissed WOMP's efforts as the self-indulgent fantasies of alienated intellectuals.[49] In my own estimation, however, the WOMP publications are extremely stimulating and thought-provoking, and continue to serve the useful functions of interesting students, scholars, and citizens in the important issues of global political theory and of generating awareness of the need for a theory (or theories) that will enable humankind to discern and evaluate the new realities of collective life on a global scale.

The development and widespread acceptance of such a theory (or theories) can probably only occur over the longer term. Meanwhile, there is the more immediate problem of assuring humanity's survival and development in the short run. Global political theorists can also play a useful role here. First, they can illuminate and evaluate the world-order assumptions and values that underlie the actions of specific countries, leaders, political groups, and international organizations. Robert Johansen's *The National Interest and the Human Interest* provides a provocative example of this approach applied to U.S. foreign policy.[50] Second, global political theorists can continue to remind policy-makers and policy-oriented theorists that simple, unified conceptions or images of world order are insufficient for the complex transition period in which we live today. Stanley Hoffmann's *Duties Beyond Borders* provides a good example of this sort of theorizing.[51] Third, global political theorists can endeavor to provide the eclectic approaches that this transition period seems to call for with at least some degree of direction.

Perhaps it would be useful to conceive of ourselves as moving about somewhere in the space between an interstate society and a cosmopolitan world, but still saddled with the dangerous baggage of the state of war. The larger field of global policy studies, of which global political theory is a part, could then conceive of itself in terms of the practical problems both of defusing this baggage and divesting humanity of as much of it as possible, and of exploring the possibilities and limits of the quasi-society, quasi-cosmopolitan space in which we find ourselves. Global political theory has an important role to play in this exploration in terms of the development and evaluation of the ideas through which the exploration is carried forward.

NOTES

1. Martin Wight, "Western Values in International Relations," in Herbert Butterfield and Martin Wight, eds., *Diplomatic Investigations (Cambridge: Harvard University Press, 1966), pp. 92-102; Hedley Bull, The Anarchical Society* (New York: Columbia University Press, 1977).

2. Bull, *Anarchical Society*, p. 24.

International Relations," *World Politics*, 24, 1 (1971), pp. 80-105; Wight, "Western Values," pp. 93-94.

6. Bull, *Anarchical Society*.

7. Edward H. Carr, *The Twenty Years' Crisis, 1919-1939* (New York: Harper & Row, 1964); James E. Dougherty and Robert L. Pfaltsgraff, Jr., *Contending Theories of International Relations* (Philadelphia: Lippincott, 1971), pp. 3-13, 65-101.

8. See, for example, John W. Burton, *World Society* (London: Cambridge University Press, 1972); Richard A. Falk, *This Endangered Planet* (New York: Random House, 1971); Chadwick F. Alger and David G. Hoovler, *You and Your Community in the World* (Columbus, OH: Consortium for International Studies Education, 1978); Beitz, *Political Theory*.

9. See, for example, Robert W. Tucker, *The Inequality of Nations* (New York: Basic Books, 1977); Bull, *Anarchical Society*.

10. Tucker, *Inequality of Nations;* Beitz, Political Theory; Bull, *Anarchical Society*.

11. Martin Wight, "Why Is There No International Theory?" in Butterfield and Wight, *Diplomatic Investigations*, p. 33.

12. Tucker calls the cosmopolitanism of the Western liberals "the new political sensibility." See Tucker, *Inequality of Nations*, pp. 56-57.

13. *Ibid.*, p. 61.

14. *Ibid.*, pp. 107, 200.

15. Beitz, *Political Theory*, p. 179.

16. *Ibid.*, p. 180.

17. *Ibid.*, p. 176.

18. John Rawls, *A Theory of Justice* (Cambridge: Harvard University Press, 1971).

19. Beitz, *Political Theory*, p. 181.

20. Bull, *Political Theory*, pp. 4-5.

21. *Ibid.*, pp. 67-68.

22. *Ibid.*, pp. 258-260.

24. Glenn Tinder, *Political Thinking: The Perennial Questions* (Boston: Little, Brown, 1973).

25. *Ibid.*, pp. 14-15.

26. Bull, *Anarchical Society*, p. 68.

27. *Ibid.*, p. 51.

28. *Ibid.*, p. 276.

29. Stanley Hoffmann, *Duties Beyond Borders: On the Limits and Possibilities of Ethical International Politics* (Syracuse, NY: Syracuse University Press, 1981), p. 164.

30. Tucker, *Inequality of Nations*, p. 201.

31. Seyom Brown, Nina W. Cornell, Larry L. Fabian, and Edith Brown Weiss, *Regies for the Ocean, Outer Space, and Weather* (Washington, DC: Brookings Institution, 1977).

32. Lester Brown, *The Twenty-Ninth Day* (New York: Norton, 1978).

33. Richard J. Barnet, "Challenging the Myths of National Security," *New York Times Magazine*, April 1, 1979.

34. Beitz, *Political Theory*, p. 155.

35. Ervin Laszlo, *The Inner Limits of Mankind: Heretical Reflections on Today's Values, Culture and Politics* (Oxford, England: Pergamon Press, 1978), p. 37.

36. For an overview of the World Order Models Project, see Saul H. Mendlovitz, ed., *On the Creation of a Just World Order* (New York: Free Press, 1975).

37. Rajni Kothari, *Towards a Just World*, Working Paper No. 11, World Order Models Project (New York: Free Press, 1974); "World Politics and World Order: The Issue of Autonomy," in Mendlovitz, *Just World Order*, pp. 39-69.

38. Gustavo Lagos and Horacio H. Godoy, *Revolution of Being: A Latin American View of the Future* (New York: Free Press, 1977); Gustavo Lagos, "The Revolution of Being," in Mendlovitz, *Just World Order*, pp. 71-110.

39. Lagos, "The Revolution of Being," p. 84.

40. *Ibid.*, p. 90.

41. Robert C. Johansen, *Toward a Dependable Peace: A Proposal for an Appropriate Security System*, Working Paper No. 8, World Order Models Project (New York: Institute for World Order, 1978).

42. Ali A. Mazrui, *A World Federation of Cultures: An African Perspective* (New York: Free Press, 1975); "World Culture and the Search for Human Consensus," in Mendlovitz, *Just World Order*, pp. 1-38.

43. Mazrui, "World Culture and the Search for Human Consensus," pp. 4, 6.

44. Johan Galtung, *The True Worlds: A Transnational Perspective* (New York: Free Press, 1980).

45. *Ibid.*, p. 89.

46. For example, see Hoffmann, *Duties Beyond Borders*; Bull, *Anarchical Society*.

47. Mendlovitz, *Just World Order*, p. xiii.

48. Miriam Steiner, "Conceptions of the Individual in the World Order Models Project (WOMP) Literature," *International Interactions*, 6, 1 (1979), pp. 27-41; "Human Nature and Truth as World Order Issues," *International Organization*, 34, 3 (1980), pp. 335-353.

49. Tom J. Farer, "The Greening of the Globe: A Preliminary Appraisal of the World Order Models Project (WOMP)," *International Organization*, 31, 1 (1977), pp. 129-148.

50. Princeton, NJ: Princeton University Press, 1980.

51. Hoffmann, *Duties Beyond Borders.*

2

Development and Global Challenges

HAN S. PARK

Development has been a central topic in the study of comparative politics and international relations. As all societies are in a constant state of change, the pursuit of knowledge in the causes, processes, and goals of such change has become an integral part of social sciences in their quest for universal generalizations. Development as a course of social change has recently ascended as a focus of social studies since a large number of Third World nations have attained independence and become influential members of the global community. At a time when "social engineering"[1] and "problem-solving"[2] are considered important goals of social knowledge, a study of development is required to discover laws governing the process and dynamics by which such a developmental change occurs.

The initial problem in the study of development lies in conceptual ambiguity, resulting in a lack of definitional clarity as well as confusion in the selection of units of analysis. Different units and various levels of social complexity have been suggested almost at random. The state of theory building in the area of political development is virtually primitive.

With or without scholarly achievements in the study of development, however, the existential process of "development" has affected every society in such a way that a number of sequential global problems pose a serious threat to the very survival of humankind throughout the world. One intriguing nature of contemporary global problems is the fact that it is often the success of "development," rather than the absence of it, that may be responsible for the emergence of these problems.

In this chapter, I shall first examine various conceptual elements commonly used in defining the nature of development with the intent of discerning the direction in which different societies have evolved and are expected to continue their developmental journey. In this context, I shall propose that most definitions available in the literature of development have actually been partial descriptions of the same phenomenon, namely, industrialization. Subsequently, an attempt will be made to explain (discover the causes of) the origin and process of industrialization. Finally, some major problems that have resulted from industrialization will be discussed in the hope to alert the reader that an unchecked industrial development could eventually lead to human extinction.

Development: Definitional Diversity

The concept of development has been frequently defined at different levels of social complexity ranging from the micro individual to the macro society. A brief survey of these definitions may help us understand the common characteristics underlying the apparently incongruous definitions of and views on the nature of development.

Development as Human Attributes

Long before political scientists ever attempted to define "development," Talcott Parsons introduced a taxonomic scheme for the purpose of differentiating "traditional" societies from modern societies when he elaborated what is now known as the pattern variables.[3] These pattern variables refer to mutually exclusive value orientations held by members of the society: (1) ascriptive versus achievement orientation, (2) functionally diffused versus functionally specific roles, (3) particularistic versus universalistic values, (4) collectivity versus self-orientation, and (5) affectivity versus affective neutrality. In each of these dichotomies, the former is taken as characteristic of traditional society and the latter is typical of modern (hence, developed) society.

Numerous approaches have utilized this Parsonian dichotomous scheme: to cite a few, McClelland's "achievement orientation" as a measure of modernity,[4] Lerner's "mobile personality" as a personality found in developed societies,[5] and Apter's "instrumentality"[6] as characteristic of value orientation observed in industrial societies.

In attempting to provide a cross-cultural assessment of national development, McClelland compared the content of various children's story books. The contents of the stories were taken to be a measure of the extent to which the cultures of the various societies were grounded in achievement-oriented values.

One of the earliest attempts at comparing different societies by a similar individual-level conceptual framework, although it was far from being as systematic as McClelland's attempt, was the work of Daniel Lerner. He used the concept of mobile personality or "empathy" as the common yardstick with which to compare and explain the developmental dynamics of several Middle Eastern countries. Here, development was defined as the movement of individuals toward this personality type. In a comparative study in Turkey, Egypt, Lebanon, Syria, and Iran, Lerner and his associates found that there were regularities in the life situations of individuals in these countries, thus making generalizations possible concerning the relationship between personality types and development.

In his approach to comparative analysis, Apter juxtaposed "instrumental value orientations" to "consummatory value orientations." The former is to be held by people in industrial and modern societies and the latter by members of traditional societies. Instrumentality here is perceived as a concept comparable to secularity, rationality, or specificity.

A more ambitious comparative research project was conducted by Verba and Almond, culminating in the publication of *The*

Civic Culture in 1963.[7] Known as the "five-nation study," this research compared the United States, the United Kingdom, Germany, Italy, and Mexico in terms of people's political perceptions and attitudes as revealed by survey research methods.

While these descriptions of personality types and value orientations are accurate representations of what is known to be the Western man, they fail to explain (that is, identify the causes of) these types. Moreover, to the extent that they are unable to generate composition laws integrating individual members of the society into a systemic unit, they fail to theorize the process of *societal* change. In an effort to remedy these and other problems with the individual-based conceptualization of development, an array of theoretical formulae have been proposed under the rubric of structural-functionalism.

Structural-Functionalism

With the growing realization that dichotomous schemes juxtaposing modern elements to traditional elements are unable to meet the scientific requirement of universal generalizability and explanatory-predictive capability, scholarly efforts began to shift to the idea of "transitional systems." This new focus emerged from the realization that societies possess attributes of both the modern and the traditional ideal types.

Generally regarded as the founder of structural-functionalism in the discipline of political science, Gabriel Almond states his assumption in terms of some "characteristics that all political systems have in common" and that thereby constitute the basis for the comparison of political systems.[8] He asserts that all political systems have structures, which he defines as the legitimate patterns of interaction by which the order of society is maintained. Systems may be compared, then, in terms of the degree and form of *structural specialization.* These structures derive their *raison d'etre* from their performance of certain *functions.* As a further basis of comparison, Almond postulates that there are certain functions that are performed in all systems. His "universal functions" on the input side include (1) political socialization, which involves the transmission of political culture from one generation to the next; (2) political recruitment, whereby the new incumbents of political roles are selected and trained; (3) interest articulation, by which demands are identified and transmitted from the masses to the decision-making elite; (4) interest aggregation, whereby these demands are consolidated into a manageable form for the elite to act upon; and (5) political communication, which is the process by which information is transmitted within the political system and between the political system and its environment. On the output side, there are functions of (6) rule-making, (7) rule application, and (8) rule adjudication, which correspond to the legislative, executive, and judicial functions in the democratic political system as it is commonly perceived. Beyond this, Almond assumes that all structures, no matter how specialized, will be multifunctional in some sense and to some extent. Additionally, all political systems are "mixed" systems in the cultural sense, in that no system is completely "modern"; nor are there any "all primitive," or traditional, systems. In general, comparison is made within this framework in terms of the probabilities of performance of the specific functions by the specific structures, and in terms of the differences in the styles of their performance. Development is conceived of as the system's increase in the *effectiveness* of the performance of these functions.[9] The criticisms directed at Almond's initial formulation are numerous and multifaceted. They point to, among other things, the lack of definitional clarity evident throughout this framework, weakness in the logical structure of the model, and questions concerning its capability to depict meaningfully the process of change that must be central to any model of development.

Furthermore, if the increase in the effectiveness in performing these functions is what constitutes development, some criteria by which performance is evaluated must be available if development is to be explained. This is particularly so when development is commonly perceived as a concept involving some important identifiable changes other than the evolution of "more structures" performing the same functions "more effectively."[10] In other words, goal-orientedness inherent in the concept of "development" is totally absent, perhaps to maintain value neutrality.

In an attempt to correct some of the theoretical and conceptual deficiencies attributed to his earlier formulation, Almond presented a much revised version of his functionalist model of development when he co-authored *Comparative Politics: A Developmental Approach.*[11] Most important, he expanded his set of functional categories and attempted to establish relationships between them in an effort to infuse his model with the capacity to account for the procedural phenomena of developmental change. In particular, Almond asserts that political systems must be evaluated in terms of three different "levels of functioning," which, ostensibly, are products of certain patterns of interrelationship among the various functional categories. On one level are the capability functions (regulative, extractive, distributive, and responsive) that determine the performance of the political system in relation to its environment. Second, there are the conversion functions (the input-output functions of the previous formulation) that are internal to the political system and involve the system's ability to meet demands (inputs) with authoritative decisions (outputs). The third level is that of the system maintenance and adaptation functions of political socialization and recruitment, whereby the system enhances its own continuity.[12]

Under this construction of the model, political development is given impetus when certain environmental conditions give rise to significant changes in the magnitude and content of political inputs. Such changes are deemed "significant" when it becomes apparent that the existing structural and cultural makeup of the political system is incapable of satisfactorily processing the new demand load. In such a situation, political development occurs when the political system undergoes the processes of *structural differentiation* and *cultural secularization* to the extent that the needed increase in systemic capabilities is achieved, so that the new demands can be dealt with effectively.[13]

By means of these changes in the logic and conceptual content of his model, Almond has ostensibly answered the criticism that his earlier model was inherently static—dealing only with the comparison of system states—and therefore unable to explain the dynamics of a process such as development. The new model apparently addresses the question of the "what" and "how" of development: Development is the acquisition of greater capabilities by means of the processes of structural differentiation and cultural secularization. The definitional clarity of Almond's conceptual framework is sharpened somewhat by virtue of the greater number of concepts that are now explicit in the model.

Another example of the structural-functional approach is the work of David Apter.[14] However, Apter's use of "structural requisites" and his more empirically based classification scheme for transitional societies distinguish his use of the functionalist mode from that of Almond. As might be expected, the theoretical propositions he generates within this framework differ from those of Almond with respect to both the analytical aspects of the development process and the conceptualization of these phenomena.

To begin with, Apter limits his analytical concern to the process of "modernization," which he terms a particular case of the more general process of social development. He lists three preconditions for the inception of modernization: a social system (1) that can absorb innovation without disintegrating; (2) in which there are flexible, differentiated social structures; and (3) with the capacity to provide the skills and knowledge necessary for living in a technologically advanced world.[15] What Apter alludes to here is *industrialization,* the definitive economic and technological aspect of modernization. Hence, modernization is defined as the increasing complexity of social patterns resulting from the differentiation and integration of new functional roles, and, particularly, the spread and use of "industrial type roles in a nonindustrial setting."[16]

In order to analyze this process, Apter begins by proposing a typology of transitional systems which, in their fulfillment of the above-mentioned conditions, represent four analytically distinct, alternative starting points for the modernization process. These "ideal type" constructs are distinguished according to whether they have a *pyramidal* or *hierarchical* authority structure, on the one hand, and whether their political actions are guided by *con-*

summatory (that is, sacred or "ultimate") goals or *instrumental* (that is, secular) goals, on the other.[17]

Apter attempts to specify what activities must be performed in order for the system to maintain itself as a unit. He terms these "structural requisites" rather than "functional requisites," although it appears that what he means to imply by use of this term is the institutionalization of the performance of what others would designate as functions. Apter's primary structural requisites are (1) the structure of authoritative decision-making and (2) the structure of accountability. These two correspond roughly to what he calls the functional requisites of government, which are "coercion" and "information." Thus, in Apter's framework, functional requisites are the minimum tools a political system needs in order to perform the functions implied in the list of structural requisites.[18] He later increases his list of structural requisites to include the structure of coercion and punishment, the structure of resource determination and allocation, and the structure of political recruitment and assignment.[19]

Yet another researcher using the general framework of structural-functionalism is Fred Riggs.[20] He developed a more highly structured concept of the "developing nation" by proposing that all transitional societies go through the stage of the "prismatic society." A prismatic society is one in which the social and political functions of institutions have been diffused but not yet integrated. Hence, the degree of development of a nation may be described and compared in terms of the extent to which its institutional functions have become rationalized and specialized. Accordingly, Riggs defined development as "a gradual separation of institutionally distinct spheres, and differentiation of separate structures for the wide variety of functions that must be performed in any society."[21] Thus, role differentiation or institutional specialization has been proposed as the unit for comparing degrees of development. Huntington, Diamant, and Deutsch might also be included in this school of thought, since they too use "institutionalization" and system's capability as the barometer of development.[22]

As we have seen in the paradigms of structural-functionalism, there are certain concepts that are consistently being used to define the process of development. These include "structural differentiation," "cultural secularization," "functional specialization," and "system capabilities" to cope with the changing demands of the people. These attributes are the institutional characteristics of the *industrial* society, and they result inevitably from the process of industrialization. We shall turn to this point later in the chapter, but for now it is sufficient to point out that the definitions of development under the rubric of structural-functionalism are by and large descriptions of the institutional and organizational characteristics of the industrial society.

Stages of Societal Change

To the extent that "development" is a system-relevant concept, neither the individual-based conceptions nor the structural-functional stipulations are sufficiently broad to include all levels of societal change. Given this and other problems with the individualist and functionalist analyses, several authors have turned their attention to the development of stage theories. In this manner, not only was the idea of change built into the theory, but qualitatively discernible changes could be represented, instead of the simple movement along a single dimension such as increasing structural differentiation. Rostow's and Organski's theories have been selected to represent this school of thought in our discussion here.

Given the historical experience of the United States, Rostow proposed a five-stage process of development as follows:[23]

(1) *Traditional society*. At this stage, society is characterized by low levels of technology, a static, agrarian economy that is labor-intensive.
(2) *The preconditions of take-off*. Here, scientific discoveries (or the intrusion of the West) are translated into technological advances.
(3) *Take-off*. Self-sustaining economic growth is achieved through increased investment, industrialization, and the commercialization of agriculture.

(4) *The drive to maturity*. Outputs begin to exceed the increased demand generated by population growth.
(5) *Mass consumption*. The leading sectors of production shift to the production of durable consumer goods and service-oriented activities.

While Rostow's theory is useful in delineating various historically observed stages of development in the West, it only refers to the process of economic development. To this extent, Rostow's model has limited applicability to the broader concept of societal development. In an effort to remedy this limitation, Organski introduced a paradigm, in which industrialization constitutes only one stage. His stages are:[24]

(1) *Primitive unification*. The creation of national unity.
(2) *Industrialization*. The accumulation of capital at the expense of mass living standards.
(3) *The politics of national welfare*. Protection of people from the hardships of industrial life.
(4) *The politics of abundance*. Characterized by the beginning of a new industrial revolution—the revolution of automation.

Unlike Rostow, Organiski succeeds in characterizing political styles and social life at various stages of development, although he too bases his analysis on the process of industrial maturity. However, both Rostow and Organski have accurately described what has happened in the history of the presently industrial societies, especially the United States.

We have selectively examined a sample of definitions and conceptualizations of "development" in an effort to discern common denominations, if any, inherent in the literature of development. As alluded to previously, it is the contention here that most definitions of development have evolved around the process of industrialization. By using esoteric terms such as "empathy," "rationality," "prismatic society," "functional requisites," "structural differentiation," "cultural secularization," "take-off stage," and "politics of abundance," the authors we have discussed are simply telling us what industrialization is all about.

Nations have striven to industrialization under the name of "development" plans. Never has a developmental plan been instigated by a "developing" nation that is not primarily aiming at a greater degree of industrialization. There may be cultural variations and indigenous adjustments, but all societies have been changing from the state of *agraria* to the state of *industria*. This process is reflected in all arenas of the life-world, including politics, economy, psychology, religion, and even the arts.

Industrialization may have been under the veil of "development," but it has indeed shaped humankind and society in such a powerful and uniform manner that the outcome of industrialization will seldom allow cultural and regional variations. Human civilization is becoming more homogeneous, patterned after what industrialization dictates. To be sure, its dictatorship is omnipotent and merciless. If global problems challenging us today have in any way resulted from "development" (that is, industrialization), as will be argued here, we are compelled to study the structure and function of industrialization in order to explain and cope with the resulting problems.

The Leisure Thesis of Industrialization

The economic thesis of *profitability* has been a prevalent and powerful explanation of the cause of industrialization. Invention of tools and more sophisticated machines, division of labor and role specialization, and rapid capital circulation of the industrial economy have been considered important motives and justifications for industrialization, for they facilitate profitability and economy of production. While the economic thesis still underlies the expansion of any industry, it cannot fully account for some noneconomic aspects of *industrial life*, particularly in postindustrial societies.

As an alternative explanation of industrial development, I shall propose a psychological thesis that it is the human desire to create and expand leisure that propels humankind toward industrialization. By doing this, we might be able to account better for social and political issues emerging in the more mature industrial and postindustrial societies.

The Psychology and Sociology of Leisure

> I never met a blacksmith who loved his anvil.
>
> —*Kurt Vonnegut*

Though perplexity may characterize the question of whether human beings have an inherent desire to work, human history tells us that a more consistent desire has been to avoid rather than to look for more.[25] Workers demanding longer vacations and fewer working hours in all societies constitute an unmistakable indicator of the human desire for more leisure time. This is not to suggest that a person without work is in the ideal situation. What is being suggested here is that it is not work itself that a person desires when and if he does work; rather, it is what work brings to the individual by way of securing physical survival and psychological comfort that is the source of work motivation. The needs for survival and comfort in this context may be considered to be more urgent and basic than the leisure need; thus, the former are expected to be pursued at the expense, if necessary, of the latter. In any event, the present analysis is based on the assumption that people pursue leisure as soon as they are assured of more basic needs, and that this characteristic of human beings might well be universal, unrestricted by cultural norms, ideologies, or social differences.

Congruous with the definition offered by Weis,[26] leisure time is defined as "that portion of the day not used for meeting the exigencies of existence." Those who just manage to live on a subsistence level or those who are seriously ill, thus devoting all their energies to the task of staying alive, cannot be said to have leisure time. As Weis suggested, leisure time is time made available by work, not time in which work is made possible. It is, therefore, different from time for relaxation or rest to recover from work and for more work. In this sense, leisure involves the consumption of time, energy, and other resources. Leisure is a commodity whose value is measured by the amount of free time and the amount of nonessential commodities available for enjoyment during that time.[27]

People's desire for a more leisurely lifestyle has been a driving force for the invention of tools. Tools help them finish their work in a shorter period of time with less energy, and the more efficient use of both time and energy is vital for leisure as well as increased productive ability. As the agricultural sector's share of total employment decreases (or the share of the work force engaged in industrial and service activities increases), the average or typical number of work hours will be reduced. This trend is expected to be the case in all industrializing societies, as labor-intensive agriculture is replaced by capital-intensive industry.[28] According to one study, leisure time for the Americans has increased steadily since 1900, whereas their work hours declined over the same period, indicating a close linkage between industrial development and the amount of leisure time consumed (Table 2.1). In Table 2.1, a grand total of 1329 billion hours for 1950 was computed based on the total population of 151.7 million people in the United States, each of whom had twenty-four hours each day, for 365 days of the year. Based on numbers of people in each age and occupation group and the typical pattern of daily activity, a total budget of time was prepared for 1900 and 1950, and estimates were made for 2000. The amount of leisure time was increased from about 27 percent in 1900 to 34 percent in 1950, whereas worktime decreased from 13 percent to 10 percent during the same period. At the same time, as industry expands, there will be a greater demand for new laborers, enabling previously unemployed or seasonally unemployed workers to find more secure and better-paying jobs. as a result, family income will increase, and the added income will help family members use their available leisure time in more "efficient" and enjoyable ways. In order to expand leisure activities, workers will demand material consumption beyond the level of basic needs, and industry will respond with the production of goods designed to enhance the leisure lifestyle. For example, in a farm family in a nonindustrial society, one or more members of the family may spend an entire day out of each week washing by hand the family's laundry. This is an activity that is highly labor-intensive and time-consumptive yet produces virtually no increase in the family's wealth. By contrast, a factory worker in an industrial society may buy a washing machine that will do the family's laundry with less human labor and in less time. Thus, the family members whose

TABLE 2.1 National Time Budget and Time Division of Leisure, 1900, 1950, and 2000 (billions of hours annually)

Use of Time	1900	(%)	1950	(%)	2000	(%)
Total time for entire population	667	(100)	1,329	(100)	2,907	(100)
Sleep	265	(39.7)	514	(38.7)	1,131	(38.9)
Work	86	(12.9)	132	(9.9)	206	(7.1)
School	11	(1.6)	32	(2.4)	90	(3.1)
Housekeeping	61	(9.1)	68	(5.1)	93	(3.2)
Preschool population, nonsleeping hours	30	(4.5)	56	(4.2)	110	(3.8)
Personal care	37	(5.5)	74	(5.6)	164	(5.6)
Total, accounted for above	490	(73.5)	876	(65.9)	1,794	(61.7)
Remaining hours, largely leisure	177	(26.5)	453	(34.1)	1,113	(38.3)
Daily leisure hours	72	(10.8)	189	(14.2)	375	(12.9)
Week-end leisure hours	50	(7.5)	179	(13.5)	483	(16.6)
Vacation	17	(2.5)	35	(2.6)	182	(6.3)
Retired	6	(.9)	24	(1.8)	56	(1.9)
Other, including unaccounted	32	(4.8)	26	(2.0)	16	(.6)

SOURCE: Adapted from James C. Charlesworth, ed., *Leisure in America* (Philadelphia: The American Academy of Political and Social Science, Monograph 4, 1964), p. 10.

time and energy were once consumed in washing clothes now can invest that time and energy in other activities, some of which may well be leisure activities, such as playing tennis or watching television. Automobiles perform the same function: They reduce the amount of time and energy consumed in various activities, thus creating additional time and energy to be invested in productive or leisure activities. The growth in the proportion of women in the work force and of two-income families has been made possible in part by the proliferation of such products of industrialization. The same can be said of the growth of the "leisure industry," which produces such things as televisions, sports equipment, movies, video games, and a myriad of other nonessential leisure goods.

The shift from an agrarian economy to an industrial one will eventually lead the society to a more complex class structure organized along the line of achievers and nonachievers in the command of skills and technology.[29] Those who have skills and technological know-how will enjoy more leisure time, and those who do not will continue to be engaged in labor-intensive occupations, thus having less leisure time. It is expected that unskilled laborers in industrializing societies will struggle at the bottom of the social strata for little more than physical subsistence, whereas skilled technicians and white-collar workers will develop the culture and lifestyle that are suitable for satisfying the leisure desire, as they attempt to ensure what Lenski refers to as "creative comfort."[30] At the same time, technological innovations and modifications will be designed to make the commodities even more convenient and less time- and labor-consumptive. The "industrial man" eventually will become totally dependent on machines, and by this time the age of "push-buttons" and "disposables" will be imminent.

Leisure and Division of Labor

As Durkheim observes, "an industry can exist only if it answers some need. A function can become specialized only if this specialization corresponds to some need of the society." The emerging imperative for the industrializing society lies in the expansion of commodities designed to make more leisure time available to the consumer. Thus, new specialization is aimed at increasing and improving productivity so that more goods can be made with fewer man-hours.[32]

Division of labor, in a sense, can be viewed as social expression of "simplifying work" when work is unavoidable. By engaging in only limited segments of production, one expects to make the work routinized and easy to perform. As a result, the division of labor facilitates role specialization and professionalization. Acquiring role expertise is viewed as highly desirable in a society whose members are appraised by the *performance* of their functions. This is especially true in a new urban community whose members are assigned their relative status not on the basis of their ascriptive characteristics but by virtue of their achieved positions.

In short, the desire for leisure inherent in human nature may have been a powerful facilitator for the invention of tools, technological development, and industrialization. Industrial growth, in turn, led to extensive social and cultural change, directly in the forms of role differentiation and functional specialization and indirectly in a number of other more profound ways.

Industrialization and Social Change

The kind of social change induced by industrialization tends to be most drastic and profound, for this change is likely to unravel the very fabric of the conventional social and cultural structure. It is a common historical experience that industrialization is inevitably accompanied by urbanization, the expansion of market culture, and eventually the growth of a middle class. Furthermore, as the industrial economy crosses national boundaries and penetrates into the world market, a global community will emerge with a patterned network of economic interaction. The much-referred-to North-South nexus, replacing the ideological polarization of East-West hostility, indicates this development.[33] In this process, world cultures will become increasingly similar and mutually integrated as traditionally different peoples come to experience similar problems and generate homogeneous aspirations for industrialization and material prosperity. In this process, the "rational man" is born, becoming the modal personality type. We shall discuss some dynamics and implications of these aspects of social change, which may be ultimately responsible for many of the emerging global problems.

Mass Consumption and Marketing

The desire for leisure and "conspicuous consumption" is an effective impetus for continuous industrialization.[34] The industrial economy is fundamentally different from the agricultural economy in that it possesses the capability for virtually unlimited production of consumer goods, and these goods, unlike most agricultural products, are usually not essential for basic subsistence. Rather, industrial goods are intended for the more leisurely living desired by the consumer who has already secured the basic needs for survival.

For the survival of industry itself, the economy will be compelled to sell new products to the leisure-minded "conspicuous" consumer. This requires advertisement and marketing. At this stage of social change, a huge amount of resources is invested in this relatively new sector for market expansion. The survival of an industry will depend on its ability to sell what is already produced, and to make "better" products continuously, so that "old" products can be replaced and mass consumption may be maintained. The automobile industry in America, for example, will not survive unless the consumer is looking for new models coming out every year. It is not in the industry's interest to encourage the consumer to retain his or her present automobile for a prolonged period by making them durable and keeping the same style year after year. The same logic is applied to a variety of other consumer goods, ranging from appliances to clothing fashions.

In order to induce the masses to consume, the industry will devise new marketing strategies on a continuing basis. A few such strategies prevalent in the United States employ coupons toward the purchase of goods, rebates, trading stamps, discount sales, catalogue sales, allowances on trade-ins, and deceptively marked price tags (for example, $9.99 instead of $10.00). Advertising techniques are extremely sophisticated in all industrial societies where marketing is an integral part of economic and social life.

As mass consumption necessitates commodity advertisement in a way that the public can be reached, mass media will become a powerful instrument for the expansion of demand for industrial products. Commercials dominate newspaper pages. Radio broadcasting airs every program with a multitude of sponsors. Television commercials alone in the United States reportedly cost some $30 billion annually. Indeed, the mass media themselves are completely reliant upon advertising sponsors. Although the mass media have always carried advertisement, the extent to which the advertising of consumer goods overwhelms the media themselves is a relatively recent phenomenon, expected only in mature industrial societies.

I have made a comparative examination of Sears Roebuck catalogues in selected years—1900, 1920, 1940, 1960, and 1980—in an effort to observe the pattern of emphasis on consumer goods. In the 1900 catalogue, there was virtually no item that we might identify as leisure-oriented. The closest thing was fishing equipment, which might not have been for leisurely fishing alone. In 1920, however, some sporting items, such as baseball and archery equipment, appear, but only on a few pages in the catalogue. By 1940 we see consumer emphasis on domestic commodities such as furniture, rugs, refrigerators, stoves, washing machines, and kitchen accessories, but in limited variety. A major change in consumer goods was observed in the 1960 catalogue, where a variety of sporting goods are listed, including golf, billiards, weight lifting, croquet, tennis, badminton, basketball, and of course fishing equipment. There was even a variety of children's toys. Additionally, there were for the first time fourteen pages of camping equipment, indicating that an increasing number of people had the time and resources to enjoy leisurely camp-outs. Commodities geared for convenience and time-saving were prevalent in the 1960 book: vacuum cleaners, rug shampooers, washer/dryers, freezer/refrigerators, electric kitchen appliances, dishwashers, electric stoves, and even adding machines. Some eight pages were concerned with swimming pools and their accessories. The 1980 book is distinctly characterized by electronic and computorized consumer goods. The microwave oven appearing in this book dramatizes the importance of time-saving. It might be noted that these commodities have new looks and more sophisticated features in each subsequent volume.

Credits and the "Precarious Consumer"

By the time society is deeply into the process of industrialization, the masses are likely to have jobs with limited and fixed incomes. Here emerges a social dilemma in that the masses are encouraged to consume a wide variety and larger quantities of goods, yet their income may not warrant such a consumption. At the same time, the industry needs to sell commodities in volumes that the consumer cannot afford.

To ease this dilemma, banking and credit systems develop to allow the consumer to spend on credit and loans of all types. Due to the relative stability of this stage of society, the creditor can extend loans to be repayed over an extended period of time. Buying a house on a thirty-year loan, which is a common practice in the United States and other industrial nations. is something unheard of in many countries, particularly those in the Third World. The magic of credit buying induces the consumer continuously to seek yet more current commodities and more convenient items. Consumer debt in the United States, and most likely in all industrial countries, has been steadily rising in support of the "buy now, pay later" syndrome.[35] By making credit easily available in large amounts, banks and other lenders offer additional purchasing power with which one can buy and enjoy now. To the fashion-minded consumer, it is difficult to refuse such an offer for, among other things, people have a time preference for goods now rather than later. Their propensities are, of course, to go the quick route, the easy route, to consumption. Coincidentally, government policies at this stage of social development encourage credit use as a way of stimulating buying power and higher levels of economic activity.

The bank credit card, "plastic money," offers safety and convenience to the consumer, who is attracted by the tempting offers of the credit companies. To business, the simple fact is that debt is profitable—an end in itself for businesspeople and bankers. Indeed, in a mature economic situation such as that of postindustrial society, merchandise and service sales are becoming a means to sell debt. In this credit economy, one can live rather comfortably, consuming far more than one's income or social status warrants.

However, when consumers acquire comomodities through credit buying, and therefore do not truly "own" them, their state of mind has to be different. At the end of each month, when they are forced to pay bills, they must be reminded of the fact that their possessions are not entirely their own property. This could have profound psychological implications for credit buyers, in that they might feel uneasy and uncomfortable, although their physical comfort may appear to be secure. Thus, as consumers become addicted to convenience and to the relaxed use of credit that lenders are eager to offer, they will be psychologically uneasy yet conspicuously comfortable-looking. This kind of consumer may be called a "precarious consumer" because his or her state of mind is "precarious" with the fear of default and the burden of debt.

Money Addiction and the Slave of Convenience

With the expansion of the market culture, where every commodity and every form of service are translated into the single yardstick of money, people's overwhelming aspirations center on enriching themselves. Unlike smoking or drug addiction, where health warnings and social sanctions work as prohibitive forces, money addiction is virtually unchecked. In fact, a unique feature of money addiction is that more money is always looked at as something to be desired, whereas other forms of addiction are not usually admired or desired by the nonaddict.

People get addicted to drugs because drugs do "wonders," which only the addict fully appreciates. But one does not have to be an addict to know what wonders money can do in the industrial market society. It is hard to think of many things that money cannot buy, which is the irresistible source of money's power.

At this level of industrial maturity, however, money is not earned for accumulation but for consumption of industrial commodities that are designed to appeal to leisure-seeking consumers. Indeed, consumers rarely make enough money to accommodate their desire for conspicuous goods that themselves are being constantly replaced by new patterns and more convenient models.

I once asked some college students to make a list of consumer goods that they thought were designed primarily for convenience and for the expansion of leisure time. The following were some of the most frequently mentioned items:

electric garage doors	remote-control televisions
hair appliances: blow	electric knives

dryers, curling irons, rollers
hot shaving cream dispensers
sun lamps
electric can openers
dishwashers, dryers, washing machines
garbage disposals
automatic nail buffers
drive-up windows (at banks, restaurants)
microwave ovens
automatic ice makers
electric toothbrushes
automatic telephone dials
home computers
moving sidewalks
escalators
cruise-controlled cars; power windows; electric trunk openers
riding lawn mowers
digital watches
golf carts
"super glue"
electric hand dryer in bathroom
jogging boards
tennis machines
shower massagers
giant screen televisions

In light of the fact that the sample consumer goods are subject to constant refinement and "improvement," keeping up with the current products requires an enormous amount of resources. Furthermore, as alluded to earlier, the industry has by now acquired a lifestyle of its own, its survival depending on its ability to innovate new styles and more appealing products and thus to promote sales on a continuing basis.

In addition, the time-saving and convenience commodities to which the leisure-seeking consumer is attracted include a variety of disposables. The list of disposable household items has been expanding steadily in industrial societies: cups, dishes, utensils, diapers, razors, hats, umbrellas, lighters, pens, towels, tissues, bottles, thermometers, and vacuum cleaner bags, to name a few.

Bureaucratization and Alienation

The process of industrial production, with its foundation in the division of labor, forces social institutions to transform their organizational structure from a hierarchical structure, which is typical of an agrarian community, to a pyramidal structure. In the pyramidal structure, as typified by bureaucracy, social interaction is compartmentalized and peer interaction is restricted.[36]

Such an industrial bureaucracy will spread to all other social organizations and political institutions where roles become specialized and performed by line experts. As discussed earlier, this phenomenon of role specialization will contribute to the development of a "diffracted" society, to use Rigg's metaphor, as the previously "diffused" society will undergo a structural and functional transition analogous to the "prismatic" effect whereby a ray of light breaks into a series of discernibly different rays as it passes through a prism. In an organization with this kind of structure, we would expect an incremental process of decision-making in which synoptic or innovative decisions on the part of the organization as a whole will be unlikely. This would affect the practice of government bureaucracy in such a way that its role can be limited to caretaking and maintenance. Any kind of drastic change is likely to provoke serious dissent and turmoil, as we witness in the industrial societies where sweeping government organizational changes are highly impractical and improbable. Government authority at this point will experience a transformation of its basis of legitimacy from traditional or charismatic persuasion to "rational" persuasion.[37]

In the operation of a bureaucratic organization, work performance will be rewarded on the basis of *efficiency* in terms of tasks defined in a narrow job description, rather than on the basis of *effectiveness* in meeting the broader objectives of the organization as a whole. A person who works on an assembly line is not expected to comprehend the entire process of production or to appreciate its final output. On the contrary, the assembly-line worker tends to dig a small hole in which to find peace and privacy, although boredom may prevail. An "industrial person" therefore becomes gradually alienated from other members of his or her own organization, as well as from his or her product. As Berger suggests, alienation seems almost complete when one can say with honesty and moral conviction, "I am not what I do; do not judge me by what I do for a living," and turns to nonworking life for values and identity.[38] If workers in industrial and commercial bureaucracies are indeed psychologically alienated, the Marxist indictment of capitalism as an agent alienating humans from things is indeed applicable to all bureaucracies.

Tyranny of Technology and New Victims

Schumacher, in his seminal work, *Small Is Beautiful*, laments that "technology, although of course the product of man, tends to develop by its own laws and principles. . . [It] recognizes no self-limiting principle."[39] As individuals become helpless cogs in a machine, they lose control over the machinery. Furthermore, when the machine gets more sophisticated, workers are compelled to adapt themselves to it by obtaining new skills and technical know-how, or they will lose their jobs. Thus, as ironical as it may sound, human beings become subjected to machines, and technology controls people rather than the converse.

Technological sophistication is assumed to be unlimited because without it no industry can survive. Unlike agriculture, industry came only to expand, and industrial expansion is made possible by an increasing demand for industrial products. As discussed earlier, technological innovations on a continuing basis are necessary for producing commodities that will appeal to the eyes of the leisure-minded masses and the "precarious consumer." The growth of technology itself is virtually unlimited and, more important, it is unchecked. Technology transcends national boundaries or ideological differences. There is no such thing as capitalist technology as opposed to socialist technology. For that matter, there is no American technology that will be repudiated in the Soviet Union simply because of its origin. In this sense, as Boorstein observes, we may be drifting into the "republic of technology," where civilization will become increasingly homogeneous and humankind will experience common problems of a common life environment.[40] In the triumphant march of technological growth, all humans will end up as the victims, since they will be subservient to machines.

In a society where technocrats prevail and new technical innovations are so swift that no one can acquire sufficient skill to enjoy them throughout his or her life, the elderly will be sure victims because they are not as able and motivated as younger people to retrain themselves. As a result, older people will easily be elimi-

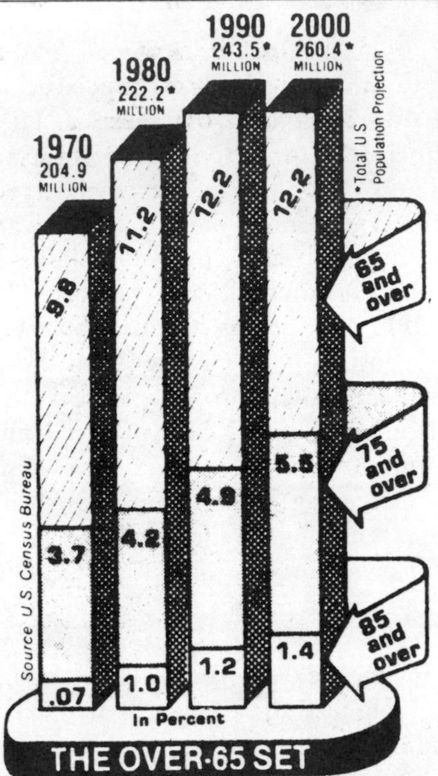

Figure 2.1 Structure of Elderly Population in the United States

SOURCE: From James C. Hyatt, "Aging Americans: As Lives are Extended, Some People Wonder If It's Really a Blessing," *The Wall Street Journal*, October 25, 1979. Reprinted by permission of *The Wall Street Journal*, © Dow Jones & Company, Inc., 1979. All rights reserved.

nated from the work force, and those who remain will be discriminated against.

In 1976, there were 22 million adults who were 65 or older; one out of every ten persons in America belongs to this group, which is rapidly growing due to prolonged life and the declining birthrate.[41] As Figure 2.1 shows, not only will the group aged 65 or older grow, but the older segment of population within that group will increase, exacerbating the problem. Historically, the elderly have been dependent on the family for survival. But the spread of industrialization and urbanization has changed the institution of family, separating the places of work and home and leaving fewer roles for the elderly. The extended family system has been replaced by the nuclear family. Houses have become smaller, women work, mobility has increased, and family care for the elderly has become more of a burden.

In a typical society, the increase of the aging population leads to a transfer of functions from the family to government. Over the last fifty years or so, there has been a profound growth of this shift of functions in the United States and European societies. This period corresponds to the time of active industrial development in the Western world.

As Sussman correctly observes, for some tasks primary groups such as the family can be more effective than bureaucracy.[42] These tasks include (1) the acquisition of general knowledge and communication with respect to one's physical needs (eating, dressing, and the like); (2) personal problems and issues that bureaucracy cannot meet, such as human relations, emotional issues, and the values a person should pursue; and (3) idiosyncratic events, such as dealing with car accidents. These functions are better performed by family members and intimate friends, rather than institutions and government bureaucracies.

As a result, the elderly maintain a precarious lifestyle: one-fourth of American senior citizens fall below the federal poverty level and more than 10 percent of them are as vulnerable and defenseless as children.[43] Furthermore, the elderly suffer psychological and social alienation, many of them turning helplessly to the crutch of drugs and alcohol.

Overurbanization

While urbanization is a natural outcome of industrialization, some cities increase their populations without industrial development, exerting a parasitic effect on social stability.

Hauser characterizes "overurbanization" as involving a situation in which "a larger population of people lives in urban places than their degree of economic development justifies."[44] As implied here by Hauser, the concept of overurbanization is defined only in relation to the level of economic development, rather than the sheer number of people residing in a city. Breeze directly relates overurbanization to the "gap between urbanization and industrialization that makes it possible to provide employment to all persons coming to urban areas."[45]

Many other authors advance the notion that overurbanization can occur when the size of a city is unrealistically large, as though there is an optimal city size. According to this view, the relationship between a city's efficiency and the size of its population is curvilinear, in which a growing city is expected to contribute to economic development and social stability only to a certain point. An overly grown city would have an adverse effect on its socioeconomic and political development. Estall and Buchanan assert that at "some time or other most of the world's great industrial complexes have been thought to be beyond the point where economics are offset by the extra cost incurred in various ways."[46]

Still others maintain that the phenomenon of a primate distribution of cities will be harmful to the society. The primate distribution phenomenon will occur when one or a few core cities grow rapidly, thus slowing down the growth of smaller and middle-sized cities. This will accelerate modernization of core cities at the expense of the rest of the country. It is believed that a tendency toward the primate distribution of cities is not only destructive for the balanced growth of the cities themselves, but also harmful to the political stability of the nation. Conversely, this would mean that a "rank distribution" of cities of varying sizes existing simultaneously is conducive to the development of the nation.

In any case, mechanization of agriculture combined with the apparent promises shown by new industrial jobs facilitates the process of overurbanization of one sort or another, contributing to urban unemployment and other social dislocations. The influx of incoming population would make the government hard to control effectively. Such cities would become subjected to increasing urban crimes and violence, as may be easily seen in large cities everywhere.

The Middle Class

As a direct consequence of industrial development, one should never forget the emergence of the middle class, a class that was not foreseen by Karl Marx when he evaluated the process of social change accompanying the market economy. What made the middle class different from the proletariat was their ability to influence the mechanism of production as both the producers and the consumers. Industrial workers managed to develop their expertise and claim their fair share through collective bargaining and strikes. Thus, the blind exploitation on the part of the capitalist was not as natural a result as Marx predicted.

The middle-class person is by and large a self-supporting person with a job security and a constant income, usually as a salaried worker. As such, he or she is a typical consumer in an industrial society, without much control over personal income or production. The volume of consumption on the part of the middle class, however, can be so large that the industrial sector becomes completely dependent upon them. It is by their collective purchasing power that they give appropriate recognition, which helps them to improve their social and economic position. We discussed earlier how dependent the industry would be upon continuous consumption by the masses, and it is the middle class who have the purchasing power and develop mass consumption.

A middle-class person is likely to be socially and psychologically alienated from others, typically residing in an urban apartment cell. The middle class may have prevented a proletarian revolution, which Marx would have loved to see, but this class has contributed to the emergence of ill symptoms of the industrial society. These symptoms include the absence of public regardingness, selfishness, alienation, and laziness. We shall discuss some of these problems later in this chapter.

Thus far, we have discussed the idea that the human desire for leisure may have paved the way for technological development and industrialization, and subsequently for behavioral and social change. We shall now examine the impact of such development on societal institutions.

Deterioration of Institutions

It has been maintained that industrialization is a comprehensive process of social change in which the traditional community is rapidly dismantled. In this process, some farmland will be destroyed and converted into industrial parks, highways, and parking lots, resulting in a sharp decline in farm population, although not in agricultural productivity.[47] The military will undergo a process of declining relative importance as it becomes subservient to industrial pressures and yields the way to the broader "military-industrial complex." The family as a primary institution will experience a profound transformation endangering the very foundation of its existence. Education will have to adapt itself to the new cultural and societal demands. Even religious organizations will become more secular and commercialized. We shall examine some of these changes in more detail.

Agriculture: A Perennial Loser

It seems almost as though farmers are the perennial losers in all societies. Since what the farmer can do is limited to the production of food and basic necessities, his function will be appreciated less and less in societies where people's imminent needs are beyond those necessities. Furthermore, as agricultural productivity is restricted in part by the amount of arable land available and other natural conditions, agriculture can offer little competition to industry in generating and expanding resources for a society geared to the expansion of leisure commodities. On the other hand, industrial output is relatively free from national boundaries, so long as market expansion accompanies that output.

As the farmer's function becomes more peripheral to the nation's economy, agriculture also suffers in its relative importance in the culture. Many farmers in agrarian societies enjoy a prestigious position in a culture where farming is regarded a sacred job, only to find that the wave of industrialization overwhelms them with social change.

Unlike urban industrial workers, farmers are tied to their land and have little mobility. They lack bargaining power because they seldom have alternative employment. Work boycotts are not realistic bargaining tools because they cannot afford to lose a whole year's worth of crops, since most of them are already impoverished or at least deeply in debt. With these problems and weaknesses inherent in the agricultural sector, farmers are forced to drift away from the mainstream of the industrial society.

The Military-Industrial Complex

Once industrialization gets under way, it is difficult to contain its expansion, since industry faces the dilemma of "growth or death." Industrial economy is such that firms can seldom accommodate reductions in their operation. Thus, the forces for industrial expansion are fierce and will spill over into every other aspect of the society. The military can hardly be an exception.

The institution of the military, despite its sacred and exclusively assigned function of territorial defense, can be impaired by industrial intrusion.[48] Realizing that the military is a unique institution for which there can be no economic recession, industry will be eager to benefit economically by penetrating into the operation of the defense apparatus.

The phenomenon of the military-industrial merger is more apparent in capitalist industrial societies, where weapons are manufactured by industries upon terms of contracts. In this case, the parties to the contract represent two different behavioral entities: While the government is a publicly funded organization that does not have to be "rational" or profit-motivated, industry is a profit-maximizing institution. This leads to contract terms favoring the industry without personally costing the government personnel, who have a virtually unlimited source of funds in taxes. Given the magnitude of the cost of building aircraft, tanks, and other weapons for the military, we can easily imagine the volume of economic interest on the part of industry.

In the case of the United States, there were as of the 1960s some 22,000 prime contractors doing business with the Department of Defense, all advocates of the free enterprise system. However, 90 percent of all weapons procurement is now done without competitive bidding. Initially the contractor will make a low estimate, but will often spend two or three times as much as estimated without worrying about the Pentagon cancelling the order. This is a form of "private socialism" in which the public takes the risk and the companies the profit. At least 68 weapons systems, worth

$59 billion, have had to be abandoned as unworkable, including the nuclear-powered plane, of which $514 million was lost, the B-70 Superbomber (a loss of $1.5 billion), the Snark Robot Bomber ($678 million), and numerous others. Such cases of wasteful spending and inefficiency would make any normal business or government agency stagger, but when it comes to defense spending, the nation has become accustomed to such waste.

In fiscal 1968, the hundred companies that did more than two-thirds of the prime military work held on their payrolls 2072 retired military officers. Many of the same men who negotiated the deals with private business had worked for the Pentagon. After they retired, they used their influence and knowledge to land profitable jobs working with defense companies. As an example, Litton Industries has 49 retired high-ranking officers on its payroll. With all these doors opening into the right Pentagon office, it is little wonder that Litton jumped from thirty-sixth largest prime defense contractor in 1967 to fourteenth in 1968.[49]

Due in part to the syndrome of ever-expanding industry, military buildup in collaboration with industry can also be unlimited, as we witness in the unending process of the arms race between industrial giants. As a way of promoting the endless process of military buildup, military superpowers are often compelled to become merchants themselves when they cannot consume all the hardware the industry wishes to produce. This would involve selling arms to surrogate countries and even enemies of the surrogates. Indeed, it often appears that it is in the interest of the superpowers to facilitate conflicts and wars around the world so as to meet domestic industrial demand. We should not be misled into believing that the arms race toward the alleged balance of power has necessarily contributed to global security. In fact, many wars and regional conflicts during the cold war era were "sponsored" by the superpowers themselves, often for the domestic reasons of the military-industrial complex. One need not be a critic of the United States to be able to see the formidable role of industry in shaping American military policy.

The Family: The Last Resort Threatened

The extended family system was commonplace in agrarian communities, for it was conducive to organizing and mobilizing the labor force, and the practice of uncalculated mutual aid within the family was beneficial to labor-intensive farming. But as the community opened its doors to industrialization and urbanization, the institution of the extended family system was the first to be affected. As youthful members of the family were attracted to urban centers, their allegiance and loyalty to the extended family came to a gradual end. At the same time, the new young members of the city were left with the awesome responsibility of forming a new family without the close guidance and protection of the more experienced members of the extended family. As Mead observes in the American context, "thousands of young couples are living together in some arrangement and are wholly dependent on their private, personal commitment to each other for the survival of their relationship."[50]

In the urban setting, where there may be little social interaction and communal congeniality, the nuclear family becomes the sole source of psychological comfort for individuals who seldom find a sense of attachment to their work environment. Thus, the socially isolated and emotionally lonesome "industrial person" seeks and expects the psychological comfort of belongingness in the small nuclear family itself. But in industrial society, both spouses are likely to be providers, though often failing to become mutual providers. This and other complications contribute to the proliferation of divorce, which epitomizes the crisis faced by the family in industrial society.[51]

Furthermore, families that manage to avoid breaking up through divorce are not necessarily performing their proper function in protecting the children and comforting their belongingness need. It is no longer shocking news that children are breaking away from homes. What is shocking is the fact that a majority of these children are from relatively well-off families, by economic and social standards. The soaring suicide rate among the young people in relatively affluent societies may be attributed in part to the breakdown of the family.[52]

Industrial development changed the family institution in a number of ways; for instance, the relative roles of men, women, and children have undergone profound transition. In the preindustrial society, many men worked at crafts and farming in or near the home. They were around and nearby to eat meals with the family and share their workloads with other members. This contrasts with the industrial men, who are expected to be physically away from home to work and whose work is in isolation from that of their families.

The role of women has changed perhaps more than that of men. In the past, housewives' tasks included the manufacturing of clothing, soap, bread, and other staples. In addition, they expected to educate children when public education was limited. These types of work required creative efforts on the part of women. In industrial society, women's jobs at home became somewhat easier and less time-consuming, thanks to automated appliances and ready-made foods. As a result, they could go out and become wage earners.

The role of children has also changed drastically. Instead of being babysitters and helpers around the house, they now spend long hours away from their families and often become wage earners themselves. Indeed, in the early expansion of industrial work demand, children became a source of the labor force, as we witnessed in the United States and Great Britain, where the government had to intervene with child labor laws to curtail the unjust exploitation of children.

As the industrial society penetrates the family, in such a way that its members become wage earners, relations among the members are likely to be defined in terms of "give and take," which is essentially a contractual relationship. In industrial and postindustrial societies, compensating children for their daily chores and other household work is hardly perceived as unusual. Keeping separate banking accounts and the legal definition of property shares between the husband and wife are no longer considered unusual. In fact, the family has ceased to be a primary institution. It is becoming more of a contractual and legal association that is readily subject to the intervention of the court.

Education: An End to the Total Person

With the necessity to respond to industrial demand, educational curricula will gradually do away with liberal arts and philosophy and incorporate technical and scientific training. This trend is rapidly reinforced by the ascent of the technocrat in the community power structure. As Bell observes, "with the rise of the technician has come the belief that advanced industrial society would be ruled by the technocrat."[53] In response to the changing status of the technocrat, education as training for the total person is replaced by technical training, and education will be viewed as a tool for obtaining more attractive (better-paying) jobs, which tend to be in the technical area. Whereas fields such as philosophy and ethics lose popularity and in some cases vanish for lack of students, new fields and disciplines will emerge from areas dealing with technology and management. In many societies the traditional function of primary education has been one in which children learned norms and beliefs predominant in the society, so that they could join the mainstream of the cultural system. But industrialization has completely altered the meaning of education; education here is little more than vocational training intended to prepare the student for a particular job. Indeed, technical schools and vocational junior colleges will draw more students, and only a small number of "deviant" people will still study the liberal arts and humanities. A layperson's observation of educational institutions in developing Third World countries will convincingly testify to the shift to technocratic training.

Religion: Secularization

As with all organizations, religious organizations are expected to have the social function of providing a sense of belongingness to their members. In this respect, religion has secular functions. Nevertheless, the religious organization is different from all others in that its primary *raison d'être* lies in its pursuit of visions beyond the affairs of this world. Yet, churches in the industrial and postindustrial society become seeking enterprises themselves, and many members profess to be "believers" on utilitarian grounds.

Furthermore, because of the failure of the family institution and problems with education in the industrial society, the masses are easily attracted to religious sects that appear to be more paternal and intimate in human relations among the members. These sects have proven to be as much business organizations as religious entities as we have seen in many recent cases in the United States such as Jim Jones and the Unification Church of Sun Myung Moon.

The story of Reverend Moon is truly an incredible one. With a limited education, Moon tried to establish a Christian denomination of sorts in his own country, Korea, but never succeeded. His church was merely one of many frequently emerging religious sects. Unlike most of his competitors, Moon held a strong nationalist appeal for the Koreans, in that he proclaimed them to be a chosen people. This aspect of his religion helped him gain lukewarm political support from President Park, who was himself an ardent antiforeignist.

Reverend Moon's expansion in the United States, Japan, and Western Europe was indeed an unexpected surprise, even to the church leaders themselves. Why young people, many of whom were of a rather affluent social background, were helplessly and passionately absorbed into the family of Reverend Moon remains a mystery. The most plausible explanation would be that the social context of the industrial societies is such that many young people develop a deep sense of alienation, especially from family. The Unification Church, with its doctrine that all members are brothers and sisters and belong to the same family, was quickly appreciated by the lonely youth. They found the rare opportunity to show their devotion to altruism by living, working, and sharing together. Altruistic and brotherly living is much discussed in conventional churches, but idealistic and innocent youth may never find the preaching to be convincing. Thus, they become highly suspicious of the religious associations that the industrialized and "rationalized" church offers. In this sense we might even say that if something is responsible for the religions sect, it is the society, the broken family institution, and the inhumane industrial culture itself that should be held liable more than anything else.

This analysis is not meant to condone and sanctify the religious sects we have witnessed in recent years. In fact, churches themselves are failing. Of all conceivable deceptions, deceptions in the church may be most grave. Despite the acclaimed brotherhood and equality before God, how many churches in the United States are making serious efforts to have racially integrated memberships? Indeed, few social groups are as segregated and closed as churches. In order to belong to a certain church, you have to belong to a certain secular status group first. How can one justify this in the name of God?

The Rational Person and Immoral Politics

When people are helplessly swept up by the wave of industrialization and the accompanying social changes, they are forced to alter their attitudes, values, beliefs, and even behavioral patterns.

The Evolution of the Rational Person

With the breakdown of traditional social systems such as the extended family and the rural community, members of the newly forming urban society will lose the sense of communal bonding, and they will experience social and psychological alienation. The new life environment will eventually force them to develop a reverence for privacy and individualism.

Furthermore, the worker's job environment is such that reward is in proportion to individual achievement, and his or her work relationships are limited essentially to the employer, curtailing group orientation and collective behavior. Workers participate in collective bargaining or strikes not to promote collective interests but in the calculated consideration of self-interest. Thus, mass movements are not expected to succeed when such movements mean a high degree of risk to the participant and the payoff is not readily translated into tangible and immediate individual gains. This may be a partial explanation for the lack of mass political organizations and revolutionary social movements in industrial societies. The group-oriented phenomena of mass movements are most prevalent at the political integration stage, when individuals in sufficient numbers are willing to sacrifice their individual interests for collective good.

The concept of human rationality has evolved in a most intriguing way. Following medieval times, when legitimacy of power had little to do with "people's consent," with the introduction of the "social contract," along with the concurrent development of philosophical individualism and *laissez-faire* economics in the ensuing decades, philosophers and political thinkers raised the issue of the state of human nature as an ultimate source of justification for different types of politics. Machiavelli, Hobbes, Locke, and Rousseau, to name only a few, had varying perceptions concerning the state of human nature, and hence, different views of legitimate forms of government. Nevertheless, they all seemed to agree that "rationality" is virtuous and desirable, although they interpreted the degree of human rationality differently. Further, they agreed that the rational person is benevolent and altruistic. Selfishness was regarded as irrational, and it laid the foundation for tyrannical theories of political order as espoused in Machiavelli's *Prince* and Hobbes's *Leviathan*.

As the industrial economy with its market culture swept Western civilization, the economic conception of rational man overpowered the traditional philosophical version of human rationality. The economic rational man was ironically the traditional "irrational man." A man motivated to maximize benefit by minimizing the cost is defined as being rational, and this very man would have been regarded as irrational for his selfish motivation. In the mature industrial society, "selfishness" disguised as "rationality" is hardly considered a vice. Thus, hedonistic utilitarianism is accepted as a norm, and anything unselfish is typically viewed as irrational and abnormal.[54] In short, the industrial society made man not only selfish but justified his selfishness as not immoral and naturally expected of any reasonable person.

Government as an Agent of Conflict Management

People are never content with what they have. Human desire knows no limit. With all the industrial fruits and prosperity of the affluent society, people will be still unhappy as long as they have a sense of "relative deprivation," that is, as long as they feel that others are doing better than they are. Human satisfaction is perfected only when one's achievement is relatively "better" than that of other members of the society, yet no society can become fully developed if all of its members are completely satisfied, because someone's achievement of satisfaction in this context requires someone else's failure to achieve.

In a society where a substantial majority of the people have acquired a comfortable lifestyle as a result of industrialization, they will start pursuing a competitively superior position by way of "conspicuous consumption" or seeking power positions. This inherently conflictual situation dictates the government to become a peacekeeping agent and direct its efforts to facilitate a distributive system that is "just."

In agrarian society, where people's needs were met—through the production of food and other necessities—by exploring the natural environment, social conflict was seldom of a mutually exclusive kind, since people could always explore the unexplored resources. But in a society where people compete for the sake of "winning," people's needs cannot be met without producing loss; thus, the winner's satisfaction will be offset by the loser's suffering. Social and political competition in the mature industrial societies is generally of this kind, namely, a zero-sum game.[55] It is for this reason that societies that may have reached a mature stage of industrialization tend to shift their policy emphasis from production to redistribution.

In this regard, it is not surprising that definitions of politics offered by scholars of Western postindustrial origin tend to focus on the function of redistribution, as we witness in Easton's "authoritative allocation of values"[56] and Lasswell's "who gets what, when, and how."[57] These definitions of politics presuppose the existence and availability of "values" to be allocated and resources to be acquired by someone in the first place.

As members of the society compete for superiority in relative social and economic positions, the role of government will inevitably shift to the generation of more "equitable" distribution as long as it needs to maintain popular support in order to stay in power. This emphasis on equity is a common phenomenon in the postindustrial societies, where social and economic inequality has been exacerbated as a result of industrialization. People of lower status in the economic and social structure will claim their "legitimate" share by placing demands on the government since they themselves are incapable of challenging the establishment. People at the top, on the other hand, will by now have established a solid political and economic base that cannot be easily altered. Thus, the established class will not yield the way to a more equitable distribution as long as it affects them adversely. In this situation the middle class becomes most vulnerable and subject to government manipulations.

As alluded to earlier, members of the middle class in industrial societies are individualistic, private-oriented, and thus likely to be apathetic about politics; further, they would find it very difficult to know how to express their views effectively, despite channels to express public opinion. Even in participatory democracies, effective participation is barred by issue complexity, voter apathy, and a number of other factors. As a result, government efforts to calm down the noisy "underdog" are mainly aimed at extracting resources from the middle class for reallocation, rather than promoting equitable redistribution by taking away from the rich and privileged. To illustrate this point, let us look at the situation in the United States. When we compare the pattern of family income distribution in 1947 with that in 1977 (Table 2.2), it is evident that there has been virtually no change, indicating a constant pattern of income distribution in the last three decades, despite all the rhetoric and alleged government efforts. This indicates that, in a society whose members are primarily concerned about "just" distribution, the government will have little incentive to change the status quo in a drastic way, because any redistribution will spur criticism unless everyone becomes better off as a result of the redistribution. Since satisfying everyone through redistribution is untenable and logically impossible, the government chooses to maintain the "optimality" by refusing change. By failing to take action, the government can at least avoid generating new groups of unhappy people.

TABLE 2.2 Distribution of Family Income, 1947-1977

	Shares (%)	
	1947	1977
Lowest quintile	5.0	5.2
2nd quintile	11.9	11.6
3rd quintile	17.0	17.5
4th quintile	23.1	24.2
Highest quintile	43.0	41.5

SOURCE: U.S. Bureau of the Census, *Current Population Reports, Consumer Income 1977*, Series P-60, no. 118 (March 1979), p. 45.

TABLE 2.3 Distribution of Wage and Salary Earnings for Persons

	1948 (%)	1977 (%)
Lowest quintile	2.6	1.7
2nd quintile	8.1	7.7
3rd quintile	16.6	16.1
4th quintile	23.4	26.4
Highest quintile	49.3	48.1

SOURCE: U.S. Bureau of the Census, *Current Population Reports, Consumer Income 1977*, Series P-60, no. 118 (March 1979), pp. 226-227.

Government policies to promote redistributive justice have failed in the United States (a country Daniel Lerner regards as a prime example of the postindustrial society) and it is clear that the magnitude of inequality has, indeed, increased when we analyze the structure of wages and earnings during the last three decades (Table 2.3). The degree of unequal distribution becomes even more severe when we compare *wealth* distribution rather than income distribution. Although data on distribution of wealth are less accessible than those on income, occasional measurements have been made. In 1962 the Federal Reserve Board conducted a survey of the ownership of all private assets. According to that survey, the wealthiest 20 percent of population owned over 75 percent of all private assets, while the poorest 25 percent of all families had no net worth (see Table 2.4). The wealthiest 8 percent of the population owned 60 percent of all private assets; the wealthiest 1 percent owned over 26 percent of all assets. This kind

TABLE 2.4 Family Distribution of Net Worth in 1962

Net Worth Class ($1000)	Cumulative Distribution of Families	Cumulative Distribution of Total Net Worth
Negative	8.1	−0.2
$0–1	25.4	0.0
1–5	42.7	2.1
5–10	56.9	6.6
10–25	81.3	23.8
25–50	92.5	40.9
50–100	97.6	55.9
100–200	98.6	61.3
200–500	99.5	74.2
500 & over	100.0	100.0

SOURCE: Lester C. Thurow and Robert Lucas, "The American Distribution of Income: A Structural Problem," in Lee Rainwater, ed., *Inequality and Justice* (New York: Aldine, © 1974), p. 82. Reprinted with permission of the publisher.

of unequal distribution is not going to be easily altered; government policies in the United States have favored the wealthiest at the expense of the low and middle classes.

Thus far, it has been observed that in a mature industrial or postindustrial society the question of redistribution overrides that of production, and that equitable redistribution is not expected, despite the need for a rhetorical campaign for it. Further, we have suggested that as competition becomes an essential feature in a society where people pursue "winning," the role of a popular government is not to suppress or resolve competition and conflict completely, but rather to maintain them to such a degree that the society will not break down. A government capable and willing to eliminate conflict completely will lose its basis of legitimacy because it needs to demonstrate continuously its function of conflict resolution, which necessitates the continuous presence of conflict itself. In this sense, one might assert that government is a conflict-creating agent as much as a conflict-resolving one.

Global Ills: Dilemmas and Challenges

As a theme of this chapter, we have noted that industrial expansion behind the cosmetic veil of development has contributed to many social problems, ranging from moral decay to environmental deterioration. The emergence of an integrated economic order and rapid technology transfer, among other things, will only facilitate industrialization on the surface of this planet. This being the case, it is not difficult to predict a truely gloomy course of social change in that the global problems will only be intensified.

In the hope that we might be able to discern some ideas that might be useful in devising strategic measures to alleviate some of the problems, we shall examine the question of who will pay the price for problem-solving. Subsequently, we shall see if there can be any remedial solution, even of a theoretical nature.

Who Will Pay? The Supreme Dilemma

As alluded to earlier, most global problems in the area of environment, food, population, and energy are of a "public" nature, benefiting or hurting everyone regardless of one's contribution to their creation or solution. In this regard, the heart of the issue lies in the fact that a rational individual will be unwilling to sacrifice for the "public" benefit, since this is exactly what he or she is not supposed to do as a rational person. In the case of pollution, for example, clean air is a commodity that does not distinguish those who have contributed to its creation or preservation from those who have not. It would be perfectly rational for some people to avoid paying the cost of clean air if they expect that others who need clean air more desperately will pay for it. The benefit will reach them anyhow.

The problem of food shortage is seen by those who do not starve as a foreign problem which has little to do with them. They, as rational and private-regarding individuals, will find perfect justification in believing that what the poor have is what they have earned, and they will be least likely to sacrifice for the solution of someone else's problem. Similarly, the population problem has its own dilemma. The question of this planet's capacity to accommodate the population explosion is not seen as an intimate, personal question at all, as long as individuals can afford and believe in benefiting from having more children. It is in the labor-intensive agricultural and underdeveloped countries, where having more children may be considered beneficial, that the problem of population increase is most serious. In those societies where an increasing labor force is not desirable, people believe in the wisdom of having small families. Thus, the vicious cycle of poverty cannot be easily overcome in less developed societies, and as a result they are compelled to contribute to intensifying world population problems.

To fight energy shortages in recent years in the United States, drivers have been sufficiently informed of the bleak energy future and asked to drive less. But the public did not respond effectively until gasoline prices went up. This price-response behavior indicates that individuals will only behave "rationally" and cannot be persuaded with the noble idea of public regardingness or altruism.[58] As long as the "rational person" is taken for granted, global problems will persist. There may be short-term relief, but human competition for more production, more allocation, and more consumption will eventually make the planet uninhabitable. Furthermore, if the government, which presumably generates and protects "public" goods, is unwilling and unable to do anything about the problems, the future of the global community will be bleak indeed.

What Can Be Done?

If, indeed, global problems confronting us today are essentially industrial products, and industrial development is prompted by the human desire for leisure, a logical inference would be that we need to change human nature. This calls for a cultural revolution in which the moral value of human "rationality" may be reassessed and attempts may be made to change such a psychological orientation. In the entire spectrum of socialization processes, systematic and painstaking efforts should be made to reorient ourselves. Anything less than this may well lead to the grave consequence of human extinction.

However, one might speculate on another line of thinking that theoretically could eliminate the necessity for such a cultural revolution. This may be termed a dialectical synthesis of human beings and their environment, in that one becomes the essence of the other: If people come to realize that there is nothing that is theirs only that "private" goods are at the same time "public" goods—global problems as "public" issues could be resolved by the same mechanisms and processes that hedonistic individuals use to pursue their rational interests. When the meaning of "public goods" is such that not only the creation of them but also their destruction will directly affect private individuals, as in the case of ecological imbalance, people will be concerned about the protection of such public goods and thus be willing to pay for solving public problems. But this remains a theoretical solution; even if public goods and private goods merge, it is probable that the seriousness of global ills may already be too extensive to reverse their course of development.

Summary

In this chapter, I have attempted to develop the following ideas:

(1) A survey of the literature on development indicates that definitions and conceptions of development have generally been partial descriptions of the dynamics of industrialization. This being the case, ramifications and consequences of development, many of which constitute global problems, can best be analyzed and explained by a study of the causes, structure, and consequences of industrialization.

(2) As an ultimate contributor to industrialization, we have proposed a leisure motive of human nature. We observed that human desire for leisure might have prompted the invention of tools and mechanization, division of labor, and eventually industrialization.

(3) It is industrialization that has forced social and cultural change through its accompanying developments of urbanization and the expansion of the market. In this process, humans have become "rational," institutions bureaucratized, the life-world deteriorated, and politics immoral.

(4) Industrial maturity and the development of postindustrial societies made members of the society mutually competitive and conflictual as social and political dynamics became increasingly zero-sum oriented.

(5) The global problems surrounding food, population, environment, and energy are essentially of a public nature, and the hedonistic and rational member of the industrial and postindustrial society is not willing or able to solve them.

(6) Thus, the prospect for planetary health and quality of the life-world appears to be gloomy indeed. As we attempt to draw some ideas intended to remedy these global problems, we might trace the sequence of events that led to their formation, and suggest that leisure- and victory-seeking human nature must be altered throughout the entire spectrum of the socialization processes.

NOTES

1. For a discussion of "social engineering," see Eugene J. Meehan, "What Should Political Scientists Be Doing?" in George J. Graham, Jr., and George W. Carey, eds., *The Post-Behavioral Era* (New York: David McKay, 1972).

2. David Easton, "The New Revolution in Political Science," *American Political Science Review*, 63, 4 (1969), pp. 1051-1061.

3. Talcott Parsons, *Essays in Sociological Theory* (New York: Free Press, 1949), pp. 24-112.

4. David C. McClelland, *The Achieving Society* (New York: Free Press, 1961).

5. Daniel Lerner, *The Passing of Traditional Society* (New York: Free Press, 1958).

6. David E. Apter, *The Politics of Modernization* (Chicago: University of Chicago Press, 1965).

7. Gabriel A. Almond and Sidney Verba, *The Civic Culture* (Boston: Little, Brown, 1963).

8. Gabriel A. Almond and James S. Coleman, eds., *The Politics of the Developing Areas* (Princeton, NJ: Princeton University Press, 1960), p. 11.

9. *Ibid.*, p. 59.

10. For an excellent discussion along this line, see Lawrence C. Mayer, *Comparative Political Inquiry* (Homewood, IL: Dorsey Press, 1972).

11. Gabriel A. Almond and G. Binghorn Powell, Jr., *Comparative Politics: A Developmental Approach* (Boston: Little, Brown, 1966).

12. *Ibid.*, pp. 28-30.

13. *Ibid.*, p. 24.

14. Apter, *Politics of Modernization.*

15. *Ibid.*, p. 67.

16. David E. Apter, *Some Conceptual Approaches to Modernization* (Englewood Cliffs, NJ: Prentice-Hall, 1968), p. 334.

17. Apter, *Politics of Modernization*, pp. 19-24.

18. Mayer, *Comparative Political Inquiry*, p. 157.

19. Apter, *Conceptual Approaches.*

20. Fred W. Riggs, *Administrations in Developing Countries* (Boston: Houghton Mif-flin, 1963).

21. Joseph LaPalombara, ed., *Bureaucracy and Political Development* (Princeton, NJ: Princeton University Press, 1963), p. 122.

22. Samuel A. Huntington, "Political Development and Political Decay," *World Politics*, 17 (1965), pp. 386-430; Alfred Diamant, "The Nature of Political Development," in Jason L. Finkle and Richard W. Gable, eds., *Political Development and Social Change* (New York: John Wiley, 1966); Karl W. Deutsch, "Social Mobilization and Political Development," *American Political Science Review*, 55 (1961), pp. 493-514.

23. W. W. Rostow, *The Process of Economic Growth* (New York: Norton, 1952).

24. A.F.K. Organski, *The Stages of Political Development* (New York: Knopf, 1965).

25. To the Greeks, leisure was concerned with those activities that were worthy of a free man, activities we might today call "culture." Work, on the other hand, as instrumental and productive activity was regarded as below the dignity of a free man. Since then, the work ethic may have changed significantly but the unmistakable fact is that it is leisure, not work, that people have sought and largely earned in the course of human history. For a concise discussion of this thesis, see Bennett M. Berger, "The Sociology of Leisure," *Industrial Relations*, 1, 2 (1962).

26. Paul Weis, "A Philosophical Definition of Leisure," in James C. Charlesworth, ed., *Leisure in America*, American Academy of Political and Social Science Monograph 4 (Philadelphia: 1964), p. 21.

27. For a further analysis on the measurement of time allocation, refer to Gary S. Becker, "A Theory of the Allocation of Time," *Economic Journal* (September 1965).

28. In this respect, I challenge the Marxist overture that human effort to eliminate labor is not to increase leisure but to maximize profits and the opulence of the capitalists.

29. Michael Young, in order to depict this aspect of class structure, discusses the emergence of "technocracy" in industrial societies in his book, *The Rise of the Meritocracy*; see also A. Rahman, "Science and Technology for a New Social Order," *Alternatives*, 4, 3 (1979).

30. Gerald E. Lenski, *Power and Privilege* (New York: McGraw-Hill, 1966), p. 38.

31. As Lenski specifically points out, leisure not only requires free time but, equally importantly, "the production of various kinds of nonessential goods" (Lenski, 1966: 121).

32. Emile Durkheim, *The Division of Labor in Society* (New York: Macmillan, 1933), p. 272.

33. For a landmark study on this proposition, see Willy Brandt, *North-South: A Program for Survival* (Cambridge: MIT Press, 1980). On the formation of a homogeneous culture, see Ali A. Mazuri, "World Culture and the Search for Human Consensus,"in Saul H. Mendlovitz, ed., *On the Creation of a Just World Order* (New York: Free Press, 1975), pp. 1-37.

34. The term "conspicuous consumption" was introduced by Thorstein Veblen in *The Theory of the Leisure Class* (New York: Modern Library, 1931).

35. Consumer debt outstanding, including mortgage debt, was $1.6 trillion in the United States as 1978 ended, representing an increase of 13 percent over the previous year.

Repayments needed to service debt required 23 cents of each dollar of after-tax disposable income.

36. David Apter utilizes the concept of pyramidal/hierarchical authority structure in building a typology of society, where the pyramidal structure is implied as being in industrial market systems. See Apter, *Politics of Modernization.*

37. For the three bases of legitimacy, I am using Max Weber's authority types; see Weber, *The Theory of Social and Economic Organization* (New York: Free Press, 1947), ch. 3.

38. Bennett M. Berger, "The Sociology of Leisure," in Erwin O. Smigel, ed., *Work and Leisure* (New Haven, CT: College and University Press, 1963).

39. E. F. Schumacher, *Small Is Beautiful* (New York: Harper & Row, 1973).

40. Daniel J. Boorstein, *The Republic of Technology* (New York: Harper & Row, 1978).

41. Rockhelle Jones, *The Other Generation* (Englewood Cliffs, NJ: Prentice-Hall).

42. Marvin B. Sussman, *Family, Bureaucracy, and the Elderly* (Durham, NC: Duke University Press, 1977).

43. For these and other data, see Louis Harris et al., *The Myth and Reality of Aging in America* (Washington, DC: National Council on the Aging).

44. Philip Hauser, "The Analysis of 'Over-Urbanization,' " *Economic Development and Cultural Change*, 12 (1964), pp. 113-122.

45. Gerald Breeze, *Urbanization in Newly Developing Countries* (Englewood Cliffs, NJ: Prentice-Hall, 1966), p. 6.

46. R. C. Estall and R. Ogilvie Buchanan, *Industrial Activity and Economic Geography* (London: Friedman, Milton, 1961), p. 107.

47. According to a report by a presidential advisory commission in 1981, some 12 square miles of farmland are being converted into highways and parking lots every day in the United States. The same report warns that if this trend continues, we will have a serious food shortage by the year 2000.

48. A long list of books taking this position could be cited. Among them: Richard J. Barnet, *The Economy of Death* (New York: Atheneum, 1969); Richard J. Barnet and Ronald E. Miller, *Global Reach: The Power of the Multinational Corporations* (New York: Simon & Schuster, 1974); William Domhoff, *The Higher Circle* (New York: Random House, 1970); and Anthony Sampson, *The Sovereign State of ITT* (New York: Stein & Day, 1973).

49. For these and other facts about the military-industrial complex, see Caroll W. Pursell, *The Military-Industrial Complex* (New York: Harper & Row, 1972); Benjamin F. Cooling, ed., *War, Business, and American Society* (New York: Kennikat Press, 1977); Gavin Kennedy, *The Economics of Defense* (London: Western Printing Service, 1975).

50. Semlser, in his analysis of industrial impact on the family, summarizes: "As the family ceases to be an economic unit of production, one or more members leave the household to seek employment in the labor market. The family's activities become more concentrated on emotional gratification and socialization." This observation reinforces the contention that the family has become an organization from which its members seek to satisfy the belongingness need more than from any other social group. The quotation of Mead is from *U.S. News and World Report*, October 27, 1975.

51. In the United States, there were 26 divorces for every 100 marriages in 1960, 48 divorces in 1975, and 63 expected by 1990 (*U.S. News and World Report*, October 27, 1975).

52. For suicide statistics for American and selected European countries, refer to Walter A. Lunden, *The Suicide Cycle* (Montezuma, IA: Sutherland Printing, 1977).

53. Daniel Bell, *The Coming of Post-Industrial Society* (New York: Basic Books, 1973), p. 78.

54. For a classical exposition of this thesis, see Milton Friedman, *Essays in Positive Economics* (Chicago: University of Chicago Press, 1953).

55. Refer to lester C. Thurow, *The Zero-Sum Society* (New York: Basic Books, 1980).

56. David Easton, *The Political System* (New York: Knopf, 1953).

57. Harold Lasswell, *Politics: Who Gets What, When, How* (New York: Meridian Books, 1958).

58. Many of these dilematic problems are insightfully analyzed by Blaney, by authors in the Club of Rome studies, and in publications of the World Order Models Project. Refer to Harry Clay Blaney III, *Global Challenges* (New York: New Viewpoints, 1979); Donella H. Meadows et al., *The Limits to Growth* (New York: Universe Books); and Saul H. Mendlovitz, ed., *On the Creation of a Just World Order* (New York: Free Press, 1975).

3

Comparative Analysis

Economic Well-Being and the Global Human Condition

GARY K. BERTSCH

One-fourth of the planet's population—over one billion human beings—live in absolute poverty. Absolute poverty, so described to distinguish it from the kind of poverty we know in the West, has been described by Robert McNamara as a condition of life so limited as to prevent the realization of the potential of the genes with which people were born; a condition of life so dehumanizing and degrading as to be an insult to human dignity. But this is only one small element of the human condition in the modern world. What else do we know, and need to know, about the human condition on the planet Earth? Is the state of being, or human condition, of coal miners in Poland less desirable than that of their counterparts in Appalachia? How do we know? If it is true, why? This chapter examines the role that comparative analysis and global policy studies can play in explaining the human condition in the contemporary world. It investigates one dimension of the human condition—economic well-being—and examines some of the attributes that represent it and some of the forces that affect it in villages, social groupings, and nation-states around the world.

While economic well-being is only one component of the human condition—other important dimensions include peace, social justice, and various spiritual elements—it is a significant one. The elements implicit in economic well-being—health, safety, services, goods, and comfort—are important to people around the globe. The purpose of this chapter is to suggest how we can begin to describe the state of well-being globally and to help explain why the state of well-being is what it is. The chapter is intended to help define the broad parameters within which more productive comparative research might be conducted. More specifically, it will utilize comparative analysis (1) to identify, describe, and compare selected indicators of well-being and some attributes related to it around the globe, and (2) to examine the impact of certain forces upon these indicators and attributes and upon governmental policy and policy outcomes related to economic well-being. Perhaps this will be of some use to other students of global policy studies who will want to analyze the human condition further as well as to those who may want to change it.

Since data on the human condition, and economic well-being, are most often collected, aggregated, and made available on the nation-state level, our comparative analysis and discussion will tend to be cross-national. This cross-national emphasis is, therefore, to some extent a matter of necessity and does not mean that the comparison of individuals, ethnic or economic groups, and certain social groupings is unimportant. Indeed, we would prefer to compare individuals in almost all cases, if that were possible. In addressing the human condition we are talking about individuals. When we analyze and discuss the human condition of national populations such as Polish and Iranians or of urban dwellers and peasants in the Third World, we make certain simplifications. Obviously, the human condition of specific individuals can and usually does vary markedly within such groupings. Therefore, while there are reasons for comparing groups, the comparison of individuals is our ultimate concern.

The Nature of Comparative Analysis

In a historical review and stock-taking exercise, Eckstein and Apter contend that "the field of comparative politics has a long and honorable past."[1] They note that the pedigree reaches as far back as Aristotle, and to Cicero, Polybius, and Tacitus among the Romans, to Machiavelli in the Renaissance, to Montesquieu in the Enlightenment, and to such figures as Tocqueville, Marx, Mill, Bagehot, and Mosca in the nineteenth century. The comparative analysis of political systems, structures, and institutions, the classification of types, and the study of political development, change, and revolution are concerns that have drawn considerable attention over the years. While the study of comparative politics may have an honorable past, it, like other areas of scholarly activity, is open to certain criticisms. One such criticism is that the work of comparativists has not been particularly relevant to the practical and pressing problems of humanity. It is my opinion that comparativists have been insufficiently concerned with the most urgent and pressing human problems confronting the world in which they live. While social scientists should strive for objectivity and intellectual honesty, they should not avoid addressing problems with strong normative and ethical implications. The most urgent problems of our time—food and starvation, war and peace, racism and community—require the best we have to offer in normative, scientific, and prescriptive analysis. It is unfortunate that most comparativists have failed to provide it. This is particularly disappointing because of the important contributions that comparative analysis can make to addressing the challenges of the modern age.

For example, comparative analysis can contribute to a simple, descriptive understanding of what states are or are not doing to improve the human condition of their peoples. We ought to know that some European governments (those of Sweden and West Germany, for example) invest nearly 50 percent of their national budgets in social security and welfare, while others in Europe (such as Finland and the United Kingdom) invest only one-half of that. How do these expenditures affect the human condition? We also ought to know that many Middle Eastern governments spend a high percentage of their GNPs on defense (44 percent for Egypt in 1976), while the defense expenditures of European governments as a percentage of GNP are significantly less (around 3.5 percent for West Germany and Czechoslovakia in

1976). Such "univariate" comparison of governmental expenditures can tell us what countries are investing in human welfare and how much they are putting into defense, foreign aid, and so forth. One issue that should particularly concern us is how governments spend limited resources with particular focus on the magnitude and nature of government involvement in the welfare of its citizens. Of course, we have to use indicators of governmental involvement and support for human welfare with careful judgment. Later, I shall discuss some problems of comparison. For the present, I am simply suggesting that governments are making choices that affect the human condition and human dignity, and we ought to know more about what they are.

Univariate comparisons can be made of important attributes in addition to governmental expenditures. For example, we can compare certain indicators of the human condition around the world. Data of the Overseas Development Council can be used to compare the percentage of a nation's population living in absolute poverty (around 75 percent in Bangladesh and Ethiopia, compared to 5 percent in Iran and Venezuela).[2] We can utilize the work of Morris D. Morris to examine the physical quality of life in various countries,[3] or the work of Ruth Sivard to compare the economic-social standing or dietary standards of countries around the world.[4] Of course, comparative inquiry should take us beyond the mere description of attributes.

A second example of comparative analysis involves the comparison of relationships. For example, what is the relationship between economic development and the physical quality of life, or ideology and defense spending, or public policy and poverty? What explains the fact that the quality of life and defense expenditures vary so markedly across nations? Why did defense expenditures constitute 44 percent of Egypt's national budget in 1976, while Israel's defense expenditures were 27 percent and Sudan's 2 percent? Why is the physical quality of life reasonably high in Costa Rica and relatively low in Saudi Arabia, even though their per capita incomes are similar? And why did Iran and India have about the same physical quality of life scores in the 1970s, even though Iran's per capita income was nine times that of India's?

These questions and the suggested emphasis on exploring relationships take us in the direction of explaining the causes and consequences of the human condition. If comparativists can link certain domestic and global forces (variables) to policies such as defense or welfare spending, or policy outcomes such as the quality of life, we can better understand why states act and perform as they do and what might be done to change both their behavior and their performance.

Another example of comparative studies and one that I would like to encourage involves the monitoring, assessment, and evaluation of governmental performance.[5] Using evaluative criteria such as quantitative indices (e.g., the Physical Quality of Life Index), international standards (e.g., the Universal Declaration of Human Rights), or national goals (e.g., the Soviet Five Year Plan), comparativists can monitor and evaluate aspects of governmental performance. By examining bi- and multivariate relationships, such as the impact of certain policy programs on human welfare, while controlling for the level of economic development or certain global forces, comparativists can help explain why some states appear to be more successful than others. In what follows, I shall discuss some examples of comparison and their importance in global policy studies by reviewing some relevant research and suggesting additional research that can be done to understand more fully the many forces affecting the human condition in the contemporary world. Although we can be critical of much of what has been done in comparative politics, it is important to know and assess what has been done in order to avoid past mistakes and, perhaps more important, to build upon that which is useful. There is no need to "reinvent the wheel." As we shall see, a considerable body of research and literature is relevant to the evolving field of global policy studies.

Comparative Analysis and Global Policy Studies

I conceive of global policy studies as the study of forces that affect the human condition. I am proposing an ethically moti-

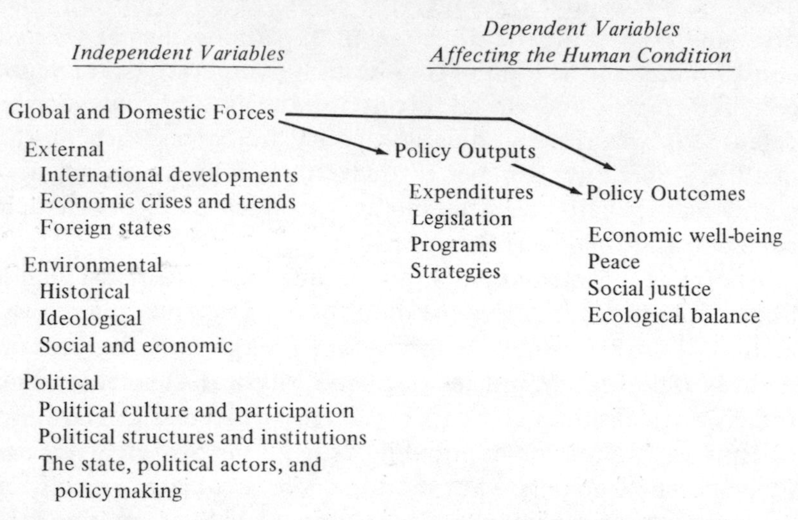

Figure 3.1

vated, scientifically grounded, multidisciplinary, international effort to understand better and to improve the human condition on the planet Earth. Figure 3.1 represents a simplified description of some elements of the field of inquiry I am proposing. The conceptual framework suggests a set of independent variables, global and domestic forces, and two sets of dependent variables, policy outputs and policy outcomes. The *global and domestic forces* are intended to call attention to some of the most important influences of governmental policy and the human condition. *Policy outputs* represent those decisions (expenditures, legislation, programs, strategies, and so on) made by governmental units impacting on the human condition.

The arrows in the framework are suggestive and are intended to portray and clarify the elementary relationships to be addressed in this chapter. The relationships among forces, outputs, and outcomes in the real world are considerably more complex. Like other models, however, Figure 3.1 represents a simplified description of reality. Obviously, the various forces are interactive and interrelated. For example, social and economic forces impact on political culture and political culture on policymaking. Similarly, policy outcomes, conceived of as components of the human condition, influence one another. Some believe that increases in economic well-being often come at the expense of ecological balance. Certainly, the countries with the most impressive scores on the Physical Quality of Life Index are among those that have done the most damage to the environment. Also, the framework does not include arrows describing the feedback loops that are obviously at work. That is, while we use the framework to suggest the impact that external, environmental, and political forces have on governments, policy outputs, and the human condition, we do not mean to imply that governmental policy and the human condition do not, in return, influence these forces. They obviously do. Close examination of these more complex relationships would bring further clarification and explanatory value to the model. For the present, our concern will be addressed to the more elementary relationships portrayed in Figure 3.1. We now have a list of variables organized in what is intended to be a logical fashion. In the future we want to work toward the development of a testable model.

The framework is intended to aid the comparativist in identifying the most important attributes (forces, outputs, and outcomes) and relationships between and among these attributes for examination and study. While the model suggests a wide array of forces, few have attempted to deal with all or many of them simultaneously. As the discussion in succeeding sections of the chapter will indicate, many scholars have been involved in univariate analysis (for example, comparing political attributes, or public expenditures, or economic well-being across systems). Others have utilized bivariate analysis to look at such relationships as those between economic forces and expenditures or political forces and certain policy outcomes. Far fewer have engaged in multivariate analysis incorporating three or more variables from the framework. No one has utilized all of the variables in a sophisticated, interactive model. Perhaps this should be a goal for the true globalist.

Political scientists, of course, have traditionally focused on the political variables and relationships. Economists have concentrated on the economic and sociologists on the sociological. As

Phil Meeks argues in Chapter 4 of this volume, global policy studies is truly a multidisciplinary enterprise.[6] Hence our framework should attempt to include all relevant variables.

How does the comparative analysis I am suggesting relate to the field of global policy studies? I think it does in a number of important respects. For example, we want to know what the human condition is across the planet; and we want to know why it is what it is in slums in New Delhi, ghettos in New York, cities in Europe, communes in China, and so forth. Our concern is also global in the sense that it strives to include all relevant variables in an explanatory system. We are trying to move away from the parochialism of our disciplines and the parochialism of our countries. To carry out global policy studies requires us to do more than political science and to study more than the United States or Europe. The cross-national study of forces, outputs, and outcomes I am proposing can also help take us away from the more parochial concerns of case and area studies. While such studies make an important contribution to global studies, they do not allow global analysis. On the other hand, cross-national, comparative studies do by aiding our search for generalizations and universals. Finally, our concern with the human condition is a global concern. The suggested components of the human condition—economic well-being, peace, social justice, ecological balance—are global challenges and cry out for global solutions. We recognize that both challenges and solutions stretch beyond national borders. You cannot improve the human condition unless you come to grips with the complex forces that operate outside the local environment and often outside the borders of the nation-state. It seems to me that if we can make some progress in understanding the forces that improve the human condition and those that deteriorate it, we are making an important contribution to the field of global policy studies.

Comparing Attributes

As noted above, one necessary task involves the simple global comparison of certain characteristics or attributes related to the human condition. What is the state of the human condition and factors related to it around the world? In order to begin to find out, we can compare a variety of indicators including the physical quality of life, governmental policies (on expenditures, for example) intended to improve the quality of life, and other such variables. For purposes of this analysis, the human condition will be defined as an individual's or group's state of being. Of course, an individual's state of being has many different dimensions. The concept of human condition I am suggesting represents a value-centered approach based on the assumption that the human condition can be conceived of and evaluated in terms of values that people consider important. Numerous scholars have suggested value frameworks to organize such inquiry. Harold Lasswell has offered and utilized an eight-value scheme including power, respect, rectitude, affection, wealth, well-being, skills, and enlightenment.[7] Robert Johansen has suggested four values: peace, economic well-being, social justice, and ecological balance.[8] It is assumed that the higher the presence of these values within an individual or group, the better the human condition. An individual who has ample amounts of all values would be characterized by a more desirable human condition than one who enjoys fewer. Some suggest that a preferred distribution of these values for an individual or society represents human dignity.[9] Since human dignity means different things to different people, and preferred value distributions will vary across individuals, groups, and societies, there will never be universal agreement on the ideal distribution of values. Yet, it is clear that there are values that people around the globe seem to desire (such as well-being or peace) and the way these values are distributed does have an impact on the human condition.

Such value-centered approaches usually raise the following question: Are such values universally applicable? My own response is they may not be, but they can be used profitably for analysis if the analyst uses them sensibly and, specifically, does not assume that there is only one ideal distribution of values in the world. This value-centered approach to comparative global policy studies rests, then, on three important assumptions. First, human needs and values should be the guiding focus of our studies. Second, while we shall look across political units for patterns and trends, we are guided and motivated by an overriding global concern. Third, by gaining a fuller understanding of the present, we may be better prepared to deal with the future.

Perhaps one of the most fundamental of all values in today's world is economic well-being. A sizable portion of the world's population is going without adequate diet, health care, social services, and physical security and comfort. I am not suggesting that well-being is the most important value, or that it means the same thing to all people, or that individual or national conditions on this variable form a good predictor of their status on other values. The various values and dimensions of the human condition are complex. Sometimes they may be related; in other cases they are not. As mentioned earlier, some have posited an inverse relationship between economic well-being and ecological balance. Others have suggested a positive relationship between social justice and economic well-being. At this point, we simply want to note that there are a variety of complex and important dimensions of the human condition. But, to limit and better define my analysis in this chapter and to attempt something manageable, I have chosen to focus on economic well-being.

Table 3.1 provides data on the economic well-being, and factors related to it, of individuals living in 140 countries around the globe. The first few columns in the table tell us something about the state of well-being across the 140 states. Drawn from Ruth Sivard's handbook, *World Military and Social Expenditures 1980*, the first column represents an index of economic-social standing. The index is based upon eleven different indicators: GNP per capita, five indicators of educational standing, and five indicators of health standing.[10] Unfortunately, the Economic-Social Standing Index tells us almost nothing about the distribution of well-being among individuals within countries. For example, only one of the eleven indicators in the index (the percentage of girls in total high school enrollment) begins to reflect the *distribution of values* within societies.

The next two columns in Table 3.1 reflect the rank and levels of GNP per capita across states. Although national data such as these are notoriously unreliable, particularly in some countries, they can be helpful if used with care. The GNP per capita indicator calls attention to the great contrasts between the developed states of the North and the developing states of the South ($5853 versus $548), between the United States and some of its neighbors ($8743 versus $641 for El Salvador and $216 for Haiti), and among other combinations of states. Although a possible indicator of the economic and social well-being of populations, it also suffers because of its insensitivity to the investment and distribution of resources within countries. For example, the distribution of wealth may vary considerably among both individuals and groups in a society, and the proportion of GNP invested in the social realm may vary markedly from one country to another. Although countries may have identical GNP per capita levels, some may distribute and invest the resources rather equally among their populations, while others may distribute them very unequally. Furthermore, some states may spend most of their resources in the military sector while others invest the majority in social programs. Although useful in some respects, the GNP per capita indicator is not sensitive to these investment and distribution issues.

The next six columns in Table 3.1 allow us to compare other indicators of well-being—namely, certain dietary characteristics—across states. Like other social and economic indicators, the data call attention to the great contrasts in the world. While 98 percent of the American people have access to safe drinking water, less than 15 percent of their South American neighbors in Haiti and Paraguay do. It seems to me that this does tell us something of fundamental importance about the human condition. Think about it the next time you go to the water fountain. Still, these dietary indicators, while helpful for cross-national comparison, obviously do not tell us all we need to know. For example, maldistribution of safe water and food within countries may mean that individual diets and safe drinking vary significantly from the national averages.

What are governments doing to improve the human condition and the value of well-being in their societies? The next few

(Text continued on p. 108)

TABLE 3.1 Military and Social Indicators of Economic Well-Being (140 countries, 1977)

		GNP		NUTRITION				WATER	
	Economic-Social Standing[1]	per Capita		Calorie Supply per Capita[2]		Calories as % of Requirements		% Population with Safe Water	
	Avg. Rank	Rank	U.S. $	Rank	Number	Rank	%	Rank	%
WORLD			1,838		2,581		108		53
Developed			5,853		3,387		132		93
Developing			548		2,320		100		39
AMERICA									
North America			8,712		3,518		133		98
United States*	5	8	8,743	7	3,537	15	134	8	98
Canada*	7	10	8,428	24	3,346	27	126	8	98
Latin America			1,260		2,550		107		57
Argentina	33	45	1,848	23	3,359	25	127	50	66
Barbados	36	48	1,659	35	3,048	11	136	8	98
Bolivia	78	76	677	97	2,134	110	89	84	34
Brazil	54	53	1,443	60	2,522	61	106	59	55
Chile	47	55	1,250	51	2,644	58	108	47	70
Colombia	69	71	758	84	2,255	86	97	53	64
Costa Rica	50	51	1,444	65	2,477	51	111	44	72
Cuba	42	73	752	52	2,636	47	114	56	56
Dominican Republic	67	68	823	102	2,107	99	93	59	55
Ecuador	63	66	854	101	2,109	100	92	81	36
El Salvador	79	80	641	105	2,075	104	91	61	53
Guatemala	77	65	856	93	2,166	78	99	76	39
Guyana	60	87	515	69	2,431	60	107	33	84
Haiti	117	113	216	115	2,040	106	90	108	12
Honduras	88	96	426	106	2,074	100	92	74	41
Jamaica	46	50	1,456	49	2,663	38	119	31	86
Mexico	60	58	1,153	48	2,668	46	115	54	62
Nicaragua	68	62	927	67	2,453	55	109	56	56
Panama	42	56	1,166	73	2,357	70	102	37	77
Paraguay	71	74	710	43	2,779	36	120	107	13
Peru	65	71	758	78	2,286	86	97	68	47
Trinidad and Tobago	42	40	2,631	46	2,684	51	111	21	93
Uruguay	38	51	1,444	34	3,098	42	116	25	92
Venezuela	40	39	2,633	63	2,480	76	100	41	75
EUROPE									
NATO Europe			5,261		3,332		130		91
Belgium*	17	13	8,195	4	3,565	11	135	28	88
Denmark*	4	7	8,910	17	3,432	23	128	1	99
France*	10	16	7,214	12	3,458	8	137	14	97
Germany, West	6	11	8,415	22	3,362	27	126	1	99
Greece	32	33	2,901	16	3,441	6	138	52	65
Iceland*	8	12	8,387	40	2,939	49	113	1	99
Italy*	24	28	3,360	11	3,462	8	137	31	86
Luxembourg*	18	6	9,419	4	3,565	11	135	8	98
Netherlands*	15	14	7,710	25	3,324	32	124	14	97
Norway*	3	9	8,592	32	3,126	40	117	8	98
Portugal	42	47	1,764	18	3,424	2	140		na
Turkey	73	59	1,142	41	2,916	42	116	48	68
United Kingdom*	16	24	4,388	26	3,305	20	131	1	99

TABLE 3.1 (Continued)

HEALTH		EDUCATION			MILITARY			
Public Expenditures per Capita		Public Expenditures per Capita		Health and Education Expenditures as Percentage of GNP	Public Expenditures per Capita		Defense Expenditures as Percentage of GNP	Physical Quality of Life Index
Rank	U.S. $	Rank	U.S. $		Rank	U.S. $		
	62		98	13.2		86	4.7	60
	230		336	9.7		274	4.7	na
	8		21	5.3		26	4.7	na
	319		568	10.2		436	5.0	
12	304	8	557	9.8	7	465	5.3	94
6	460	3	676	13.5	22	167	2.0	95
	15		42	4.5		19	1.5	
57	14	64	44	3.1	52	46	2.5	85
37	64	30	144	12.5	116	4	0.2	89
83	7	77	28	5.2	82	12	1.8	43
59	13	74	33	3.2	76	16	1.1	68
50	25	65	43	5.4	53	45	3.6	77
83	7	91	16	3.0	103	7	0.9	71
70	10	40	95	7.3	92	9	0.6	85
48	32	44	76	14.4	53	45	6.0	84
68	11	94	15	3.2	80	14	1.7	64
78	8	68	37	5.3	66	26	3.0	68
73	9	85	22	4.8	85	11	1.7	64
83	7	94	15	2.6	85	11	1.3	54
63	12	67	40	10.1	88	10	1.9	85
124	1	138	1	0.9	127	2	0.9	36
63	12	91	16	6.6	92	9	2.1	51
41	49	40	95	9.9	85	11	7.6	84
78	8	58	56	5.5	92	9	0.8	73
57	14	80	26	4.3	71	22	2.4	54
54	18	51	67	7.3	96	8	0.7	80
113	2	103	11	1.8	88	10	1.4	75
73	9	82	25	4.5	70	23	3.0	62
42	48	39	99	5.6	106	6	0.2	85
59	13	68	37	3.5	71	22	1.5	87
34	74	31	142	8.2	56	43	1.6	79
	272		287	10.6		194	3.7	
11	329	9	532	10.5	14	255	3.1	93
2	573	6	602	13.2	17	207	2.3	96
9	398	15	416	11.3	11	281	3.9	94
4	477	19	345	9.8	10	282	3.3	93
31	83	62	49	4.5	23	164	5.6	89
3	486	23	275	9.1		–	–	96
23	165	28	168	9.9	34	88	2.6	92
32	81	12	511	6.3	35	81	0.9	92
5	461	5	655	14.5	13	273	3.5	96
6	460	4	660	12.8	12	276	3.2	96
40	53	53	65	6.7	45	59	3.3	80
73	9	55	62	6.2	43	63	5.5	55
20	209	21	281	11.2	16	213	4.8	94

(*continued*)

TABLE 3.1 (Continued)

	Economic-Social Standing[1]	GNP per Capita		NUTRITION: Calorie Supply per Capita[2]		NUTRITION: Calories as % of Requirements		WATER: % Population with Safe Water	
	Avg. Rank	Rank	U.S. $	Rank	Number	Rank	%	Rank	%
ALL NATO (incl. U.S. and Canada)			6,747		3,412		131		94
Warsaw Pact			3,392		3,470		135		60
Bulgaria*	26	35	2,840	3	3,594	1	144		na
Czechoslovakia*	20	26	4,234	13	3,450	2	140	35	78
Germany East*	14	22	5,094	2	3,610	6	138	34	82
Hungary*	29	32	3,094	9	3,494	17	133	72	44
Poland*	27	30	3,303	1	3,647	5	139	68	47
Romania*	31	37	2,780	21	3,368	25	127		na
USSR*	24	29	3,326	14	3,443	15	134		na
Other Europe			4,314		3,295		130		83
Albania	55	77	665	53	2,624	55	109		na
Austria*	11	20	6,375	6	3,547	11	135	28	88
Finland*	9	21	6,245	31	3,130	42	116	44	72
Ireland*	21	34	2,883	8	3,519	2	140	43	73
Malta	33	46	1,846	33	3,103	30	125	42	74
Spain	28	31	3,205	27	3,210	21	130	35	78
Sweden*	1	5	9,460	29	3,168	39	118	1	99
Switzerland*	2	4	10,025	20	3,386	27	126	18	96
Yugoslavia	40	43	2,094	10	3,469	8	137		na
AFRICA			506		2,262		97		30
Algeria	75	60	1,119	73	2,357	80	98	37	77
Angola	112	107	287	111	2,063	115	88		na
Benin	119	118	199	95	2,153	94	94	84	34
Botswana	86	82	560	107	2,070	110	89	70	45
Burundi	129	128	136	83	2,260	86	97		na
Cameroon	104	99	390	70	2,408	65	104	87	32
Central African Rep.	127	121	191	86	2,250	76	100		na
Chad	137	132	121	131	1,793	131	75	90	26
Congo	90	89	481	88	2,234	74	101	78	38
Equatorial Guinea	105	93	442		na		na		na
Ethiopia	140	134	109	130	1,838	129	79	113	8
Gabon	57	38	2,638	71	2,403	67	103	116	1
Gambia	121	116	202	79	2,281	90	96	108	12
Ghana	95	84	540	119	2,014	115	88	82	35
Guinea	125	119	196	126	1,921	124	83	104	14
Ivory Coast	97	70	808	57	2,563	51	111	104	14
Kenya	100	105	293	112	2,060	110	89	98	17
Lesotha	99	111	256	96	2,138	94	94	98	17
Liberia	102	92	446	72	2,374	67	103	103	15
Libya	33	19	6,478	38	2,946	30	125	30	87
Madagascar	101	112	219	63	2,480	55	109	91	25
Malawi	128	127	150	79	2,282	80	98		na
Mali	138	134	109	100	2,114	106	90		na
Mauritania	125	106	289	128	1,894	126	82	98	17
Maurilius	58	75	700	58	2,557	49	113	55	60

TABLE 3.1 (Continued)

HEALTH		EDUCATION			MILITARY			
Public Expenditures per Capita		Public Expenditures per Capita		Health and Education Expenditures as Percentage of GNP	Public Expenditures per Capita		Defense Expenditures as Percentage of GNP	Physical Quality of Life Index
Rank	U.S. $	Rank	U.S. $		Rank	U.S. $		
	292		407	10.4		298	4.4	
	78		154	11.4		276	8.1	
39	57	37	110	5.4	42	68	2.4	91
24	135	33	128	6.2	25	126	3.0	93
28	112	25	204	6.2	19	190	3.7	93
34	74	34	119	6.2	40	69	0.2	91
27	117	36	111	6.9	30	108	3.3	91
42	48	47	70	4.2	53	45	1.6	90
36	70	27	169	7.2	8	348	10.5	91
	190		226	9.6		103	2.4	
70	10	74	33	6.5	47	55	8.3	75
12	304	17	352	10.3	39	73	1.1	93
10	352	13	467	13.1	32	92	1.5	94
22	173	26	179	12.2	50	62	1.8	93
38	63	52	66	7.0	75	21	1.1	87
29	94	45	74	5.2	48	54	1.7	91
1	644	2	798	15.2	9	325	3.4	97
9	356	10	522	8.8	18	206	2.0	95
32	81	37	110	9.1	31	96	4.6	84
	6		25	6.1		20	4.0	
63	12	42	93	9.4	63	28	2.5	41
89	5	107	10	5.2		–	–	16
104	3	66	41	23.1	124	3	1.5	23
63	12	107	10	3.9		–	–	51
124	1	68	37	27.5	124	3	2.2	23
104	3	124	4	1.2	106	6	1.5	27
104	3	99	14	8.9	116	4	2.1	18
124	1	115	8	7.4	106	6	5.0	18
78	8	129	3	2.3	87	25	5.2	27
94	4	101	13	3.8	71	22	5.0	28
124	1	133	2	2.7	111	5	4.6	20
46	42	32	138	6.8	61	29	1.1	21
89	5	110	9	6.4		–	–	25
89	5	85	22	5.0	57	42	7.8	35
94	4	103	11	7.6	116	4	2.0	20
59	13	49	69	10.1	96	8	1.0	28
89	5	94	15	6.8	88	10	3.4	39
113	2	110	9	4.3		–	–	48
78	8	94	15	5.2	116	4	0.9	26
30	84	18	350	6.7	27	125	1.4	45
94	4	110	9	5.9	111	5	2.3	41
113	2	124	4	4.0	124	3	–	30
124	1	122	5	5.5	116	4	0.4	15
104	3	89	17	6.9	60	30	10.4	17
52	20	61	52	10.3	132	1	–	71

(continued)

TABLE 3.1 (Continued)

		GNP		NUTRITION				WATER	
	Economic-Social Standing[1]	per Capita		Calorie Supply per Capita[2]		Calories as % of Requirements		% Population with Safe Water	
	Avg. Rank	Rank	U.S. $	Rank	Number	Rank	%	Rank	%
Morocco	98	82	560	56	2,568	61	106	63	51
Mozambique	130	129	135	125	1,930	126	82		na
Niger	135	123	172	113	2,051	119	87	89	27
Nigeria	103	81	570	77	2,291	86	97		na
Rwanda	124	125	164	81	2,277	80	98	48	68
Senegal	118	101	355	89	2,228	94	94		na
Serra Leone	122	117	200	103	2,101	104	91	108	12
Somalia	131	131	131	98	2,129	100	92	78	38
South Africa	72	97	424	39	2,945	36	120		na
Sudan	109	102	348	87	2,247	90	96	65	50
Swaziland	87	85	530	80	2,281	80	98	80	37
Tanzania	108	115	208	104	2,089	106	90	76	39
Togo	110	108	279	116	2,035	115	88	102	16
Tunisia	76	69	822	50	2,657	51	111	67	49
Uganda	110	104	327	107	2,070	110	89	82	35
Upper Volta	139	133	112	120	1,997	121	84	91	25
Zaire	112	122	183	75	2,312	65	104	96	19
Zambia	95	94	441	118	2,018	119	87	73	42
Zimbabwe	93	90	475	59	2,545	61	106		na
ASIA									
Middle East			1,878		2,753		112		73
Bahrain	38	25	4,291		na		na	1	99
Cyprus	51	44	1,868	36	3,047	33	123	20	95
Egypt	85	86	520	45	2,716	58	108	21	93
Iran	64	42	2,102	28	3,193	18	132	63	51
Iraq	66	49	1,594	76	2,306	90	96	40	76
Israel*	22	27	4,110	30	3,145	34	122	1	99
Jordan	81	78	657	110	2,067	121	84	37	77
Kuwait	23	3	12,518		na		na	27	89
Lebanon	53		na	62	2,495	74	101	25	92
Oman	74	41	2,570		na		na	62	52
Qatar	30	2	13,000		na		na	14	97
Saudi Arabia	56	15	7,335	66	2,472	70	102	14	97
Syria	80	66	854	54	2,616	64	105	46	71
United Arab Emurates	49	1	14,416		na		na		na
Yemen, Arab Rep.	123	95	435	92	2,179	106	90	115	4
Yemen, People's Dem. Rep.	106	103	343	127	1,897	129	79	21	93
South Asia			152		1,982		89		32
Afghanistan	133	114	212	122	1,974	128	81	112	9
Bangladesh	133	137	75	124	1,945	121	84	56	56
India	114	126	154	123	1,949	115	88	88	31
Nepal	136	136	101	107	2,070	94	94	113	8
Pakistan	119	120	192	84	2,255	80	98	91	25
Sri Lanka	84	109	262	114	2,043	100	92	96	19

TABLE 3.1 (Continued)

HEALTH		EDUCATION			MILITARY			
Public Expenditures per Capita		Public Expenditures per Capita		Health and Education Expenditures as Percentage of GNP	Public Expenditures per Capita		Defense Expenditures as Percentage of GNP	Physical Quality of Life Index
Rank	U.S. $	Rank	U.S. $		Rank	U.S. $		
83	7	71	36	7.7	59	38	6.8	41
124	1	133	2	2.2	111	5	3.7	25
113	2	119	7	5.2	127	2	1.2	13
83	7	84	23	5.3	63	28	4.9	25
124	1	124	4	3.0	116	4	2.4	27
94	4	102	12	4.5	96	8	2.2	25
104	3	115	8	5.5	127	2	0.1	27
94	4	119	7	2.4	88	10	7.5	19
89	5	56	61	15.6	36	80	18.3	53
104	3	103	11	4.0	80	14	4.0	36
70	10	76	31	7.7	127	2	0.4	35
94	4	107	10	6.7	96	8	3.8	31
104	3	87	21	8.6	103	7	2.5	27
52	20	60	55	9.1	65	27	3.3	47
94	4	110	9	4.0	96	8	2.4	40
124	1	129	3	3.6	116	4	3.6	16
113	2	110	9	6.0	106	6	3.3	32
59	13	78	27	9.1	106	6	1.4	28
73	9	89	17	5.5	61	29	6.1	46
	30		108	7.4		237	12.6	
21	180	29	164	8.0	29	112	2.6	61
51	24	57	59	4.4	58	41	2.2	85
78	8	78	27	6.7	28	119	22.9	43
47	33	35	118	7.2	15	222	10.6	43
73	9	58	56	4.1	24	138	8.7	45
25	127	22	280	9.4	2	1,045	25.4	89
68	11	80	26	5.6	40	69	40.5	47
19	231	11	520	6.0	6	659	5.7	74
	na	73	35	na	67	25	na	79
44	47	43	91	5.4	4	844	32.8	na
18	235	1	2,131	18.2	1	1,257	9.7	31
26	125	7	561	9.3	3	939	12.8	29
94	4	63	48	6.1	25	126	14.7	54
15	264	20	288	3.8	5	822	5.7	34
113	2	124	4	1.4	76	16	3.7	27
94	4	99	14	5.2	67	25	7.3	33
	2		4	3.8		5	3.2	
124	1	129	3	1.9	116	4	1.9	18
124	1	138	1	2.7	132	1	1.3	35
113	2	122	5	4.5	111	5	3.2	43
124	1	133	2	4.9	132	1	1.0	25
124	1	124	4	2.6	82	12	6.2	38
94	4	115	8	4.6	127	2	0.8	82

(continued)

TABLE 3.1 (Continued)

		GNP		NUTRITION				WATER	
	Economic-Social Standing[1]	per Capita		Calorie Supply per Capita[2]		Calories as % of Requirements		% Population with Safe Water	
	Avg. Rank	Rank	U.S. $	Rank	Number	Rank	%	Rank	%
Far East			850		2,413		103		43
Burma	115	130	133	90	2,211	70	102	98	17
Cambodia	116		na	129	1,857	124	83	70	45
China	82	100	378	68	2,439	70	102		na
Indonesia	107	110	259	99	2,115	80	98	111	11
Japan*	11	18	6,517	42	2,847	34	122	8	98
Korea, North	82	79	648	44	2,730	40	117		na
Korea, South	69	63	879	47	2,682	47	114	50	66
Laos	132	138	86	121	1,979	110	89	74	41
Malaysia	58	61	969	55	2,594	42	116	84	34
Mongolia	52	64	870	61	2,510	67	103		na
Philippines	92	91	455	94	2,155	93	95	65	50
Singapore	37	36	2,794	37	3,039	18	132	18	96
Taiwan	62	57	1,160		na		na		
Thailand	98	98	422	91	2,193	78	99	91	25
Vietnam	93	124	167	117	2,032	94	94	104	14
Oceania			5,558		3,418		129		58
Australia*	11	17	7,028	19	3,413	23	128		na
Fiji	48	54	1,279		na		na		na
New Zealand*	18	23	4,440	14	3,443	21	130	21	93
Papau New Guinea	91	88	505		na		na	19	20

columns in Table 3.1 tell us how much money governments spend annually per capita on health, education, and the military. Among other things, these indicators tell us something about a country's priorities and what it is trying to do. When we examine U.S. expenditures per capita across the three sectors, we find that relatively similar amounts are invested per capita in each ($304 in health, $557 in education, and $465 in military). In contrast, the emphasis in the USSR is decidedly on the military ($70 in health, $169 in education, and $348 in military), while in Sweden it is on health and education ($644 in health, $789 in education, and $325 in military). The data also tell us something about what countries have available to spend. While the United States, the USSR, and Sweden have considerable resources to invest in all three sectors, a country like Haiti has little to invest annually in any sector ($1

TABLE 3.1 (Continued)

HEALTH		EDUCATION			MILITARY			
Public Expenditures per Capita		Public Expenditures per Capita		Health and Education Expenditures as Percentage of GNP	Public Expenditures per Capita		Defense Expenditures as Percentage of GNP	Physical Quality of Life Index
Rank	U.S. $	Rank	U.S. $		Rank	U.S. $		
	23		40	7.4		25	3.0	
124	1	133	2	2.3	111	5	3.8	51
	na		na	na		na	na	40
88	6	94	15	5.6	71	22	5.8	69
113	2	119	7	3.5	96	8	3.1	48
16	247	16	363	9.4	44	60	0.9	96
113	2	88	19	3.2	45	59	9.1	na
113	2	83	24	3.0	49	53	8.0	82
124	1	133	2	3.5	92	9	10.5	31
55	17	53	65	8.5	51	49	5.1	66
63	12	47	70	2.4	38	78	9.0	na
104	3	115	8	2.4	82	12	2.6	71
45	43	46	71	4.1	21	179	6.4	83
113	2	103	11	1.1	33	90	7.8	86
104	3	91	16	4.5	79	15	3.5	68
124	1	129	3	2.4	76	16	9.6	54
	246		347	10.7		138	2.5	
12	304	14	443	10.6	20	184	2.6	93
49	29	49	69	7.7	103	7	0.5	80
17	238	24	254	11.1	37	79	1.8	94
56	16	71	36	10.1	96	8	1.6	37

SOURCE: Data reprinted with permission from *World Military and Social Expenditures 1980*, by Ruth Leger Sivard, © 1980 World Priorities, Leesburg, VA 22075. Physical Quality of Life figures are reprinted with permission from *Measuring the Conditions of the World's Poor*, by Morris David Morris, © 1979, Pergamon Press.

*Developed; — none or negligible; na = not available.

1. Represents average of ranks for GNP per capita, education, and health.
2. Per capita supply of food, including fish, in calories.

per capita in health, $1 in education, and $2 in military). The developed countries spend an average per capita of $230 on health, $336 on education, and $274 on military, while the developing countries spend $8, $21, and $26 respectively. As we shall discuss later, the level of economic development is a powerful predictor of public expenditures.

Another useful way of looking at what governments do that affects the human condition is to examine their expenditures as a percentage of GNP. The next two columns in Table 3.1 provide

TABLE 3.2 Government Expenditures as Percentages of GNP, 1977

	Health/Education Expenditures (%)	Defense Expenditures (%)
Sweden	15.2	3.4
United States	8.8	6.0
Switzerland	8.8	2.0
USSR	7.2	11.9
Saudi Arabia	9.3	12.8
Iran	7.2	14.2
Israel	9.9	27.7
Egypt	6.7	44.3

data on health and education expenditures and defense expenditures as percentages of GNP. The summary figures in Table 3.2 select a few cases for closer examination and comparison.

While most states listed invest relatively similar amounts of their GNPs in health and education (Sweden is clearly the deviant case, spending twice the percentage as some others), there is considerable variation in the defense figures. The countries in the Middle East (particularly Egypt and Israel) spend a much greater amount of their GNPs on defense. While their expenditures in health and education do not appear to suffer unduly, one must question how this level of defense spending is affecting the human condition.

Looking at these expenditure figures in more global terms also suggests some important and interesting findings and trends. Surprisingly, military expenditures internationally constitute a relatively small amount of global GNP and actually decreased from 7.06 percent in 1960 to 5.21 percent in 1976. Although this might belie apparent trends toward an escalating global arms race, the decrease is concentrated in heavily industrialized nations. Defense expenditures as a percenage of GNP increased 300 percent from 1.78 percent to 5.38 percent during the 1960-1976 period for developing countries. The implications of these figures are therefore most significant for the Third and Fourth World countries in their early stages of development. Increasing defense spending and militarization of many developing societies may inhibit their economic potential and do further damage to the human condition of their people. The military sector competes with the civilian sector for scarce scientific and management talents, raw materials and resources, and transportation facilities. In summary, comparative examination of public expenditures, both cross-temporal and cross-national, can draw attention to some important indicators of and variables related to the human condition.

The final column in Table 3.1 contains data purporting to reflect the "physical quality of life." The indicator is based on infant mortality, life expectancy, and basic literacy data and is claimed to be an unbiased, nonideological, and nonethnocentric index reflecting important elements that should be included in a humane existence.[11] How do states compare on this indicator of well-being? How do various groups and individuals within states compare?[12] Rankings and scores of countries worldwide on the index range from a high of 97 for Sweden to lows of 18 for Afghanistan and 12 for Guinea-Bissau. When looking within countries, we find that white Americans had a Physical Quality of Life Index (PQLI) score of 95 in 1974, while nonwhites had a score of 88. Although the reasons for these differences and the relationships between the PQLI and other variables such as socioeconomic development will be examined in greater detail in the next section of the chapter, we should note here that poor countries tend to have low PQLIs, while high-income countries tend to have high PQLIs. Yet, the relationships between GNP and PQLI are not all that close. Deviations exist at all levels of income, but they are particularly evident at the upper and lower levels of the per capita income range. This raises some important questions for the comparativist. For example, what explains these deviations? For the present, we shall simply note that the index supplements our judgments of well-being and does provide a useful variable that allows cross-national and cross-temporal analysis of relationships. In the next section we shall examine why the quality of life varies so significantly across states.

There are obviously far more data sources reflecting on the human condition than included in Table 3.1. There are those prepared by international organizations, such as the UN's various yearbooks[13] and other UN-related publications.[14] Since 1948, the International Monetary Fund has published *International Financial Statistics* providing standardized and detailed data on operations of central governments and summary data for state and local governments.[15] While researchers should be cautious about errors and distortions, national governments publish extensive data on social, economic, and demographic issues. Finally, academic efforts such as the Yale Political Data Program,[16] the *Cross Polity Survey*,[17] and SUNY's publications [18] add to the wealth of data on the human condition, and on governmental policies and other domestic and global forces related to it.

Again, we should note that aggregate data, such as those reported in Table 3.1 and mentioned above, poorly define and often obscure real individual needs, aspirations, and achievements. While they help define the human condition of large groups of people, they often tell us little about the econmic, social, and psychological characteristics of individuals. These characteristics and issues should not be ignored, and more should be done to develop better indicators for comparing individuals. It should be noted that there have been some noteworthy efforts to collect and analyze such individual-level data over the years. Hadley Cantril's work, *The Pattern of Human Concerns*,[19] Daniel Lerner's *The Passing of Traditional Society*, Philip Jacob's *Values and the Active Community*, and Alex Inkles's *Becoming Modern*,[20] and other studies are important efforts to delve into the individual dynamics of social change, values, and the human condition. In addition, worldwide public opinion polling using the latest survey research methods, even in communist states, is adding more individual-level data to our data banks.[21] The cross-national use of individual-level data in conjunction with aggregate data is an important and rewarding application of contextual analysis. For example, what impact do rapid socioeconomic change and improvements in the physical quality of life have on certain spiritual and psychological dimensions of the human condition? Such questions can be asked and at least partially answered given present data resources.

Perhaps it is appropriate to conclude this section by noting that while there are considerable data telling us something about the state of well-being across states and what governments are attempting to do to promote it, we should be sensitive to the gaps and problems in the data and endeavor to do something about them. While there are far more data problems than we have time to discuss here, a few should be mentioned.

For example, there is the problem of *reliability*. Are the data reliable and accurate? Did those reporting and tabulating make any errors? Were there any willful distortions by governments or individuals to mislead others about their countries? There is also the issue of *validity*. Does the indicator actually reveal what it is supposed to reveal? Just as a thermometer measures only bodily heat and not the overall state of individual health, public expenditures for health do not tell us about the overall state of health care in a country. Public expenditure data often mask the influence of the private sector. Quality health care can be provided in the absence of impressive expenditures. There are groups of caring people who support, nurse, and nourish one another in the absence of modern hospitals and costly "cat scanners." Quality education can also be provided in the absence of modern facilities, expensive equipment, and other things that require lavish expenditures. There are good schools that meet in the open air of tropical countries, and effective teachers who earn less than $1000 a year. One way to improve the validity of measurements is to avoid single indicators and attempt to include qualitative, nonethnocentric indicators in a more comprehensive index.[22]

Another problem in comparative studies is that of *functional equivalence*. Do the indicators tap the same underlying dimension in different countries? When examining expenditures for social welfare, for example, we must recognize that social welfare means rather different things in different countries. In addition, some countries support welfare through government expenditures, while others tend to do it privately, through families, voluntary associations, and the like. Other indicators and conceptions of the human condition—for example, human rights—incur the problem of functional equivalence and are often susceptible to ethnocentrism. Comparativists must take care to measure and compare what they say they are measuring and comparing.

Comparing Relationships

What do we know about forces impacting on the human condition? Why is the state of economic well-being higher in some states than in others? Why do some governments appear to be more supportive of the welfare of their peoples than others? Why have some governments been able to raise the physical quality of life in settings of economic stringency, while others in similar settings have had little or no success? Our search for answers and explanations requires us to focus on "cause-and-effect" relationships. For example, what is the relationship between economic development and the quality of life, or ideology and public expenditures?

Before we begin to examine some of the forces that impact on governmental policy and the human condition, we should be reminded of some of the potential pitfalls encountered in this line of comparative inquiry. Of foremost importance is the problem of inferential fallacies. To avoid the *ecological fallacy* we must remember that correlatives of aggregated data for a group may not hold for individual members of that group. Robinson's classic example pointed to a highly negative statistical correlation between levels of literacy and percentage of black inhabitants.[23] The hasty conclusion that blacks tend to be illiterates would be false, since the correlation of data on the individual level washes out the relationship almost entirely. This fallacy is a troublesome one when using aggregated data such as those listed in Table 3.1.

The opposite of the ecological fallacy is the *individualistic fallacy*, which would attribute to a group the characteristics of an individual. To assume that motivation among individuals will universally produce citizens with a higher quality of life does not mean, necessarily, that the nation with the most motivated citizens will have the highest quality of life. Third, the *universal fallacy* occurs when the analyst fails to notice that the presence or absence of a statistically significant relationship between a pair of variables for a universe may cover up a rather different relationship for the same variables within subgroups. A good example of this fallacy is the following. The correlated relationship between PQLI and per capita GNP for the universe of 114 countries is .79. However, when the universe of 114 is broken into four subgroups, the following relationships are found:

Low-income countries (N = 35)	.17
Lower-middle-income countries (N = 28)	.24
Upper-middle-income countries (N = 45)	.45
High-income countries (N = 29)	.28

GNP per capita is obviously a better predictor of PQLI in some countries than it is in others. Finally, there are other inferential fallacies—selective, contextual, historical, and cross-sectional—of which the comparativist focusing on relationships should be aware.[24]

Many of the variables and relationships of interest to the comparativist lack quantitative indicators. The comparativist should attempt to develop functionally equivalent concepts and variables no matter how primitive. Furthermore, comparativists must be able to make judgments when few or no data exist. Many of the concepts with which we work are not easily amenable to quantitative operationalization.

Global Forces

What impact do global forces have upon the human condition? While states are powerful actors, much of what happens to their citizens today is beyond their control. The impact of the world energy crisis upon domestic economies and economic policy and the impact of the superpowers upon client states are but two examples in a long list of external forces. The literature, some of which is summarized below, reflects a growing recognition of the importance of the forces outlined in Figure 3.1.[25]

International developments such as wars obviously have a powerful effect on states, governmental welfare policies, and people. Maurice Bruce has noted that "the decisive event in the evolution of the [British] welfare state was the Second World

War."[26] The war brought about both nationalized industry and social insurance and services. British social service spending rose from 37.6 percent to 46.1 percent of total government expenditures between 1938 and 1950. Defense spending fell from almost 30 percent to less than 20 percent of total spending in the same period. Others agree with Bruce and suggest that World War II was the decisive event bringing a flowering of the welfare state.[27] Still others argue that the war brought about the national security or "warfare" state.[28] While the causative role of World War II in the "welfare-warfare nexus" is complex and much of the research is open to question and further investigation, we cannot deny or disregard the impact of wars. The influence of Vietnam on the Great Society programs in the United States and of the cold war on defense spending in East and West suggest that more limited wars can also impact in significant ways on governmental policies and welfare outcomes.

Comparativists should also examine the impact of international economic crises and trends upon a nation's physical quality of life, economic-social standing, and public expenditures. The struggle of the Third World nations for a "New International Economic Order" is based on the assumption that the structure and operation of the existing international economic system has a negative, discriminating impact on less developed states. The contemporary global energy shortage, inflationary trends, and patterns of international monetary exchange are impacting on the economies, policies, and well-being of peoples in developing and developed states alike. Kindleberger's study of the Great Depression brought attention to the spread across national boundaries of enormous decreases in wages and prices, in investments and trade, and other catastrophic economic consequences; and Cameron's comparative study of the public economy found that the openness of the economy (dependence on external economic conditions) is a powerful determinant of the expansion of welfare services.[29]

The influence of foreign states on the policies of others also represents a significant relationship worthy of comparative analysis. The various types of influence can be conceptualized in terms of Rosenau's penetrative, reactive, and emulative categories.[30] American penetration of Western Europe and Soviet penetration of Eastern Europe are examples of the impact of superpowers on the policies and the status of the human condition in other countries. Clearly, there have been significant relationships for decades between the desires of the United States and the USSR and the allocation of values (and choices between welfare and warfare) in other systems. The Soviet Union has had a major impact on the human condition in the East European states over the postwar era; the United States has had a powerful impact on Western Europe. However, present trends toward greater nationalism may suggest decreasing penetrative relationships and an increase in *reaction* and *interreaction.* A European Economic Community economist notes that policy choices made in the European states are strongly influenced by decisions on the other side of the Atlantic.[31] One might add that they are also affected by events and decisions on the other side of the Oder-Neisse and in Japan. Some note that the United States is reacting in important respects to the problems and policies of the Europeans and other industrialized countries.[32] Defense spending in the NATO countries in the 1970s and early 1980s has become highly interactive. *Emulation* also describes certain relationships between foreign countries and the policies of others. Albert has argued: "The American example is . . . at the root of the frame of reference adopted in Europe, especially in such matters as educational policy, the relations between industries and the universities, and a better awareness on the part of the government of its responsibilities towards workers and firms."[33] Although this may have been truer in the European past than it is in the present, emulation is still a significant influence at work in the world.

There are many opportunities for comparative studies of the relationships between external forces—such as wars, economic trends, and foreign states—and the human condition and well-being indicators such as those discussed in the preceding section and listed in Table 3.1. For example, what is the relationship between dependence on external economic conditions and welfare services? While Cameron and a few others have begun to raise these questions, much work remains to be done.

Historical and Developmental Forces

Comparative analysis of global policy studies must also consider the impact of environmental forces on the human condition. Figure 3.1 calls attention to some of these, including historical, ideological, and socioeconomic forces. Our consideration of environmental determinants is rooted in the ideas of Social Darwinism and the notion that humans (and the human condition) are creatures of their environments.

What, if anything, about a country's past helps explain contemporary policy and outcomes? Furthermore, what cultural, socioeconomic, or political forces in the history of a country are significant determinants of its physical quality of life? Table 3.3 shows changes in the PQLI for 34 countries from *circa* 1950 to *circa* 1970. Although Morris notes that these PQLIs should be used with caution, they suggest some interesting differences and relationships worthy of the comparativist's attention.[34] For example, India showed slow growth in per capita income yet exhibited significant improvement in its PQLI over the 1950-1970 period. Despite an identical per capita GNP growth rate and a level of income considerably higher than India's, Algeria exhibited considerably less PQLI improvement. Using Morris' Disparity Reduction Rate (DRR) as a standard for evaluating change, India's average annual PQLI improvement was about three times that of Algeria's during the twenty-year period.[35] Bulgaria's rate of improvement was considerably higher than both. To what extent are historical and developmental forces responsible for these differences? Morris feels that it is essential to examine each case individually in order to be able to interpret historical data.

Although such individual analyses and case studies are useful, the comparativist should attempt to identify relationships that hold across cases (countries) and across time. For example, we should examine the hypotheses of the "cultural determinists,"

TABLE 3.3 PQLI Performance and Per Capita GNP Growth Rates for Various Countries circa 1950, 1960, and 1970 (ranked by "1950" PQLI)

	PQLI			Average Annual DRR, 1950s-70s[1]	Avg. Annual Per Capita GNP Growth Rate, 1950-70
	circa 1950	circa 1960	circa 1970	(%)	(%)
India	14	30	40	1.7	1.8
Turkey	30	42	55	2.1	3.5
Egypt	32	42	43	0.8	1.2
Algeria	34	36	41	0.6	1.8
Nicaragua	42	53	54	1.2	3.2
Malaysia	47	47	67	2.2	2.3
Colombia	47	66	71	3.1	1.6
Ecuador	48	60	68	2.7	2.0
Reunion	48	60	70	3.4	–
El Salvador	51	61	64	1.5	2.0
Brazil	53	63	68	1.6	2.7
Mauritius	55	67	71	2.4	–1.9
Mexico	55	65	71	2.3	3.1
Philippines	55	60	72	2.2	2.6
Thailand	55	58	70	1.7	3.8
Venezuela	58	69	79	3.2	3.0
Portugal	62	69	80	3.2	–
Chile	62	65	77	2.8	1.5
Taiwan	63	77	87	5.1	5.3
Sri Lanka	65	75	80	3.4	1.9
Costa Rica	67	78	86	3.7	2.4
Jamaica	68	80	87	4.6	4.7
Panama	68	73	81	2.5	3.2
Trinidad	69	81	87	4.1	4.0
Martinique	72	78	86	4.2	–
Cyprus	72	82	85	2.8	3.8
Bulgaria	74	79	89	5.6	–
Puerto Rico	74	83	91	5.2	–
Argentina	77	82	85	2.1	1.9
Hungary	80	87	90	3.2	–
Greece	82	84	88	2.4	5.8
Italy	80	87	92	5.0	5.0
Israel	84	86	89	1.9	4.7
United States	89	91	93	2.1	2.4

SOURCE: Reprinted with permission from *Measuring the Conditions of the World's Poor*, p. 75, by Morris David Morris, © 1979, Pergamon Press.

1. Average annual DRRs are calculated for the actual number of years between "1950" and "1970" PQLIs.

who contend that cultural forces are significant influences of policy and policy outcomes.[36] Is there something embedded in the culture of certain countries or regions that impedes improvement in indicators of economic well-being such as the PQLI? Comparativists should also examine the views of "political determinists," who claim that political events, strong leaders of political movements, and ideas are the crucial influences affecting governmental policies and policy outcomes. This breed of historical determinists would place less importance on the culture of, say, China and Russia and more on the impact of Lenin and Leninism, Mao and Maoism.[37]

Socioeconomic structures form another constellation of historical forces worthy of greater consideration. Theda Skocpol's excellent analysis of the impact of these forces on postrevolutionary outcomes in China and the USSR is a good example of the type of comparative analysis that can be done.[38] Although the communist revolutions had significant impacts on the human condition in these two societies, Skocpol contends that contemporary policies and policy differences are tempered by the prerevolutionary societal structures. Historical analysis of this sort not only is useful in explaining the past but is also likely to be helpful in understanding the present and future. The likely outcomes of China's recent "four modernizations" program may be better understood, for example, after viewing the goals and program with Skocpol's research in mind. The difficulties already encountered by the post-Mao moderates suggest that such policy choices can be heavily influenced by historical sociostructural forces. While leaders have some latitude, they are also influenced and often significantly constrained by the past.

Some policy choices and outcomes may be less affected by the past than others. For example, although complete PQLI data are not available for the communist period in China, available information suggests that the PQLI increased significantly under Mao. The Chinese communists were apparently rather effective in promoting this dimension of human condition. Although historical forces no doubt influenced choices and outcomes, they did not rule out rapid social change. One of the central questions confronting comparativists is why some societies can undergo fundamental and rapid change, particularly in some policy areas such as economic well-being, while others appear to be so resistant to change. This and other equally important questions and relationships confront comparativists engaged in historical analysis.

Ideological Forces

What is the relationship between idcology and the human condition around the globe? Marxism and welfare? Western democratic values and human rights? Do symbols and ideas have a significant impact on the allocation of values and the course of human dignity? Although a cross-national and cross-temporal study by Lerner, de Sola Pool, and Lasswell did not address these questions explicity, the authors identified ideological trends that have important implications for global welfare. By comparing ideology—defined as the special vocabulary a government elite uses to reveal its social goals—through content analysis in five countries (the United States, the United Kingdom, France, Germany, and the USSR) over a sixty-year period (1890-1950), Lerner and his colleagues identified a disturbing trend toward a world of "garrison-prison states" and away from "a democratic international community."[39] They found this trend marked by a "parochialization of attention" and decreases in symbols naming, describing, and advocating the social goal of human dignity. Similarly, Gerald and Patricia Mische describe a world of "national security states" motivated by militaristic competition and national leaders unable to move toward more humanistic, person-centered values and public policy.[40] If these purported trends in ideology and values are real, they would seem to have obvious implications for the human condition and economic well-being. Certainly, when one examines contemporary military expenditures versus expenditures for foreign aid and international peacekeeping, the trends of increasingly militaristic ideologies are apparent, and the impact on the individual and the human condition disturbing.[41]

Other studies have taken an explicit look at the relationship between ideology and policy. Anthony King examined a variety of policy areas in West Germany, France, Great Britain, Canada, and the United States in order to determine why the policies of some were distinctive.[42] He found that, with the exception of education, the United States introduced all social services later and tended to spend less on them than did the other four Western countries. According to King, the underlying reason was the enduring antistatist orientation in the American ideology. While many agree with King that ideology has a powerful impact on policy, others are more skeptical. Harold Wilensky has sought to refute the widely held contentions about the influence of ideology on welfarism.[43] His study suggested that ideology consistently adds nothing to our understanding of variations in social security systems. Siegel and Weinberg also question the impact of ideology by noting that "most of the strong advocates of 'ideological determinism' employ no quantitative evidence."[44] While the relationships are complex and the findings of various scholars mixed, ideas and symbols appear to be important forces in the contemporary world. Their impacts on economic well-being and the course of human dignity are worthy of continued attention.

Social and Economic Forces

The social and economic settings in a country, region, or community are important determinants of the level of economic well-being. As the research of many has noted, social and economic forces are also related to other important dimensions of the human condition. In one published essay, Han Park found significant relationships between a number of social and economic forces, what he referred to as indicators of modernization, and different indicators of human rights practices around the world.[45] Other social scientists have established relationships between social and economic forces and various aspects of political life. Karl Deutsch examined the relationship between social mobilization and political development;[46] Seymour Martin Lipset, be tween economic development and democracy;[47] Han Park, between the pace of socioeconomic development and democratic performance;[48] and Benjamin and Kautsky, between economic development and communism.[49] There is a healthy tradition of empirical research focusing on the social and economic forces of politics and policy. Students of global policy studies should not ignore it, but improve it, build upon it, and fill the existing gaps.

With respect to the relationship of economic development and governmental welfare policies, a good deal of research suggests that the wealthier the nation, the greater proportion of its GNP will be spent for public consumption purposes. The comparative studies of Dawson, Robinson, and others on American states call attention to the influence of economic forces.[50] Dye's research on the linkages between economic development variables, political system characteristics, and over ninety separate policy output measures in education, health, welfare, and so forth indicated that the economic development variables were powerful predictors of policy.[51] Dye concluded that, on the whole, economic resources were more influential in shaping state policies than any of the political variables previously thought to be important in policy determination.

However, Siegal and Weinberg hold that while this general relationship holds true around the globe, a significant qualification ought to be recognized.[52] They argue that the relationship between economic wealth and policy outputs for public purposes appears to be strongest for nations undergoing the process of modernization. Why should this be the case? Frederick Pryor argues that modernizing countries confront a series of problems that leaders attempt to meet through greater public exertions.[53] The agenda for public policymaking expands dramatically as countries undergo economic development. Industrialization creates new infrastructural and social needs. However, after countries are relatively wealthy and industrialized, the impact of economic forces on governmental policy is reduced and the influence of political forces apparently expands. This suggests that decision makers in developing countries are, to a considerable extent, captives of developmental imperatives. National policies and governmental expenditures are largely determined by, or are in response to, socioeconomic forces. The ideas and strategies of leaders, the argument goes, are of relatively minor significance. If you want to change the human condition in developing countries, then, you try to change the socioeconomic situation and worry less about political ideologies, national leaders, and governmental strategies. As noted above, Black, Paige, and others would disagree with this notion, at least in part, and argue that leaders and politics can have a more powerful impact than the socioeconomic determinists suggest.[54] Obviously, more work needs to be done on what causes states and leaders to show greater concern for the welfare of their peoples.

There are others in addition to Dye and Pryor who argue that greater welfare spending is brought about by, or is in response to, socioeconomic forces. Phillips Cutright concludes that "the introduction of social security measures is a response by government o changes in the economic social order."[55] In *The Welfare State and Equality*, Harold Wilensky concludes that economic development is the root cause of welfare state development.[56] Obviously, economic development does have a good deal to do with economic well-being. Morris's study, for example, found a strong positive relationship between countries' per capita GNP and the PQLI. The data below indicate that countries with low incomes tend to have lower physical quality of life scores:[57]

	Average PQLI Score
Countries with per capita GNP under $300	40
Countries with per capita GNP $300-$699	67
Countries with per capita GNP $700-$1999	68
Countries with per capita GNP $2000 and over	92

The scatter diagram observations charted in Figure 3.2 outline the nature of the relationship between per capita GNP and PQLI. The correlation of .79 suggests that this particular economic force is related positvely to this particular dimension of the human condition. But are higher levels of economic development *always* related to higher quality of life indicator? The simple answer is no.[58] While the relationship between per capita GNP and PQLI is strong, the correlation is not 1.0. There are a number of significant deviations from the general pattern. Why? Why, for exam-

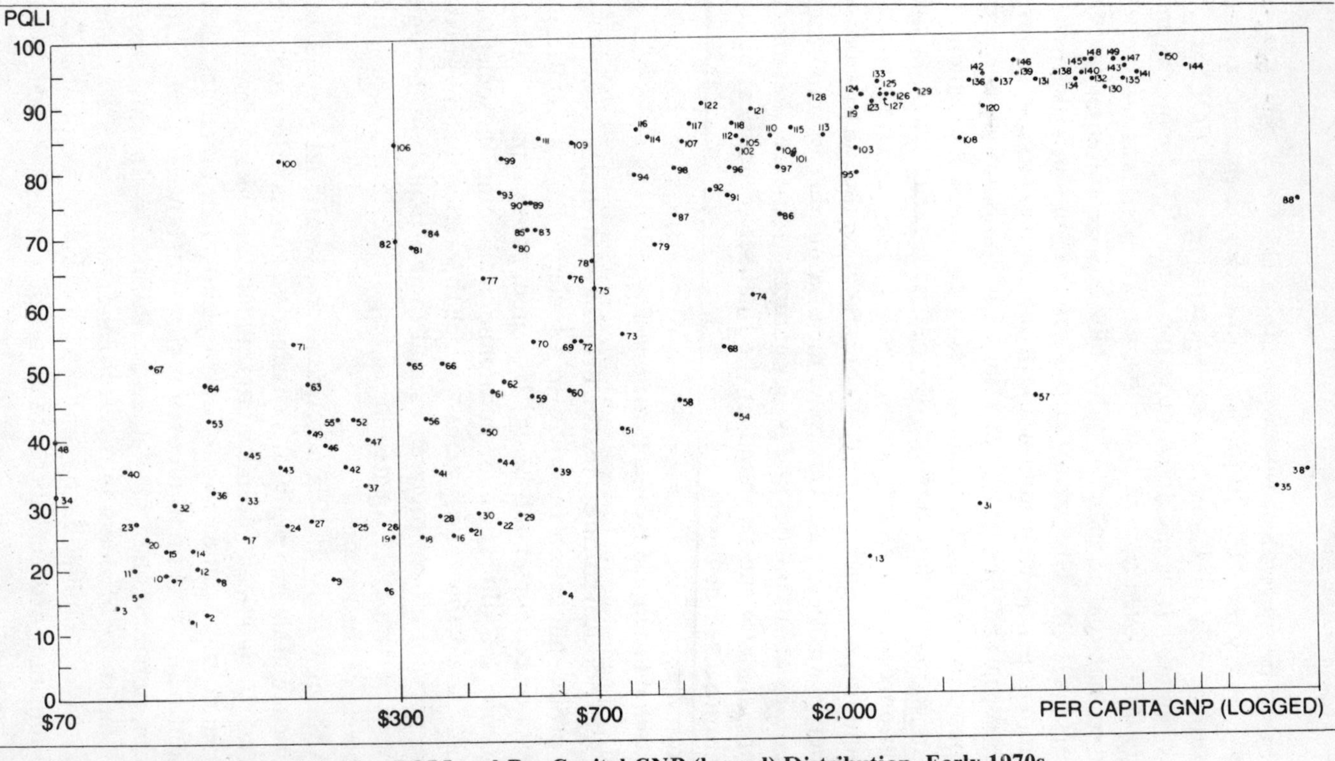

Figure 3.2 Scatter Diagram Showing PQLI and Per Capital GNP (logged) Distribution, Early 1970s

SOURCE: Reprinted with permission from *Measuring the Conditions of the World's Poor*, p. 65, by Morris David Morris, © 1979, Pergamon Press.

ple, does Saudi Arabia, with a per capita GNP of $3529, have a low PQLI score of 29? How is Costa Rica, with a per capita income of only $884, able to achieve a relatively high PQLI of 85? And why did Iran and India have the same PQLI scores in the early 1970s, even though Iran's per capita GNP was nine times higher than that of India? Finally, how has Ireland been able to achieve a PQLI equivalent to that of the United States, even though its per capita income is about one-third as large? These are interesting and important questions for comparativists. Many comparativists believe that advances in the forces of production, or in economic development, do not necessarily result in the creation of a just and equitable society. They believe that the development of such a society is contingent on the use to which a society's wealth is put. This issue raises a number of important questions about politics and policy choices. Some feel that many of the answers can be found in the final set of political forces conceptualized in Figure 3.1.

Political Culture and Political Participation

Does political culture—that is, beliefs and attitudes concerning the proper allocation of values in a society—have a significant impact on economic well-being? How does political participation influence the allocation of economic well-being in societies? Finally, are democratic systems—which theoretically show greater respect for citizen preferences and their articulation through various participatory forms—more responsive to the needs and interests of their people?

Although some have undertaken cross-national studies of political culture and political participation and have linked these forces to significant political dependent variables,[59] few have related political culture to public policy and policy outcomes such as well-being. One important study that did, however, was "The International Studies of Values in Politics."[60] In this cross-national study of values in India, Poland, the United States, and Yugoslavia, Phillip Jacob and his associates examined the relationships between the elite political culture of 400 local leaders and policy outputs in their locales. They attempted to determine why some communities grow and progress while others stagnate, and how some satisfy social needs while others fail to serve civil goals. In other words, the study sought to determine what impact the values of local leaders had upon public vitality, social progress, and economic well-being. While Jacob and his associates found that political culture and values are overwhelmed in certain cases by other forces—for example, the impetus or constraint of economic resources or entrenched political authority and opposition—they concluded that there are, in fact, important political cultural influences on policy, progress, and the human condition.

What about citizen participation? What impact does political participation have on public expenditures and indicators of economic well-being? Nie and Verba define political participation as "those legal activities by private citizens which are more or less directly aimed at influencing the selection of government personnel and/or the actions they take. . . . We are basically interested in . . . acts that aim at influencing *governmental* decisions. . . . We are abstractly interested in attempts to influence the authoritative allocation of values for a society."[61] Who has effectively or successfully linked participation to the allocation of values? No one, to my knowledge, but some, such as Jerry Hough, have suggested innovative ideas on how we might consider doing it.[62] This is an area for some exciting contextual analysis relating individual political attitudes and participatory behaviors to policy outputs, such as governmental expenditures, and outcomes, such as the PQLI. While the research will be difficult, conceptually and practically, it is a promising area for students of global policy studies.[63]

Political Structures and Institutions

Are there institutional or structural roots of public expenditures, economic well-being, human rights, or inequality? Is there anything in the realm of political structures and institutions that will help us explain why India was able to have a PQLI similar to

Iran's in the 1970s, even though its per capita income was only one-ninth as great as Iran's? Are there political-structural factors that help us explain why Bulgaria and Cuba have been able to improve their PQLI levels substantially over the last thirty years while El Salvador and Egypt have not?

There are a number of scholars who suggest the importance of political structures and institutions. Hugh Heclo describes structural characteristics that have produced different solutions and outcomes in different countries.[64] Douglas Ashford calls attention to the influence of parliamentary factors by noting that when "looking at a variety of policy developments [in Britain] over the past two decades, it is remarkable how each is affected in its conception, its evaluation, and its implementation by the needs of parliamentary governments."[65] Phillips Cutright concludes that while the level of economic development best explains variation in social service coverage, political representativeness helps explain variations in social service programs among nations at similar levels of economic development.[66] Finally, Carl Friedrich characterizes constitutions as significant politcal forces.[67] Knowing about a country's constitution may tell us something about human rights, civil liberties, and the human condition. While it is obvious that the presence of absence of a constitution, or bill of rights, does not alone determine the human rights practices of a country, the comparativist will want to ascertain why some constitutions are respected and others are not, why they have a positive impact on human rights policies in some countries and not in others.

Other scholars have explored interesting research questions that we ought to recognize and build upon in global policy studies. Some have examined the linkage between types of political systems and public policy. In an analysis of twenty-one developed and democratic systems, Guy Peters and his associates examined the relationship between four system types (depoliticized, consociational, centripetal, and centrifugal) and distributive, self-regulative, regulative, and redistributive policies.[68] The findings indicated that centrifugal political systems displayed the highest level of distributional policies and the centripetal democracies displayed the highest level of self-regulative policies. Research of this type is useful in exploring even more interesting and significant relationships between political systems and human welfare. For example, do some systems maximize the opportunities for human dignity while others impede them? Do different types of political systems do more to promote human concerns than others?

Alexander Groth has made a compelling case, in a couple of important studies, that different political systems do, in fact, produce different outcomes of consequence to individuals. In the first, Groth characterizes government types as either pluralistic democracies, innovative mobilizing autocracies, or traditional quiescent autocracies.[69] Examining both the benefits (such as public consumption expenditures) and burdens (such as taxation) of governmental policy, Groth contends that democracies distribute benefits and burdens more equitably among their citizens than either type of autocracy. Under traditional autocratic regimes, great inequalities were endemic in terms of consumption taxes, rate structures, and so forth, all of which tend to discriminate against the "have-not" sectors of societies. Furthermore, allocations to public health, education, and popular culture were found to be conspicuously low, while bureaucratic and military allocations were found to be more generous. Overall, Groth found that "the gulf between 'ins' and 'outs' tends to be greater in authoritarian regimes than in democracies."[70] He concludes that, all other things being equal, the type of political regime will affect an individual's social welfare.

In another project, Groth attempted to determine the impact of "system type" (Marxist-Leninist versus non-Marxist-Leninist) on policy.[71] Holding the level of economic development constant, Groth hypothesized that Marxist-Leninist states are likely to provide more substantive welfare benefits to industrial workers than world states generally. The hypothesis was tested comparing worker pensions and benefits in eleven Marxist-Leninist states with those of fifty-nine nonsocialist states. The comparison group consisted of all states whose GNP per capita fell between the lowest-ranking state (PRC) and the highest (Czechoslovakia). Groth concluded that Marxist-Leninist states provide higher levels of social welfare at lower direct cost to the worker than their non-Marxist counterparts and that political regime characteristics are important determinants of social welfare policy.[72]

Groth's findings relate to our earlier query about the apparent success of Marxist-Leninist states in raising their PQLI levels. Raising the level of social welfare appears to have been a high-priority goal in Marxist-Leninist states, and the centralization of political authority with Communist party systems, institutionally and structurally, has allowed a reasonably small group of political elites within Communist parties to see that it was done. This apparent success of Marxist-Leninist states in the welfare sector, however, is complemented by critical shortcomings in other areas. The events in Poland in the early 1980s indicate that there are other concerns related to the human condition that are important to people. Although Polish workers have money to spend, there often is little to buy. Meat, produce, and consumer goods in Poland and elsewhere in Eastern Europe are in short supply. Polish citizens are also concerned about certain freedoms, human rights, and the role of the individual in the political system. That these are issues very much affected by the political system is suggested by the interest of the Polish workers in making basic fundamental changes in the structure of the system. An implicit assumption of the Polish workers' movement is that structural changes will result in an improvement in the human condition.

The State, Political Actors, and Policymaking

Many political scientists feel that we underestimate the impact and power of the state, its leaders, and politics not only in affecting policy outputs, outcomes, and the human condition, but also in affecting global and environmental forces. Some, such as Ashford, even suggest that policy can be viewed as a "cause" of politics.[73] The types of policies a government pursues supposedly structure the kind of politics likely to ensue. If the government is attempting to enact redistributive measures, for example, the actors, arena, and form of interaction will be different from what would result if other types of policies were being considered.

Other scholars would encourage us to give more emphasis to the linkage between political forces and the dependent variables in Figure 3.1, and also to emphasize a feedback arrow running from the political forces to the global and environmental in order to call attention to the impact of political forces.[74] Glenn Paige argues that it is a mistake to consider politics and policymaking dependent variables and "prisoners" of their own traditions. He cites the role of politics in developing countries such as China and North and South Korea to show that political behavior can be conceived as a causal and relatively autonomous force in many cases. Others agree with Paige. Robert Vincent Daniels undertook a comparative study of the Russian and Chinese revolutions and concluded: "In present-day communism, the political structure is not a reflection of the economic base, but its creator; political power and inspired willful leadership become the prime movers of history."[75] Mao himself seemed to recognize the influence of political forces: "If we do not win," he wrote in 1945, "we will blame neither heaven nor earth, but only ourselves."[76]

As noted earlier, Anthony King has conducted some systematic research that examines a variety of political forces and relates them to public policy. One of the publications from this research asks what governments do and why they do it.[77] King notes that while the countries of North America and Western Europe are often described similarly as welfare states, there are wide divergencies among them and these divergencies need to be explained. Among other things, King examines the role of the state in the United States, Canada, Britain, France, and West Germany and asks how the states came to play the roles that they do. Modern governments in these states do a broad range of things. In addition to the conduct of defense and foreign affairs, they educate the young, provide social services, operate railways, and manufacture steel, cigarettes, and other things. In so doing, they have considerable impact on the economic well-being and human condition of their peoples.

King's research indicates that the five countries "have pursued policies that diverge widely, at least with respect to the size of the direct operating role of the state in the provision of public services."[78] As might be expected, the United States differs more from the other countries—and is likely to differ more in the years ahead —than they do from each other. For example, the United States introduced most social services later and spent less on them than did its counterparts. Why is this so? Among other forces, King examines the role that political elites and interest groups might play in explaining these differences. It could be maintained, King argues, that government plays a smaller role in the United States because, unlike the other four countries, the United States is dominated by an elite that wishes to inhibit the expansion of state activity and succeeds in doing so.[79] Although this may seem quite reasonable, particularly within the political context of the early 1980s and an antistatist Reagan administration, King argues that this elite explanation is really not plausible. The character and successful domination of elites did not seem to vary significantly among the five states during the time period King studied. Whether they will in the future and whether possible differences will be of consequence to the human condition is an interesting question. The strategy of the Reagan administration in the early 1980s seems to be more and more distinct from other Western democracies. Although the possible impact of the U.S. strategy on economic well-being is now unclear, it should be discernible in the years ahead.

King also asked whether the more limited U.S. role in social services might be explained by certain political actors, such as interest groups, that have opposed and prevented the expansion of government.[80] After examining three propositions concerning the impact of interest groups, King concludes they are not all that important in explaining the distinctive U.S. policy position. Furthermore, neither are the institutional factors he considers. King finally concludes that the most satisfactory single explanation of the distinctive U.S. policy response to the welfare state is also the simplest: "The state plays a more limited role in America than elsewhere because Americans, more than other people, want it to play a limited role."[81]

While this finding lends support to our earlier consideration of ideology, political culture, and public opinion, it seems quite reasonable to expect the other political factors King considers to have an impact on policy in certain states, under certain circumstances, in certain issue areas. We should not generalize from his limited study that public opinion is the most important determinant of policy across time and space. What King's research should tell us is that through careful comparative study, we can make some progress in sorting out the apparent forces of policy.

A final study worth mentioning in this regard is a bold cross-national (125 states), cross-sectional (1968 data) study by Gulman Haniff.[82] Haniff related such political variables as participation, party representation, competition, stability, and party system to social policy outputs (such as percentage of total national expenditures allocated to welfare programs) and social policy outcomes (such as number of physicians, average life expectancy, infant mortality, and death rates). Though political conditions were found to exert limited influence on social policy, the research does suggest some useful ways to operationalize political forces, policy outputs, and policy outcomes in line with Figure 3.1. C. Bradley Scharf's research also makes an important contribution in this regard by examining four environmental variables, four political variables, and three measures of social security in eight countries.[83] As a final note on political factors, we should call attention to the policy process itself. What impact does the way governments make policy have upon the human condition? In *Comparing Political Systems*, my co-authors and I argue that the policymaking process itself has much to do with a government's ability to achieve designated goals such as social development and economic well-being.[84] "Muddling through," the predominate mode of policymaking, seems to plague decision-making units around the world. Many in the Third World are plagued by an error-prone process of policymaking that makes it particularly difficult to mobilize national resources for desired ends. Energy, resources, and ideas are wasted as such countries confront worsening economies with obvious costs to the people and to the human condition. On the other hand, some decision-making units are able to make policy in a more planned, rational, and comprehensive way. They systematically study policy goals and challenges, carefully consider alternative courses of action, and more effectively utilize resources to serve societal goals. In my estimation, politics is the art of the possible. It does make a difference.

Evaluating and Comparing Political Performance in Global Perspective

The preceding parts of the chapter have viewed the subject of global policy studies and the human condition rather mechanistically. The discussion centered on a cybernetic approach to "inputs and outputs," or global, environmental, and political forces—policy outputs and outcomes involving the human condition. In short, the presentation was more in the tradition of "pure" or positivist global policy science. I would like to note, however, that global policy studies should do more than describe, analyze, and explain; they should do more than examine the relationships outlined in Figure 3.1. Global policy studies should also evaluate and recommend, criticize and clarify, and engage in ethical and normative commentary. These missions raise a host of important questions.

First, can we analyze and evaluate governmental performance related to the human condition? Can we determine if capitalist economies are outperforming centrally planned economies in meeting basic human needs? Are socialist or capitalist systems more successful in promoting human dignity? Is the quality of life all it is cracked up to be in Sweden and Switzerland? Do Italy, Turkey, Kampuchea, Poland, and South Africa have as serious problems as are reported? Is their governments' performance of consequence to the human condition? In order to analyze, evaluate, and compare political performance, or what governments are doing to improve the human condition, we need both logic and standards for judging performance.

Standards vary among individuals, groups, and societies around the world. What may be a reasonable level of economic well-being to a peasant in South America may be considered near poverty-level in Western Europe. In addition, values like economic well-being and social justice, peace and ecological balance, take on a rather different significance depending on the society one considers. Furthermore, problems associated with these values, like inequality or segregation, social conflict and environmental deterioration, take on a rather different meaning—sometimes these issues are not even considered problems—depending on whether we are talking about a Marxist-Leninist or a Western state, a less developed or a postindustrial country. The values and problems take on diverse meanings not only because of their varying significance in different countries but also because of the way they are viewed, analyzed, and evaluated. Inequality is considered a major problem and equality a high priority in the People's Republic of China. The same issues are viewed rather differently in the United States. How the issues are treated, what a government does to resolve problems, and how well a government performs depend very much on standards of judgment. Criteria of performance and standards of judgment are important concepts in global policy studies.

While I have argued for systematic study of global policy issues and the human condition, I am suggesting here that we not overlook some important normative issues in global policy studies. When we talk about standards and evaluating political performance, "global monitoring systems" and "measuring conditions of the world's poor," we are drawing attention to the normative elements of our field of study. Unfortunately, most research and scholarly activity in political philosophy and systematic political science go on in relative isolation. There are notable exceptions, of course, but more must be done in global policy studies to merge the normative issues of the philosophers and the scientific inquiry of the policy scientist. What is the good life? How do societies achieve it? Ideally, what we need in this emerging field are "philosopher-theorists-scientists-analysts." Policy scientists should not be blind to the unavoidable and critical normative and ethical implications of their studies.

Global policy scientists must also confront and comprehend the logic of evaluation. We must work from models and frameworks for evaluation. There can obviously be many models of appraisal. The model of the Marxist-Leninist will be different from that of the Western democrat. The model of the political scientist will not be that of the economist. The models used in law and medicine will be different from those that may be used in sociology, psychology, or philosophy. The models of scholars working in particular disciplines will not be the same as those taking a truly multidisciplinary approach. In all cases, however, we need an explicit, logically interconnected set of ideas and norms that allow us to evaluate, compare, and recommend.

These ideas, norms, standards, and criteria, then, will reflect different points of view, different disciplines, and different countries.[85] My own feeling is that the standards and logic of evaluation need not and perhaps should not be universal. Rather, they and our evaluation studies should maintain a healthy respect for the diversity found in the world and what different cultures and governments are trying to do. Charles Anderson notes: "A decent respect for the relativity of cultures and circumstances would seem to imply that an assessment of a government's intention is logically prior to an evaluation of its performance. The alternative is to risk normative ethnocentricity and ideological bias, if not sheer normative simple-mindedness."[86] Judging political performance against national goals and, on the other hand, against universal standards are both legitimate activities. However, it is important that the logic and standards of the evaluation be made explicit. As Charles Anderson writes: "It is one thing to render a judgment on a regime on the grounds that it failed to do what it set out to do, and quite another to rate it against some universal norm of political achievement. . . . Both . . . are appropriate to the agenda of comparative policy studies so long as we are clear about their implications.[87]

The proposal to establish a Global Monitoring System (GMS) and render judgments about political systems raises some interesting implications concerning the possible role of evaluation in global policy studies.[88] The proposal is noteworthy for a number of reasons, including its effort to merge systematic, scientific studies with more normative and ethical concerns. Those proposing the GMS systems suggest that policy scientists ought to contribute to the sharing and shaping of values by promoting and participating in a worldwide monitoring system. The proposed system would be designed to appraise policy formulation and execution by governmental actors on a global basis. Although the proposers talk more about evaluating national performance, they note that the idea is relevant to all levels of governance. The monitoring system they proposed would be a private, transnational organization (or, more likely, a series of competing organizations) consisting of policy scientists from all over the globe. The scientists would work to develop and use standardized indicators to monitor governmental actions and policy outcomes on professed official goals and on the attainment and distribution of basic human values.

The proponents of the Gobal Monitoring System agree with Anderson that evaluating performance and rendering judgments on the basis of professed goals and universal standards are both legitimate activities. To accomplish the former, they propose that we pay more attention to what leaders say, to the goals and standards they outline for their peoples and their own systems. Economic and developmental plans, party programs, and the like are examples of the sort of documents that ought to be studied. The proponents of the monitoring system also argue that there are universal standards against which we can legitimately appraise and compare performance. The Universal Declaration of Human Rights, or a set of basic human values, can be used as international standards for gauging performance. The idea is that there are certain things leaders are and are not doing, and that they ought to be held responsible. Appraisal involves attribution of the responsibility of governmental success and failure.

The GMS system, then, suggests the possibility of global policy scientists from around the world participating collectively in assessing governmental performance in terms of policy processes and actual outcomes. This transnational effort would undertake systematic projections of the probable consequences of current policy trends and disseminate the results of its studies on a periodic basis to concerned publics throughout the world. As a series of commentaries on the GMS proposal indicate, the idea has met with both support and optimism, and criticism and pessimism.[89] Although the GMS may not be an idea whose time has come, it is an important and provocative proposal that ought to be taken seriously by students of global policy studies. Perhaps it is an idea whose time will come, and should come, if today's students lay the necessary philosophical, conceptual, and political groundwork for the future.

A noteworthy effort that has undertaken policy evaluation and comparison on a global scale is Morris's *Measuring the Conditions of the World's Poor*.[90] Morris argues that as national and international concern for the needs of people mounts, it is becoming increasingly obvious that a new means of measuring the performance of countries is needed. Certainly, Morris argues, the traditional yardstick of economic performance—per capita GNP—does not provide adequate information about the life chances of individuals. Morris introduces a new indicator of social progress called the Physical Quality of Life Index (PQLI). As noted earlier, the PQLI can be used not only to look at relative performance among countries, but also to look at various sectors within countries. Are the needs of women being met as well as those of men? Rural and urban areas? Different ethnic groups? What changes have occurred over time? Obviously, economic resources and development have much to do with the physical quality of life. However, when used in conjunction with per capita GNP, the PQLI raises important questions that policymakers cannot ignore.

Although not without problems and shortcomings, the PQLI has much to offer policymakers and policy scientists. Among other things, it provides a reasonable measure of performance. The PQLI can be used by policy scientists in evaluation studies, by policymakers in appraising their own performance, and by others, such as foreign aid donors, in evaluating the impacts of their foreign assistance programs. The PQLI effort also provides a useful criterion for international decision-making, a tool for targeting and measuring social progress, and a stimulus for further research.[91] Obviously, there are important things the PQLI does not do. It does not measure economic growth, economic development, or total welfare. It does not measure effort, or identify the need for, or measure the results of, individual projects. Even though there are many things it does not do, and even though it may pose more questions than it answers, the PQLI offers some exciting ideas about evaluation in the field of global policy studies.

Conclusion

When a field is new or in its formative stages, much work is initiated and carried out without the necessary support of formal theory. That seems to be where we are in global policy studies. Ideally, our observations, descriptions, comparative examinations of relationships, and evaluations will be planned activities and be guided by some recognizable logic and theory. It seems to me that there are some useful theoretical notions around, and many of them are either explicit or implicit in much of the work reviewed here. Yet, more work of a conceptual and theoretical nature needs to be done. We should reexamine "old" theories and attempt to build new theories.[92] While the global problems and challenges to the human condition may magnify and become ever more urgent, we should not ignore the importance of theory. Intelligently addressing practical policy problems—welfare and warfare, health and disease, food and starvation, ecological balance and environmental deterioration—requires a theoretical basis. Good policy scientists and good policymakers are guided by theory whether they recognize it or not. To suggest that there are urgent problems crying out for solutions should not be interpreted to mean there should be a relaxation of scholarly and scientific rigor or to suggest the propriety of journalistic license and ideological polemic. Global policy scientists are different from journalists—they are not ideologues. Global policy studies must be guided by strenuous scholarly principles and rules.

Are the theoretical notions and ideas conceptualized in Figure 3.1 and described in the research and writings of others of any utility in our emerging field? Are they of any use as we engage in comparison, evaluation, and prescription? Perhaps this is for others to judge, but the preceding discussion is intended to be more than an academic exercise. To examine past research in terms of the suggested framework requires us to undertake some necessary tasks. It forces us to clarify, to analyze, to examine the contributions that others have made. I think it is important to build on the past. This does not mean that we should prolong past inadequacies and mistakes or needlessly stretch outdated work to fit the global challenges of today. But neither should we needlessly reinvent the wheel. Our scholarly inclinations for criticism and orginality can work against the sort of cumulative building process that often characterizes the growth of knowledge. Much important normative, theoretical, and applied work has been done. We should recognize it and build on it.

Obviously global policy studies as conceived in this chapter is a large order. The human condition is a broad concern and the forces that influence it nearly all-encompassing. To address this overwhelming task, our efforts must be multidisciplinary, cooperative, collaborative, and international in scope. Some efforts, like the GMS proposal or efforts to measure the conditions of the world's poor, should be macro; others will be micro. We must utilize our strengths and recognize our weaknesses. Many scholars will choose to work within the areas of their training and academic competence. Some political scientists will want to focus on political forces, policy, and the human condition. Policy-oriented economists like John Rawls may want to focus on economic issues and theories of justice.[93] Philosophers and theorists may address their attention to the meaning of the human condition,[94] and empiricists to measuring it.[95] Although global policy studies constitute a large and seemingly complex field, that field becomes much smaller and manageable if our work is intended to fit together. Relatedness is one of the assumptions of a field of study. Our work in global policy studies should be interrelated and cumulative. As in other areas of scholarly inquiry, progress will come through cross-fertilization, cooperation, and cumulative research.

If I were forced to sum up the arguments of this chapter, they might be that, first, global policy studies should strive to tell us more about the human condition. We need to know more about its meaning, its nature among individuals and groups, its causes and possible future on the planet Earth. Second, the rich traditions of comparative politics and comparative analysis have something to offer to our studies. We should recognize this work and see what it contributes to our evolving field. Third, in a broad and new field of inquiry like global policy studies, we need certain models, frameworks, and theories to define, guide, and enrich our studies. Four, we should not be impatient and expect unreasonably rapid progress. We should work independently and collectively, at micro and macro levels, on philosophical and practical problems. But if we have a field of study, we should work together. Fifth, what we do should be planned. There must be some level of agreement about the meaning and mission of the field. Efforts like the one in which we are all involved may help us achieve it.

Finally, this chapter is intended to start trains of thought, not stop them. In covering such a vast terrain I have slighted some matters, ignored others, and done injustices to many of them. However, because I view global policy studies as an evolving, cooperative area of inquiry, I am optimistic and hopeful that we can address them in the future.

NOTES

1. Harry Eckstein and David E. Apter, eds., *Comparative Politics* (New York: Free Press, 1963), p. 3.
2. George Thomas Kurian, *The Book of World Rankings* (New York: Facts on File, 1979), pp. 86-87.
3. Morris David Morris, *Measuring the Condition of the World's Poor* (New York: Pergamon Press, 1979).
4. Ruth Leger Sivard, *World Military and Social Expenditures 1980* (Leesburg, VA: World Priorities, 1980).
5. See the proposal of Richard C. Snyder et al., "A Global Monitoring System: Appraising the Effects of Government on Human Dignity," *International Studies Quarterly*, 2, 2 (1976), pp. 221-260.
6. See the chapter in this volume by Phil Meeks.
7. Harold Lasswell, *A Pre-View of Policy Sciences* (New York: Elsevier, 1971).
8. Robert C. Johansen, *The National Interest and the Human Interest* (Princeton, NJ: Princeton University Press, 1980).
9. See Snyder et al., "A Global Monitoring System"; Gary K. Bertsch et al., *Comparing Political Systems*, 2nd ed. (New York: John Wiley, 1982).
10. For the items and construction of the index, see Sivard, *World Military and Social Expenditures, 1980.*
11. Morris, *Measuring the Conditions of the World's Poor.*
12. Although the index is generally used for cross-national comparison, computations can easily be made to allow the comparison of subgroups within societies.
13. See the UN's *Demographic Yearbook* and various statistical yearbooks published annually.
14. See, for example, Wassily Leontief et al., *The Future of the World Economy: A United Nations Study* (New York: Oxford University Press, 1977), and such UN publications as *World Economic Survey, 1979-80, 1978 Report of the World Social Situation, Patterns of Government Spending on Social Services*, and *Economic and Social Consequences of the Arms Race and of Military Expenditures.*
15. *International Financial Statistics* is published monthly by the International Monetary Fund, Washington, D.C.
16. Charles Lewis Taylor and Michael C. Hudson, eds., *World Handbook of Social and Political Indicators*, 2nd ed. (New Haven, CT: Yale University Press, 1972).
17. Arthur S. Banks et al., eds., *Cross Polity Time-Series Data* (Cambridge: MIT Press, 1971).

18. See, for example, Arthur S. Banks and William Overstreet, eds., *The Political Handbook of the World—1980*; R. Peter Dewitt, Jr., and Arthur S. Banks, eds., *The Economic Handbook of the World—1981* (New York: McGraw-Hill, 1981).

19. Hadley Cantril, *The Pattern of Human Concerns* (New Brunswick, NJ: Rutgers University Press, 1966).

20. Daniel Lerner, *The Passing of Traditional Society* (New York: Free Press, 1958); Philip Jacob et al., *Values and the Active Community* (New York: Free Press, 1971); Alex Inkeles, *Becoming Modern: Individual Change in Six Developing Countries* (Cambridge: Harvard University Press, 1974).

21. There are worldwide affiliates of Gallup polls and other survey centers doing opinion and survey research on a global scale. For survey research in Communist countries, see William A. Welsh, ed., *Survey Research and Public Attitudes in Eastern Europe and the Soviet Union* (New York: Pergamon Press, 1980).

22. For an interesting discussion of this and related issues, see Norman Hicks and Paul Streeten, "Indicators of Development: The Search for a Basic Yardstick," *World Development*, 7 (1979), pp. 567-580.

23. W. S. Robinson, "Ecological Correlations and the Behavior of Individuals," *American Sociological Review*, 15, 3 (1950), pp. 351-357.

24. For a fuller discussion, see Hayward R. Alker, Jr., "A Typology of Ecological Fallacies," in Mattei Dogan and Stein Rokkan, eds., *Quantitative Ecological Analysis in the Social Sciences* (Cambridge: MIT Press, 1969), pp. 68-86.

25. For a more detailed discussion of global or external influences, see Richard L. Siegel and Leonard B. Weinberg, *Comparing Public Policies* (Homewood, IL: Dorsey Press, 1977), pp. 52-100. My discussion of global influences draws heavily on Siegel and Weinberg's fuller review.

26. Maurice Bruce, *The Coming of the Welfare States* (London: Batsford, 1968), p. 326.

27. See, for example, Alan J. Peacock and Jack Wiseman, *The Growth of Public Expenditures in the United Kingdom* (Princeton: Princeton University Press, 1961); Richard M. Titmus, *Essays on the Welfare State*, 2nd ed. (Boston: Beacon Press, 1963).

28. See, for example, Gerald Mische and Patricia Mische, *Toward a Human World Order* (New York: Paulist Press, 1977).

29. Charles P. Kindleberger, *The World in Depression, 1929-1939* (London: Allen Lane / Penguin Press, 1973); David R. Cameron, "The Expansion of the Public Economy: A Comparative Analysis," *American Political Science Review*, 72, 4 (1978), pp. 1234-1261.

30. James N. Rosenau, ed., *Linkage Politics: Essays on the Convergence of National and International Systems* (New York: Free Press, 1969).

31. M. Albert, "Repercussions of the Economic Policy of the United States on the Politics of the European Economic Community," in Charles P. Kindleberger and Andrew Shonfield, eds., *North America and Western European Economic Policies* (London: Macmillan, 1971), p. 140.

32. Richard N. Cooper, *The Economics of Interdependence: Economic Policy in the Atlantic Community* (New York: McGraw-Hill, 1968), p. 142.

33. Albert, "Repercussions," p. 66.

34. Morris, *Measuring the Conditions of the World's Poor*, p. 74.

35. The DRR measures the rate at which the disparity between a country's PQLI performance and the best projected performance (100) decreased between two periods. Thus, a high DRR indicates a rapid annual reduction.

36. See S.N. Eisenstadt and Yael Azmon, eds., *Socialism and Tradition* (New York: Humanities Press, 1975).

37. See G. D. Paige, "The Primacy of Politics," in Paul G. Lewis et al., *The Practice of Comparative Politics*, 2nd ed. (London: Longman, 1978), pp. 360-371; Cyril E. Black, "Political Modernization," in Kurt London, ed., *Unity and Contradiction* (New York: Praeger, 1962). Black notes: "The victory of Communism in Russia and China may be regarded as in no sense inevitable but rather as a largely personal achievement of Lenin and Mao" (p. 15).

38. Theda Skocpol, "Old Regime Legacies and Communist Revolutions in Russia and China," *Social Forces*, 55, 2 (1976), pp. 284-315.

39. Daniel Lerner et al., "Comparative Analysis of Political Ideology: A Preliminary Statement," *Public Opinion Quarterly*, 15 (1951/1952), pp. 715-717.

40. Mische and Mische, *Toward a Human World Order*.

41. See Sivard, *World Military and Social Expenditures 1980*. Nations of the world spend approximately 2500 times as much on the machinery of war as on the machinery of peacekeeping.

42. Anthony King, "Ideas, Institutions and the Policies of Governments: A Comparative Analysis," *British Journal of Political Science*, 3 (July-October, 1973), pp. 291-313, 409-423.

43. Harold I. Wilensky, *The Welfare State and Equality* (Berkeley: University of California Press, 1975), pp. 42-49.

44. Siegel and Weinberg, *Comparing Public Policies*, p. 230.

45. Han S. Park, "Human Rights and Modernization: A Dialectical Relationship?" *Universal Human Rights*, 2, 1 (1980), 85-92.

46. Karl W. Deutsch, "Social Mobilization and Political Development," *American Political Science Review*, 55, 3 (1961), pp. 493-502.

47. Seymour M. Lipset, "Some Social Requisites of Democracy: Economic Development and Political Legitimacy," *American Political Science Review*, 53, 1 (1959), pp. 69-105.

48. Han S. Park, "Socio-Economic Development and Democratic Performance: An Empirical Study," *International Review of Modern Sociology*, 6 (1976), pp. 349-361.

49. Roger W. Benjamin and John H. Kautsky, "Communism and Economic Development," *American Political Science Review*, 62, 1 (1969), pp. 110-123.

50. Richard E. Dawson and James A. Robinson, "Inter-Party Competition, Economic Variables and Welfare Policies in the American States," *Journal of Politics*, 25 (1963), pp. 265-289.

51. Thomas R. Dye, *Politics, Economics, and the Public* (Chicago: Rand McNally, 1966).

52. Siegel and Weinberg, *Comparing Public Policies*, p. 23.

53. Frederick C. Pryor, *Public Expenditures in Capitalist and Communist Nations* (Homewood, IL: Irwin, 1968), pp. 280-312.

54. See note 37.

55. Phillips Cutright, "Political Structure, Economic Development, and National Social Security Programs," *American Journal of Sociology*, 70 (1965), pp. 537-550.

56. Wilensky, *The Welfare State and Equality*.

57. Morris, *Measuring Conditions of the World's Poor*, p. 61.

58. An interesting study prepared for the World Bank found that only five of sixteen indicators of basic needs were significantly related to economic development. See David

Morawetz, *Twenty-Five Years of Economic Development, 1950-1975* (Baltimore: Johns Hopkins University Press, 1978).

59. Gabriel A. Almond and Sidney Verba, *The Civic Culture* (Princeton, NJ: Princeton University Press, 1963); Sidney Verba, Norman H. Nie, and Jae-on Kim, *Participation and Political Equality: A Seven-Nation Comparison* (Cambridge, England: Cambridge University Press, 1978).

60. Jacob et al., *Values and the Active Community.*

61. Norman H. Nie and Sidney Verba, "Political Participation," in F.I. Greenstein and F.W. Polsby, eds., *Handbook of Political Science*, Vol. 4 (Reading, MA: Addison-Wesley, 1975), p. 1.

62. Jerry Hough, "The Soviet Experience and the Measurement of Power," *Journal of Politics*, 37, 3 (1975), pp. 685-710.

63. See, for example, Charles R. Foster, ed., *Comparative Public Policy and Citizen Participation: Energy, Education, Health, and Local Governance in the USA and Germany* (New York: Pergamon Press, 1980).

64. Hugh Heclo, *Modern Social Politics in Britain and Sweden* (New Haven, CT: Yale University Press, 1974).

65. Douglas E. Ashford, "The Structural Analysis of Policy or Institutions Really Do Matter," in Ashford, ed. *Comparing Public Policies: New Concepts and Methods* (Beverly Hills, CA: Sage Publications, 1978), p. 86.

66. Cutright, "Political Structure."

67. Carl J. Friedrich, "The Constitution as a Political Force," in Eckstein and Apter, *Comparative Politics*, pp. 133-140.

68. B. Guy Peters, John C. Doughtie, and M. Kathleen McCulloch, "Types of Democratic Systems and Types of Public Policy," *Comparative Politics*, 9 (1977), pp. 237-255.

69. Alexander J. Groth, *Comparative Politics: A Distributive Approach* (New York: Macmillan, 1971).

70. *Ibid.*, p. 267.

71. Alexander J. Groth, "Worker Welfare Systems in the Marxist-Leninist States; A Comparative Perspective," paper presented at the International Political Science Association World Congress, Moscow, 1979.

72. For two interesting articles that conclude that countries of the socialist bloc achieve unambiguously higher basic welfare than other countries, see Branko Horvat, "Welfare of the Common Man in Various Countries," *World Development*, 2, 7 (1974), pp. 29-39; Jay R. Mandle, "Basic Needs and Economic Systems," *Review of Social Economy*, 38 (1980), pp. 179-189.

73. Ashford,"The Structural Analysis."

74. Paige, "The Primacy of Politics."

75. Robert V. Daniels, "The Chinese Revolution in Russian Perspective," *World Politics*, 18, 2 (1961), p. 230.

76. Mao Tse-tung, *Selected Works*, Vol. IV (Peking: Foreign Languages Publishing House, 1960), p. 41.

77. King, "Ideas, Institutions and the Policies of Governments."

78. *Ibid.*, p. 409.

79. *Ibid.*, pp. 410-411.

80. *Ibid.*, pp. 413-415.

81. *Ibid.*, p. 418.

82. Ghulam M. Haniff, "Politics, Development and Social Policy: A Cross-national Analysis," *European Journal of Political Research*, 4 (1976), pp. 361-376.

83. C. Bradley Scharf, "Correlates of Social Security Policy: East and West Europe," *International Political Science Review*, 2, 1 (1981), pp. 57-72.

84. Bertsch, *Comparing Political Systems.*

85. Authors representing fourteen countries have recently prepared some noteworthy essays defining, measuring, and comparing the quality of life in different countries and different historical periods. See Alexander Szali and Frank M. Andrews, eds., *The Quality of Life: Comparative Studies* (Beverly Hills, CA: Sage Publications, 1980).

86. Charles W. Anderson, "System and Strategy in Comparative Policy Analysis," in W. B. Gwyn and G.C. Edwards II, eds., *Perspectives on Public Policy-Making* (New Orleans: Tulane University Press, 1975), p. 227.

87. Charles W. Anderson, "The Logic of Public Problems: Evaluation in Comparative Policy Research," in Ashford, *Comparing Public Policies*, p. 30.

88. Snyder, "A Global Monitoring System."

89. See the commentaries included in the September and December 1976 issues of *International Studies Quarterly.*

90. Morris, *Measuring the Conditions of the World's Poor.*

91. For a fuller discussion of what the PQLI does and does not do, see Morris, *Measuring the Conditions of the World's Poor*, pp. 93-105.

92. For a more comprehensive treatment of these issues, see the chapter in this volume by Miriam Steiner on global political theory.

93. John Rawls, *Theory of Justice* (Cambridge: Belknap Press of Harvard University Press, 1971).

94. See, for example, Hannah Arendt, *The Human Condition* (Chicago: University of Chicago Press, 1958).

95. See, for example, Robert Parke and David Seidman, "Social Indicators and Social Reporting," *The Annals of the American Academy of Political and Social Science*, 435 (1978), pp. 1-22; Jan Drewnowski, *Studies in the Measurements of Levels of Living and Welfare*, Report No. 70.3 (Geneva: United Nations Research Institute for Social Development, 1970); *Measuring Social Well-Being: A Progress Report on the Development of Social Indicators* (Paris: Organisation for Economic Cooperation and Development, 1976); *The Use of Socio-Economic Indicators in Development Planning* (Paris: UNESCO Press, 1976). For an effort to broaden the spectrum of social indicators to include goals of the "political left," see Johan Galtung, *The True Worlds: A Transnational Perspective* (New York: Free Press, 1980), pp. 431-465.

4

Interdisciplinary Analysis

Scientific Humanism in an Age of Specialization

PHILIP J. MEEKS

As the issues and problems facing humankind have become increasingly complex, a strong deductive tendency of social science analysis has been to break down every problem into its most minute aspects. There has been a strong preference for methods of theory testing that imitate mathematics and physics. Problems are classified and diagnosed according to stereotypical symptoms and set aside in the hope that this will aid in a perfected reconstruction.

Some benefits derive from such an approach. Since even basic aspects of problems may be difficult to work on, specialization enables one person to handle specific aspects of complex problems. Familiarity with certain common patterns in one's field allows greater experience and efficiency in overcoming these problems. Since no one can be expected to spend the time trying to learn all of the techniques involved in processing specific problems, specialization allows more work to be accomplished by fewer people with more accuracy. When problems can be dealt with using thousands of computer-programmed simple steps, capacity can be enormously increased, with lower costs and faster processing.

The tendency of specialization has been the key to the organization and management of the factory-industrialization process begun at least 250 years ago. This tendency is also crucial to all bureaucratic organizations where policies are implemented through the hierarachical ordering of specialized functions.

Many social scientists have long recognized that social problems cannot be understood if they are arbitrarily broken down into a range of classified parts. Too often the forces that give cohesion and form to identifiable parts of problems are lost in the search for a cure. Yet the organization of the study of social issues has progressively become more specialized. Part of this trend is economically motivated. In the 1960s and early 1970s the number of faculty positions rapidly increased to accommodate the postwar boom in the university enrollment and the demand for advanced degrees. The traditional rationalization for granting a doctorate in some field of study was a person's contribution to "original" research or understanding in that field. It became obvious to many that one way to claim originality was to study some very specialized aspect of a problem that no one else had studied before.

This is not to say that these more specialized studies were less important or accurate than many of the more general studies that preceded them. Quite to the contrary, many of the assumptions and simplistic generalizations of older general studies broke down when their component parts were carefully scrutinized. However, the quest for originality often led to the atomization of fields of study and growing irrelevance of individual social research for pragmatic solving of important social problems.

Specialization has also been fostered by the predominance of behavioralism and quantitative methodologies in the social sciences in the past thirty years. The quest to be "truly" scientific has led many social analysts to seek to imitate the physical sciences. Like the physicists who break molecules down into atoms and then into smaller and smaller subatomic particles in order to understand their interaction, many social scientists have tried to break down various social behaviors into smaller parts in order to improve the scientific "accuracy" of their analyses.

It is relatively easy to break down a problem into smaller and smaller components, but to put the parts back together in some meaningful fashion, it is agreed, is difficult. In order to accomplish the latter, one must have an ideal to serve as the image of reality. In the absence of an agreed-upon image, many social scientists have tried to perfect an understanding of their own specialities and simply to add them on to everyone else's. The result of this accumulation of minuscule parts is usually hopelessly contradictory, redundant, and of little practical use to those who must deal with the hard realities of the human condition. While scientists debate and search for more marginal factors to improve the statistical measures of causality, tens of thousands of human lives may be lost or impaired.

A good example of the fragmentation of a social problem into specialized parts can be found in the theories of development and modernization of societies. After World War II, when Western attention was focused on the massive problems of the countries of Asia, Africa, and Latin America, a group of social scientists decided that the root cause of the social, political, and economic instability of these countries was in "underdevelopment." In order for these societies to prosper, it was claimed, they need to become more "modern." Modernity was soon broken down into a host of subcharacteristics, such as communications, education, urbanization, industrialization, transportation, wealth, and consumption. Measures of modernity were then calculated in terms of radios and televisions per capita, levels of literacy, percentages of people living in cities with populations over 20,000, and so forth. In order to become more modern and supposedly more prosperous, countries in the poorest areas of the world were encouraged to increase their literacy, their numbers of radios, and the number of people living in cities. The standards of the most powerful and wealthy countries were defined as the most advanced and therefore worthy of imitation. When efforts to imitate the Western countries failed to improve significantly the living standards of these poor countries, new theories suggested that series and sequences of development must be followed in order to achieve success. Some may question whether modernity is really a desirable end state or just a figment of an analytical imagination.

The breaking down of the problem of "underdevelopment" into many specialized aspects—political underdevelopment, economic underdevelopment, institutional underdevelopment, and so on—is often compounded by another problem. Models of what is "proper" development have been highly ethnocentric. It may actually do more harm than good to stimulate isolated aspects of modernity without proper understanding of how they relate to a more holistic environment.

There is little disagreement with the perspective that the problems facing humankind are very complex and difficult. One must question, however, whether complexity must always be broken down into more simplistic categories in order to understand systematically how to ameliorate these conditions. The vast problems of hunger, war, hatred, and injustice cannot be solved by passing them down a specialized assembly line of social analysis in the blind hope that after thousands of small adjustments the situation will improve. We have spent too much time devising ways of evading responsibility for dealing with complex social problems by claiming to be capable of dealing with only a very small part of the solution. Moreover, we need to be motivated by a sense of urgency, as analysts and as humans, we cannot continue to engage in mere mental puzzle-solving while ignoring the immediate effects of global problems on millions of people every day. We must learn quickly how to put things back together in effective new ways rather continue to find new ways to take things apart.

This chapter examines the manner in which interdisciplinary and multidisciplinary analysis of global policy problems can aid the process of reintegrating our currently overspecialized understandings of complex issues. Three specific points are presented:

(1) Interdisciplinary analysis has an important intrinsic value in the understanding of contemporary global problems.

(2) Interdisciplinary analysis can help in the search for a consensus on appropriate global interest values needed to implement solutions to complex problems.
(3) The chapter shows some of the ways in which interdisciplinary analysis is indispensable in aiding the understanding of general policy objectives.

The Intrinsic Values of Interdisciplinary Analysis

The systematic analysis and understanding of reality, whether physical or social, has always been a collective enterprise. The interdependence of mathematics and physics is fundamentally obvious to any scientist. Relationships are verifiable and unquestioned except at the edges of theory building. The laws of physics are established as truth because many scientists can verify the laws with documented evidence through experimentation. This is not to suggest that there are no controversies, since collective consensus is needed to legitimize a law or causal explanation. In the words of Frankel,

> Ideological bias, compulsive inattention to facts that later seem obvious, the failure to draw implications that are there, and the repeated drawing of implications that are not there—all these are part of the physical scientist's analyses as well as of the historian's or sociologist's.[1]

It is not surprising that collective consensus on the systematic understanding of reality has been difficult to achieve. In the social sciences, perspectives that emphasize particular factors are scrutinized for any personal motives the authors may have. Specialization generally enhances credibility, but it requires intense preparation in very limited areas of knowledge. Universities, which should be integrated institutions of learning, have often become bastions of specialized cliques. In times of scarce resources, colleges and departments are often forced to fight each other in order to maintain their programs and positions. Faculty are discouraged from engaging in collective teaching situations by cumbersome regulations on required teaching loads. Even though students are granted degrees in liberal arts or natural sciences, increasing attention, if not predominant importance, is given to one's departmental specialization. General studies programs virtually disappeared from within many colleges, although they have returned in others. Programs of study that bridge the social and physical sciences are practically nonexistent, so students who try to close the gap may have to get separate degrees in each.

Many of the reasons for this overspecialized structuring of knowledge and analysis were given in the introduction to this chapter. Rationalizations of originality of research, behavioral reductionism in the social sciences, and departmental fiefdom-building have all contributed to the atomization of the analysis of reality. The problems of human survival are undeniably complex, but our increasing specialization and division of labor has often prevented us from learning how to improve life on this planet in a holistic and integrated fashion.

Another important influence away from interdisciplinary studies (particularly in the liberal arts) and toward greater specialization has been the careerism of the past decade. Students have been far more motivated by short-term economic considerations and job opportunities than by interest in a well-rounded education. Thus, students have shied away from philosophy, history, arts, and languages and have moved toward skill subjects like computer programming, accounting, and business courses.

Many of our universities now have the worst of both extremes of specialization. On one hand, the faculty includes an excess of those trained in the microanalysis of particular fields whose practical relevance is questionable. On the other hand, there are far too many students who view their university education purely in terms of practical job skills and give little or no thought to the values inherent in their lifestyle choices or to the relation of their professions to the pressing needs of the global environment.

One major trend away from field specialization and toward the development of interdisciplinary analysis during the past thirty years has been the growth in area studies programs. The aftermath of World War II and the increased international responsibilities of the United States brought about the recognition of the need to understand better other regions of the world and their problems. The unprecedented demand for interpreters, policy analysts, and administrators brought together academics of all disciplines and fostered the growth of interdisciplinary area studies. The urgencies of wartime needs forced many of the disciplinary boundaries to crumble. After the war the spectacular growth of university education allowed area studies to grow and flourish, while at the same time the rapid expansion of professional training reestablished the intellectual authority of the old specializations of knowledge.[2]

As long as rapid growth in education and research resources continued, there was an uneasy ambiance between these two approaches to education. As educational growth plateaued and the demand for area specialists declined, hostilities between the traditional departments and the area studies programs became more heated. At the most abstract level, this confrontation focused on how generalized or particularized scientific knowledge about human behavior can or should be. At another level, the debate revolved around the general applicability of Western social science assumptions and biases (dominant in traditional departments) to research and understanding of social problems in non-Western areas. In most cases, the more self-conscious the social scientists became about being scientific, the more they tended to work with theories based on a narrow Western country data base.[3] Similarly, the more area specialists tried to understand the importance of cultural value differences in explaining social behavior (because of antipathy to Western biases and in lieu of much meaningful behavioral data), the stronger was the criticism about their being unscientific and merely descriptive in their analyses.

Since the early 1970s, area studies programs have declined at many universities. In some cases areas were abandoned where faculty expertise or outside funding were the thinnest. In other cases, programs attracting foreign students have been supported to offset losses by American students. The most important factor, however, which seems to hamper area studies programs (and other interdisciplinary programs) is the almost universal mandate at American universities that graduate study beyond the master's level be focused on a traditional discipline. This usually puts area studies students at a disadvantage, since in addition to language training they must also become proficient at the quantitative skills demanded by most doctoral programs. While area studies students may have considerable advantages over traditional students because of their knowledge in a variety of disciplines, this competence is often discounted by traditional departments (particularly those that are heavily quantitatively oriented).

Another major factor that has contributed to the decline of the popularity of area and interdisciplinary studies is the diminishing number of job opportunities that value general skills. Academic jobs in social science positions have become scarcer as demographic factors reduce college enrollments. Careerism has prompted a massive flight from social sciences and humanities into business programs. Fiscal problems and budgetary cuts in government spending have reduced government job opportunities both at home and abroad. In the face of all these problems, many universities have accepted the steady decline of area studies and interdisciplinary programs, viewing the whole situation as if it were merely an aberrant fad of the 1960s.

Several U.S. government reports and congressional hearings in the late 1970s have documented the glaring deficiencies in international education. In July 1978, Representative Paul Simon of Illinois, before the International Operations Subcommittee of the House Committee on International Relations, testified about several alarming trends:[4]

> In signing the Helsinki Final Act, the United States committed itself to extensive efforts in international education. Despite that call to action, American international education efforts have been drifting without national attention and commitment. . . . From 1968 to 1977, enrollments in college and university foreign languages courses have dropped more than 21 percent. Even more striking is the fact that only one in 20 undergraduates enrolls in a course considering foreign peoples or cultures in any substantial

> way. Of our so-called "experts" in foreign areas at the doctoral and post-doctoral levels, 20 percent have no competence in any foreign languages in their area of speciality. . . The State Department recently reduced its foreign language requirements for Foreign Service Officers, because there are not enough people with foreign language skills and knowledge. The results are predictable: We will make more mistakes in the conduct of our international relations than we should. When we began our involvement in Vietnam, for example, there was not a single American-born specialist on Vietnam, Cambodia or Laos in an American university. One of the main causes of many of our misguided policies in Indochina was the lack of any sensitivity to the cultural and institutional values of these countries. We interpreted everything in Western terms.

In the private sector as well, working knowledge of foreign languages and cultures is important and needs to be greatly improved. Journalists provide both decision makers and citizens with most of our information about foreign countries. They are often forced to get their "facts" sitting in hotels and bars from English-speaking natives, because they are often totally lacking in knowledge of foreign languages and cultural traditions. In many instances, the "facts" turn out to be very inaccurate and may cause incalculable damage in high-level policy circles.

The lack of foreign language skills and even general international education is also quite obvious in the business community. Senator Hayakawa of California gave the example of New York, where there are over 20,000 Japanese businessmen who speak English, whereas very few of the 1,000 American businessmen in Tokyo speak any Japanese.[5] Many American sales personnel and business leaders seem to care little about the foreign environments in which they must operate. Often this can result in embarrassing failures, such as General Motors' attempt to sell its Nova model cars in Latin America. The English reference to a star was irrelevant to people who speak Spanish, in which the term "nova" can be translated as "doesn't go." One job in five in the United States depends on overseas sales and the ratio is increasing while educational efforts in international studies are decreasing in terms of constant money.[6]

In November 1979, President Carter's Commission on Foreign Language and International Studies echoed the problems of ignorance and diminishing funding.[7] In the words of the Commission,

> Our lack of foreign language competence diminishes our capabilities in diplomacy, in foreign trade, and in citizen comprehension of the world in which we live and compete. Americans' unwillingness to learn foreign languages is often viewed by others, not without cause, as arrogance. The melting-pot tradition that denigrates immigrants' maintenance of their skill to speak their native tongue still lingers. . . . Americans' scandalous incompetence in foreign languages also explains our dangerously inadequate understanding of world affairs. Our schools graduate a large majority of students whose knowledge and vision stops at the American shoreline, whose approach to international affairs is provincial, and whose heads have been filled with astonishing misinformation. In a recent published study of school children's knowledge and perceptions of other nations and peoples, over 40 percent of the 12th graders could not locate Egypt correctly, while over 20 percent were equally ignorant about the whereabouts of France or China. At the college level, an American Council on Education study reported that at most only 5 percent of prospective teachers take any course relating to international affairs or foreign peoples and cultures as part of their professional preparation. A Gallup Poll in 1977 showed that those who graduate from an educational system so glaringly deficient in this vital area carry their ignorance with them into their adult lives: over half of the general public was unaware that the United States must import part of its petroleum supplies. . . At the advanced training and research level, the nation's network of institutions and programs suffers unremitting financial pressure. Some are in danger of imminent collapse. Although never fully adequate to growing national demands, this network of expertise was built by foundations, the government, and the universities themselves in a period of great scholarly advances after World War II. But this indispensable network is unlikely to survive, let alone maintain its quality, unless the federal government and the universities recognize their responsibilities to respond to the financial crisis, aggravated by inflation, created by the foundations' retreat from this area of support. The Ford Foundation, for example, which provided about $27 million

annually between 1960 and 1967 for advanced training and research in international affairs and foreign areas, now contributes only $3-4 million a year for similar purposes. At the same time, federal support for area centers and the Fulbright exchange program has been cut in half by a decade of inflation, and federally-financed foreign language and area fellowships declined from a peak of 2,557 in 1969 to 828 in 1978. Federal expenditures for university-based foreign affairs research declined from $20.3 million to $8.5 million, or 58 percent in constant dollars.

Overspecialization and national parochialism negatively reinforce each other's narrowness of perspective about the complex global situation. The revitalization of international studies programs that emphasize interdisciplinary and multicultural perspectives are urgently needed to prepare citizens, communicators, educators, businesspersons and policymakers alike. By focusing on global problems such as war, hunger, ecological balance, and social justice, students and professionals can transcend preoccupation with short-term domestic contingencies and become knowledgeable about longer-range, global consequences. Because global problems are complex, they require competency of analysis from several points of view, with interchange and understanding coming from language, philosophy, the humanities, and the physical and social sciences. A revitalized international studies program also calls for a problem-solving approach focused on present and future difficulties and needs. Diminished support for many international and area studies programs is often due to the lack of pragmatic policy options and practical suggestions about complex global dilemmas.

Obviously, in order for global policy studies programs to be successful, a new openness of attitudes toward interdisciplinary analysis and teaching is called for. Greater cooperation between traditional disciplines is essential if the old suspicious attitudes and bureaucratic jealousies are to be overcome. Instead of concentrating on further atomization of disciplines to pursue original research, more creative solutions can be found in the exploration of new interdisciplinary combinations. While some interdisciplinary subjects such as political economy have become well established, new subjects like social ecology, economic anthropology, and geographical psychology are attracting more interest. More important than interesting new combinations of disciplines, however, is the need for more interdisciplinary research and teaching where assumptions, biases, and techniques of analysis of different disciplines are carefully interwoven to highlight the best of each in addressing specific problems. Too often interdisciplinary courses are simply multidisciplinary, each discipline standing side by side, as it were, in isolation from the others.

Interdisciplinary and multi-cultural analysis is important for global policy studies and for understanding complex global problems in general because it avoids narrow parochialism and disciplinary jargon. At its best, interdisciplinary analysis can take a complex problem and reveal the many facets of its reality without becoming obsessed with any one of them. It creates balance, perspective, and relevance. Good interdisciplinary analysis should not only be held up as an ideal model of inquiry and understanding, but also be more vigorously promoted at all levels of education.

Interdisciplinary Analysis and the Search for Global Values

One of the most difficult tasks of our contemporary era is the formulation of a consensus on appropriate global values by which we can guide our actions in response to contemporary world problems. By global values I mean those norms and principles that enhance the quality of human life and natural environment on this planet. It would not seem too difficult at first glance to achieve universal acceptance of such values as peace, economic well-being, justice, self-respect, and ecological responsibility. Why then, is it so difficult for the people of the world to agree on the appropriate solutions to the problems that face us all?

First of all, one must deal with those beliefs which maintain that the human condition presently is not problematic. One sometimes hears statements like: "There have always been wars, famines and disease. They're part of the planet's natural defenses against overpopulation." "It is only man's ego that makes him feel as if his daily troubles are meaningful. People should accept life as it is and remember their utter insignificance as miniscule life forms on a speck of dust suspended in the universe." Holders of such beliefs and attitudes are obviously unimpressed with arguments and concerns over impending nuclear disasters and massive starvation. Theirs is a metaphysical position that may be quite accurate from some universal perspective, but it is very difficult to accept from a humanistic perspective. Even those who are firmly convinced that the human predicament is an unresolvable existentialist dilemma, however, recognize that it is better that we try to improve the quality of life on this planet even if we can not ultimately assess the cosmic meaning of our existence.

Second, one must deal with those who believe that, while there are real problems of human existence that must be addressed, such problems are primarily individual in their nature and not collective. Millions of people in the advanced industrial countries of the world have never experienced starvation or war or gross social injustice. They recognize that these problems exist, but they believe that they have little direct effect on their lives. For the citizens of the advanced industrial world, problems of inflation, taxation, and urban transportation are much more meaningful problems than those of sheer survival. Yet, in spite of the profound parochialism that is evident in many people's beliefs, we undeniably live in an increasingly interdependent age. The modern revolutions in communications, transportation, and international economic exchanges have made even the most parochial persons more aware of the conditions in the world. There may be no direct links between an affluent American or European and a starving child in the streets of Calcutta or Mexico City, but there is plenty of evidence transmitted around the world about conditions of poverty and abundance. Every day, television brings graphic awareness of the desperation of the world's starving people into the comfortable houses of the well-fed. Likewise, even though the world's poorest people may not own their own television sets, they watch pictures of bulging silos of wheat or corn flickering across the screens of televisions in various public places in cities all over the world. These images may provoke different responses in different places, ranging from pity to disgust, but the awareness of the realities of these conditions cannot be ignored. Even the most callous of observers cannot hide from the fact that nuclear war can destroy the lives of both rich and poor in a matter of minutes. Our direct experiences of the world's problems may be quite different, but our awareness of the fragility of human life and its problems will continue to increase as communications shrink the distances between our experiences.

Finally, there are those who believe that all values and all problems are relative to one's culture. They charge that much of the agenda of those concerned with global survival is simply Western projections of materialism and individualism. Since much of Eastern philosophy and religion is focused on spirituality and the denial of self, many critics argue that it is impossible to construct truly *global* values, let alone achieve consensus on how to implement them. There is some truth in these criticisms, just as in the two previous cases, but again these objections are also misleading. Eastern philosophy may not give much importance to the acquisition of material goods, but it is fundamentally focused on improving the quality of life. People with different religions and philosophical beliefs may recognize the benefits of fasting, but virtually no one extolls the pain of forced starvation. The ability to cope with pain and anxiety in creative ways may enhance one's personal character, but only the most despicable would advocate torture and humiliation as lifelong conditions of existence.

A more difficult problem exists with regard to the practical implementation of seemingly universal values. Peace, for example, appears to be desirable to persons of all cultures. In some cases, however, maintaining peace might mean the acceptance of a status-quo injustice in social or political terms. Maintaining the status quo actually may be perpetuating the "violence" of the system against one or more groups in a society. For example, a constant dilemma of world politics is the struggle to choose an appropriate response to dictatorship and political authoritarianism. Is the interest of peace served by opposing such regimes as Hitler's, Stalin's, or Amin's in an open and often violent manner, or should one always work in nonviolent ways to oppose injustice and abuse of power? Is the interest of world peace better served by disarmament or through vigilant defense systems and preparations?

Even if we could agree on what values such as peace or justice mean in their practical application across cultures, there remains the problem of value priorities. All other things being equal, is it better to have more freedom or more peace? Is it better to have more economic well-being if it means less ecological harmony? There may be good reasons why we would want individual nations to structure their own value priorities, but so often a large degree of global consensus is required in order to make meaningful improvements in any one area. It would be nice if there were a global consensus and the available resources to make important improvements on a number of different values, but inevitably the amount of energy and concentration that is required to make significant changes in any area are so great that only a few problems can be given priority.

In view of the difficulty of resolving these tough questions, it is easy to see why so few people have advocated establishing global humanistic values. In addition, there is the question of where one should focus the level of change—at the value/attitudinal level or at the structural/institutional level? Again, under ideal conditions, one should be interested in both attitudinal and structural change, but it is obviously difficult to achieve change at both levels simultaneously.

Various groups and organizations have tried to present their own models of an ideal world system. The Club of Rome, the Pugwash Conferences on Science and World Affairs, the World Order Models Project, the Council for the Study of Mankind, and the Stockholm International Peace Research Institute have all held numerous meetings and conferences and have published a multitude of articles and books dedicated to a more humane world order. Their proposals range from voluntary world fellowship and lobbying for change to elaborate schemes of global institutions. There is abundant idealism about the future yet, so far, little apparent success at achieving practical, tangible reforms.

Is there any meaningful hope, then, that such endeavors can succeed? Most global humanists are guardedly optimistic. As awareness of the world's problems grows, there is more opportunity for significant changes in global values. As value change becomes more prevalent, so will the momentum for institutional change. Once the incremental revolutions in attitudes and structures begin to reinforce each other, there should be a significant improvement in the quality of life for all.

It is logical at this point, given the focus of this chapter, to ask what role interdisciplinary analysis can play in overcoming some of the perceptual and logical problems of establishing and implementing global structural and attitudinal change. One natural advantage that interdisciplinary analysis has in aiding the construction of global value consensus is its predisposition toward integrating different assumptions about human behavior and physical reality. In political economy, for example, a great deal of attention is given to the ways in which the quests for power and resources are closely intermingled. Instead of concentrating just on the motives and acquisition of power or the efficiency with which one conserves or accumulates wealth, interdisciplinary analysis in this case can examine the ways in which power affects wealth and vice versa. In turn, one can explore and even systematically verify what effects increasing or decreasing equality or freedom may have on personal, national, or global wealth or power.

Similarly, a new interdisciplinary field like social ecology focuses on the relationship between lifestyles and their effects on natural environments. The exploration of the complex relationship between human beings and their environment inherently involves an examination of history and philosophy. Thus, once the effort to be truly interdisciplinary is begun, one can start to get a more systematic, as well as a more value-oriented, understanding of the human condition. By extending the level of generalization to the global situation, one can begin the process of recognizing common values.

It appears, however, that the awareness of values appropriate to a more global humanism is not enough. What is needed is a means by which value judgments can be made about the appropriate courses of action for the future. There is profound disagreement about whether any such means exist apart from a strictly individual set of preferences. Thus, on one hand, we have people like McClelland calling for the necessary creation of a "single, all-encompassing ordering idea."[8] On the other hand, Kothari emphasizes the "importance of maintaining a tension between some operational notion of 'world interest' and the deeply-felt value agenda of one's particular social group and geographical region."[9] At the same time, Bull warns that "there is no such thing as a science of ends or values that can establish that one course of action is objectively more right or just than another."[10]

Phenomenology and the Quest for Scientific Global Humanism

One of the most difficult problems and long-standing controversies of science and philosophy is whether there can be an "objective basis" for judging values and reality. One approach to this dilemma is to separate "facts" from values. Science is left to establish what is real, while philosophy is left to distinguish values. The rationalization for this separation is that if science is kept value-free, it can establish an objective basis for reality, whereas values are categorized as inherently subjective. Yet there is great disagreement about whether scientific inquiries about reality can ever be value-free or, indeed, whether they should be. The point of the whole discussion seems to be that there is no truly "objective" basis for judgment. But does this mean that every judgment is necessarily a totally subjective and individual decision?

While there will never be total agreement on the answer to this important question, it appears that a phenomenological perspective may provide some insights. Phenomenology claims to be

> a philosophy of man in his life-world and to be able to explain the meaning of this life-world in a rigorously scientific manner. Its theme is concerned with the demonstration and explanation of the

> activities of consciousness of the transcendental subjectivity within which this life-world is constructed. Since transcendental phenomenology accepts nothing as self-evident, but undertakes to bring everything to self-evidence, it escapes all naive positivism and may expect to be the true science of the mind in true rationality, in the proper meaning of this term.[11]

The key to understanding this philosophy of science lies in its notion of transcendental subjectivity. For Husserl, the founder of phenomenology, subjectivity parallels objectivity so closely that it is interdependent with the latter. The only reality that can have any significance is a constituted reality as perceived and formed by a conscious subject. Through repeated experience, judgments can be made, modified, or verified about the nature of perceived realities. Thus, transcendental subjectivity emerges as the repetition of experience and, consequently, gives one the confidence that one's constituted reality conforms with "objective" reality. This "transcendental" logic, therefore, is concerned with determining when a judgment corresponds with a "state of affairs" and hence is true.[12]

The basis of meaning in every science, according to the phenomenological perspective, is the prescientific life-world, which is experienced by everyone on this planet. Science, in the sense of systematic and rigorous understanding of reality, comes to exist because individuals are constantly experiencing reality and comparing it with their previous experiences. Furthermore, by sharing experiences, both individuals and scientists can establish an interdependent subjectivity. When the sharing of transcendental subjective judgments is systematized and proliferated through language and communication, a collective sense emerges about the appropriate responses to this sense of global reality, the processes of global attitudinal and structural change can be facilitated.

One of the fundamental problems of science is that there has been an overemphasis on the creation of a static set of "truths" derived through idealization and formalization. As Gunnell has argued, much of this is due to an unnecessary preoccupation with the deductive method of explanation.[13] Instead, what is called for is a constant sharing of subjective experiences without overformalizing their constituted realities.

By constantly exchanging our appraisals not only of what is but also of what ought to be we can create a scientific global humanism. This scientific humanism can overcome cultural ethnocentrism and be truly global by combining what Kothari describes as

> the scientific spirit as developed in the West based mainly on the assertion of man's primacy over other beings with the eclectic philosophical worldview of the Oriental civilization based on a recognition of the fundamental unity of all existence, thus drawing from both these past traditions with a view to meet a totally different future.[14]

As natural and social scientists, we can construct paradigms of understanding reality that are based on our shared experiences instead of on preconceived or predetermined notions wedded to narrow methods or epistemologies. We can share our knowledge of behavior and attitudes as well as its consequences. By fully comprehending the interdependent global nature of our human existence as well as our understanding of reality, we can establish a transcendental subjectivity and hence a common basis for value judgments about appropriate action for the future.

It is obvious that the phenomenological exchange of our subjective appraisals of the global human predicament is closely related to the interdisciplinary exchange of analytical perspectives. Scientists in university communities have natural advantages of common institutions and forums, where they can share their subjectivities as well as their analyses. The average person has far fewer opportunities to share his or her experiences. Yet some universities continue to build walls between disciplines and engage in petty fights over teaching credits, library allocations, and methodological nit-picking. No wonder common perceptions about universities abound with unfortunate metaphors about ivory-tower irrelevance. While many scientists, in and out of universities, have realized the inherently interdisciplinary nature of scholarship, too few have been willing to come out from the security of their little niches to engage in the collective enterprise of bettering the human condition by bettering its understanding.

Interdisciplinary Analysis and Global Policy Studies

A long-standing criticism of scientific analysis is its preoccupation with such general theories and abstract assertions that attempt to describe a state of affairs in ways that bear little resemblance to the common person's experience and thus have little to offer in the way of understanding. That is to say, many scientists believe there is an inescapable tradeoff between scientific exactness and relevant applications of understanding.

For the most part, social scientists have been much more concerned with being able to say something intelligible about human affairs, even if that relevance has come at the cost of greater theoretical precision. For many social scientists the pragmatic value of their analyses has led to the development of a methodology outside the "ideal" constructs of methods used in the natural sciences in order to achieve this intelligibility. Other social scientists, however, have disavowed the practical relevance of scientific analyses. Instead they have preferred to search for strictly causal explanations and have disdained the more probabilistic analyses of others. In some cases, the decision to concentrate on highly generalized propositions was a personal political choice. Especially after the ideological problems of the cold war and McCarthy periods in the United States, many American academics felt it necessary to avoid politically controversial research problems in the social sciences.

The problems of very general versus more specific research have been particularly troublesome for interdisciplinary area specialists. As Pye accurately recounts:

> In societies in which much was being made of plans for development, academics who were perceived to be generalists in matters of development were often welcomed, while ironically foreign scholars with deep knowledge of the indigenous languages and cultural traits were distrusted. Those who knew the past performances of the society were suspect because they tended to doubt the current

> rhetoric of development. . . As disillusionment about the prospects for rapid development spread among the leaders and intellectuals of such societies they came increasingly to resent the presence of foreign scholars, particularly those engaged in empirical investigations. Often there was a reversal in attitudes and foreign researchers were denounced for not knowing the local languages and cultural patterns. Scholars interested in earlier times and "safer" subjects became more acceptable, while those concerned with contemporary and emerging trends were suddenly suspect and questions were often raised as to their possible political motivations.[15]

We can see, therefore, that general versus specific research is more than a debate about theoretical merits. The implicit or explicit values of the researchers are always at stake. Furthermore, what is "safer" politically seems likely to change over time.

The recent explosion of interest in policy studies indicates a swing away from more general theorizing toward more practical problem-solving. Part of this interest is a reflection of the more practical "careerist" attitudes of students in colleges and universities in recent times. Another reason for this trend is probably the desire of many scientists, both natural and social, to have greater influence on policymakers in government.

This is not to say that policy studies will be any safer politically than general studies. Quite the contrary: Since policy analysts are often required or inclined to rationalize one policy alternative over others, there will be considerable controversy. Policy studies have raised a host of new problems related to the politicization of research and appropriate professional standards, which both scholars and policymakers should respect. In the areas of foreign or global policy studies the cases may be even more controversial, since the defense or criticism of an important policy program may have an important effect on a government's stability or effectiveness. Thus, we are now witnessing another wave of scholarly inclination to try to avoid all issues of political motivations and individual preferences by returning interests to the "classical" concerns of the scientific accuracy of their disciplines.

To be a humanist implies an active concern for the state of the human condition in contemporary times. To be a scientist implies an active pursuit of the most systematic understanding of contemporary and historical realities. To be both a humanist and a scientist is to try to use one's systematic understanding of reality to improve the human condition. These two roles need not be in contradiction if one is careful to keep both goals in balance. One should not become so abstract in one's research that there is no conceivable contribution to the betterment of life on this planet. Similarly, one cannot consistently ignore or deny systematically established patterns of evidence for purely idealistic reasons.

Policy analysis provides a good medium for combining the interests of humanists and scientists. Since one usually focuses upon some specific problem, there is an empirical focus of research. If the policy is concerned with any one of a number of important human problems, then one's knowledge will eventually improve living conditions in some way.

The level of one's policy analysis is often a conscious choice about where one believes practical action is the most appropriate. It may also involve examining effects that policies at one level have on conditions at other levels. Global policy studies include both of these concerns. Ideally, it allows one to focus on a particular problem at the local, national, or global level. At the same time it is concerned with the effects that such policies may have on the global environment and the effects the global environment may have on these policies.

Interdisciplinary analyses are particularly important in policy analyses. The complexity of practical problem-solving requires sharing the particular knowledge of many disciplines. Problems of war, hunger, energy, environmental balance, and social justice require interdisciplinary answers. Since simplistic policy solutions may have very complex consequences, an effort must be made to attempt to understand the effects of these consequences in many different areas of human existence. This does not mean that there will be easier choices about which benefits outweigh which costs. However, more complete and accurate information about the true nature of these costs and benefits is indispensable to the process of value judgments about appropriate policies. Interdisciplinary approaches to policy studies also provide additional safeguards against the possibility that single issues or particular concerns (such as efficiency, equality, stability, or uniformity) will totally dominate the process of policy formation and evaluation.

Policy studies is a good arena in which to bring analysts from different cultural as well as disciplinary backgrounds together. Often it takes common concerns as well as specific insights about a serious practical problem like pollution or hunger to motivate people to work together to find acceptable solutions. Sharing concern and particular aspects of knowledge builds trust, collegiality, and the basis for future collaboration on other problems. Even when conflicts arise over preferred courses of action, there will often be compromises that emerge which may anticipate (and, it is hoped, dissipate) more general social conflicts.

Conclusion

Few scholars and policymakers would deny the importance of interdisciplinary research and training in coping with complex contemporary problems. Yet many of these professionals are still unwilling to engage in more interdisciplinary work or teaching. It takes a certain amount of courage to let go of familiar paradigms, modes of analysis, and discipline-specific jargon. It sometimes involves a lot of work and requires overcoming bureaucratic obstacles to team-teach courses and coordinate different activities. Nevertheless, it seems absolutely essential that interdisciplinary programs, courses, and research be increased in the years ahead.

Global policy studies programs are natural breeding grounds for interdisciplinary analyses. These programs try to wrestle with some of the most complex and urgent problems. The search for integrating global values and practical problem solutions requires expertise from many different disciplines. History, philosophy, humanities, and natural and social sciences are all needed to bring the proper perspectives to an understanding of how to better living conditions on this planet. We really cannot afford the luxury of sitting in our disciplinary ivory towers waiting for the problems to solve themselves. None of us by ourselves may be able to bring enough of our subjective understanding to address the world's problems sufficiently. Working together, however, we can and must attempt to share our understanding in the hope that it will improve the global human condition.

NOTES

1. John Dewey, *The Case for Modern Man* (New York: Harper & Row, 1955), pp. 132-133.

2. Lucian Pye, "The Confrontation Between Discipline and Area Studies," in *Political Science and Area Studies (Bloomington: Indiana University Press, 1975), p. 5.*

3. *Ibid.*, pp. 6-7.

4. Representative Paul Simon, "The Future of International Education," *Hearings before the Subcommittee on International Operations of the Committee on International Relations of the House of Representatives,* July 18, 1978 (Washington, DC: Government Printing Office, 1978), p. 5.

5. *Ibid.*, p. 6.

6. *Ibid.*, p. 55.

7. President's Commission on Foreign Language and International Studies, *Strength Through Wisdom: A Critique of U.S. Capability* (Washington, DC: Government Printing Office, 1979), pp. 6-9.

8. C. A. McClelland, "Field Theory and System Theory in International Relations," in A. Lepawsky, E. Buehrig, and H. Lasswell (eds.), *The Search for World Order* (New York: Appleton-Century-Crofts, 1971), p. 382.

9. Rajni Kothari, *Footsteps into the Future* (New York: Free Press, 1974), p. xv.

10. Hedley Bull, "New Directions in the Theory of International Relations," *International Studies,* 15 (1975), p. 285.

11. Alfred Schutz, "Phenomenology and the Social Sciences," in Joseph Kockelmas (ed.), *Phenomenology* (Garden City, NY: Doubleday, 1967), p. 452.

12. Quentin Lauer, *Phenomenology: Its Genesis and Prospect* (New York: Harper Torchbooks, 1958), p. 101.

13. John Gunnell, "Deduction, Explanation and Social Scientific Inquiry," *American Political Science Review,* 63, 4 (1969), pp. 1233-1246.

14. Kothari, *Footsteps,* p. 37.

15. Pye, "The Confrontation," p. 15.

5

International Futures

ROBERT E. CLUTE

The study of international futures is a relatively new development. Much of the interest in future studies has been sparked by the Club of Rome reports and has been made possible by post-World War II technological developments in computers and advanced electronic equipment that have permitted a more sophisticated analysis of large quantities of data. Of necessity, it is primarily an interdisciplinary endeavor. However, a number of universities in the United States and Europe now have future studies departments and numerous journals have emerged, such as *Futures, Futuribles,* and *Futurist.* In 1968, about twelve schools in the United States were offering futures courses, but by 1972, over 200 such courses were taught.[1] Over 200 of the top 1,000 American companies use futuristic planning techniques.[2]

International futures research attempts to examine current interrelated global issues in order to project or forecast the future consequences of past and present trends and to suggest alternative scenarios in an attempt to avoid undesired consequences.[3] This work has become known as futurology, which, according to Victor Ferkiss, "combines the knowledge of the scientist, the will of the utopian and the imagination of the writer of science fiction."[4] The policy aspect of international futures is in essence an attempt at long-term planning.

There has been an enormous output of literature and research on international futures in recent years. This literature has motivated a large body of public opinion in the market economy developed nations, which has been organized into effective pressure groups with the result that these political systems have adopted a large body of legislation to remedy such problems as resource depletion, pollution, and environmental deterioration. The same pressure groups have also undoubtedly affected the foreign policies of their respective countries on these issues. Nations have also occasionally been able to attack these problems on a regional level, as has the recent agreement concluded by Mediterranean countries on pollution, for example. However, attempts to treat these problems and to formulate effective policy on a global level have been conspicuously unsuccessful.

This chapter will examine some of the obstacles to the formulation of sound global policies on international futures issues. The divergent views of the developed countries (LDCs) are reflected in their scenarios for policy outputs in international futures. These disagreements are heightened by the enormous differences in the negotiating styles and diplomatic capabilities of the LDCs and the developed nations. The cumbersome international structure whereby policy is formulated through international conferences with each nation having one vote—despite size, population, financial contributions or power—has given the LDCs such a majority control that they have often assumed unrealistic postures, resulting in policy outputs that tend to be repetitious statements of the Third World's views of a desired new social and economic order, rather than providing policy solutions to the specific problems being negotiated. An examination of selected international conferences reveals the enormous problems the global community has faced in attempting to formulate policies on international futures.

Divergent Views of International Futures Research

Futurologists have little disagreement as to the major global needs in international futures. They are: population stability, adequate supplies of energy and raw materials, sufficient food, well-being and economic equity, control of power and the use of force, and environmental protection. To this some might add issues on fundamental rights and social equity. Except for the latter, these are all subjects that lend themselves to systems analysis, computer models, and other techniques favored by future researchers in the art of forecasting.

Developed Free Market Economies

In published works in these economies, such as *The Limits to Growth*,[5] *Mankind at the Turning Point*,[6] *The Next 200 Years*,[7] *The Global 2000 Report to the President*,[8] or *Facing the Future*,[9] we find a communality of global needs but disagreement on the gravity of such needs, the time frame involved, and possible alternative scenarios. In most accounts the world will face an enormous population explosion that will occur mostly in the LDCs. There will be food shortages and mass starvation, raw materials will become depleted, and the planet will be hopelessly polluted if present trends continue. This has given rise to the "doomsday" or Malthusian writers, perhaps best represented by *The Limits to Growth*, who believe that unlimited technological-industrial growth and increasing world population will lead to a starving, polluted, resource-depleted planet by the twenty-first century. The optimists, or cornucopians, are perhaps best represented by *The Next 2000 Years*. The latter recognize the same dangers but believe that cautious economic and technological development, with innovations and proper constraints, will enable the world to meet human needs and to maintain the good life in a steady-state society, albeit at a somewhat lower standard than now exists.

On the surface it would be expected that the nations of the world would combine forces to meet these problems and to avoid a global catastrophe. This is not the case, which may be partially due to the manner in which many of these future studies were conducted. The works that have received the most attention and purport to be global in approach are, in the main, biased toward scenarios that are concerned with maintaining the systems and values of the market economy, developed states. This is not surprising, since futurologists base much of their work on extrapolations of past trends or present activities and historical analogies. This tends to hamper the emergence of innovative scenarios unencumbered by current accepted practices, structures and values. Indeed, many of the major futures studies are extremely ethnocentric and are therefore resisted by much of the world.

W. H. Clives Simmonds rightfully contends that one of the greatest difficulties in futures research is to define the problem aptly to avoid errors of the third kind—that is, solving the wrong problems by not asking the right questions.[10] For those who oppose the status quo and desire new structures or a new order, such as many of the Second and Third World countries, these works simply do not ask the right questions.

The Third World

The Limits to Growth raised the specter, which many other writers of the First World have since endorsed to a greater or lesser extent, of imposing limits on demographic, industrial, and technological growth in order to achieve a state of global equilibrium. Although *The Limits to Growth* denied the desire to freeze any status quo of economic development,[11] many nations of the Third World are not willing to accept or share this global model, since it would perpetuate their underdeveloped status. There have been some attempts in the literature to reply on the part of the Third World. The Fundación Bariloche in Argentina presented a conceptual model involving a shift to a more socialist society which indicated that basic need targets could be met in Latin America and Africa by the years 1992 and 2008, respectively.[12] One of the reports of the Club of Rome, *RIO: Reshaping the International Order*,[13] did focus on the problems of the LDCs; however, the Third World pronouncements on the New International Economic Order (NIEO), their support of OPEC, their concern over the transfer of technology, and the dangers they perceive in transnational corporations are a clear rejection of many existing futures models. The NIEO is designed precisely to challenge the economic system many futurists hope to maintain.

Tarcuata di Tella notes the existence of widespread discontent in the LDCs, which he refers to as the "demonstration effect," that is, the widely prevalent practice of comparing the poverty and deprivation of Third World countries to the prosperous lifestyle of the developed world. Di Tella contends that this situation creates support for leftist parties and "incongruent groups" which, despite social differences, have a common resentment of the status quo.[14] This intense opposition to the status quo is also reflected in the international negotiations of Third World countries, which have formed a cohesive bloc to negotiate a new global order. Third World negotiators have demanded a totally new order and have been reluctant to negotiate on issues that do not fit into their scenarios for the future. Mahbub ul Haq, a Pakistani official in the World Bank, is representative of many Third World officials when he notes, "what is at stake here is not a few marginal adjustments in the international system; it is its complete overhaul."[15] He then cites Prime Minister Burhuham of Guyana, whose attitude is quite typical of many Third World negotiators. The latter declared;

> There is another danger that needs to be guarded against if we are all serious in our commitment to programmes of positive action which will give life to a new international economic order. It is the danger of deceiving ourselves that we can somehow achieve fundamental change by marginal adjustments and devices of a piecemeal and reformist nature.[16]

Perhaps for the same reason, many Third World negotiators have not been noted for conciliatory postures that would lead to accommodation on international futures policy.

This is not surprising, as conditions and perceived needs in Third World countries are different from those in more economically developed systems. A country that is poor and has no industry may look on industrial pollution as a luxury. A woman who beats her clothes out on the rocks along the Niger River would be eternally grateful for some of the phosphate detergents that have become taboo in the United States. The perils of DDT to an underdeveloped, tropical Third World country may not be as threatening as the malaria, yellow fever, and sleeping sickness that might become rampant without DDT. If a traditional man lives in a society where there are no institutions except the family to care for him in his old age, and the infant mortality rate has always been high, it may seem completely rational to him that he should have a large family. If this were not the case, who would care for him in his old age? Who would work the fields? The LDCs have made it clear that many futurists are asking the wrong questions and providing the wrong answers. The LDCs want global economic equity, not a global equilibrium that perpetuates the present inequities.

LDCs may also resist futures research because of a phenomenon similar to that of an individual undergoing psychotherapy who will withhold or evade giving information to a practitioner that is needed to solve his or her problem.[17] Nations may wish to hide knowledge that they would consider damaging to the stability of their system. For example, futures studies stress the decline of agricultural production in developing countries relative to their growing populations. The development literature abounds with accounts of countries that have neglected their agricultural production at the expense of urban, industrial development, despite the fact that the majority of their inhabitants are farmers. In fact, the U.S. Comptroller General released a study listing forty-six developing countries that have actually created agricultural disincentives.[18] One of the more common practices is for authoritarian rulers to maintain themselves in power by subsidizing food prices of imported staples. This, in turn, brings the local price of the commodity so low that indigenous farmers cut production, because they cannot make enough to pay for the necessary seed, fertilizer, and pesticides. Burma is a case in point. Many LDCs also encourage the growth of agricultural products for export, such as cocoa, cotton, and jute at the expense of foodstuffs in order to obtain currency for industrial development. Abandonment of such policies would improve the food situation but would have a large impact on the internal systems of such LDCs. These practices cause such LDCs considerable embarrassment when food problems are discussed in international negotiations. Also, except for the People's Republic of China most Marxist-Leninist countries are not at ease with food questions in view of their agricultural production records.

Most LDCs cannot get enthused over many of the environmental problems discussed in futures research. Economic well-being and economic development are more important to LDCs than environment, just as they were in America during its early stages of development. Futures studies have been extremely critical of Brazil's development of the Amazon Basin, as the removal of the jungle may affect world weather conditions, could affect the amount of ozone in the earth's atmosphere, and will expose soil that should probably not be farmed as it will rapidly deteriorate and erode. The Brazilian response has coined the phrase, "scientific colonialism,"[19] which may be indicative of Third World attitudes toward futures research. Futures research finds that environmental protection measures being adopted will greatly increase the cost of development and, in turn, the price of finished products. For instance, Kahn calls attention to the fact that pollution-control costs could rise from about 1.5 percent of the GNP in 1971 to over 5 percent of the GNP in the year 2025.[20] Thus, the cost of pollution control in developed countries would be passed on to the LDCs in the form of higher prices for commodities needed for development. Obviously, environmental problems do not receive the same attention and response in LDCs that they receive in the developed world.

The LDCs are also not concerned over reports of dwindling mineral reserves in the developed world. On the contrary, former colonial entities were in the main left with their industrial minerals intact after the demise of colonialism. This was not the result of colonial policy, but was due to the fact that the price of such minerals was low enough that it did not pay to transport them back to the mother country. Mineral supplies in the Third World are now a valuable asset, not only to increase LDC income through price raises, but also to use the threatened withholding of such material from developed nations with depleted resources for negotiating purposes. Strangely enough, many futures studies do not include the price factor in their models.[21] It is this very price factor that the LDCs will utilize to maintain high income and larger mineral reserves. The Soviet Union makes a strange bedfellow in this process, for although the Soviets are not lacking in most of the strategic minerals, it is to their advantage to see that the flow of such minerals to the developed market economies is tightly controlled.

There is much discussion of discounting[22] in futures literature, that is, choosing alternatives that satisfy short-term needs but do not consider the needs of future generations. In fact, most futures studies are overly concerned with shortages of raw materials for future generations without seeming to be aware that they are discounting the economic future of the LDCs. For example, *The Global 2000 Report to the President* estimates that between the years 1975 and 2000, the per capital GNP of the developed countries will have grown from $4325 to $8485, whereas that of the LDCs will rise from $382 to $587.[23] Such studies examine in great detail technological developments that might alleviate shortages in the developed world, but they spend little time on how the LDCs might be helped to improve their situation. Thus, the futures studies offer LDCs little hope of global economic equity.

Finally, futures studies usually attempt cold, rational analysis on the basis of quantifiable data. Many LDCs do not have a great deal of data available to them and do not keep adequate vital statistics to determine the sizes of their populations. Not all developing countries could withstand the stresses of an accurate census. For instance, both Lebanon and Nigeria experienced bloody civil wars when it became evident that a presumed ratio between ethnic and religious groups really did not exist. Most LDCs have neither the finances nor the technological capacity to maintain expensive records and data systems. Often decisions in LDCs are made for ideological reasons rather than on the basis of data. This fact shows up on the balance sheets of many state enterprises in the Third World and in the failure of their five-year development plans to attain announced goals. One of the things that impresses an American most in discussions with university students on African campuses is the pervasiveness of rhetoric and paucity of data in their argumentation. If one examines the debates and negotiations of international conferences that have attempted to deal with futures subjects, one also notes this same abundance of rhetoric and lack of data on the part of many Third World delegates.

The Marxist-Leninist States

The Second World, composed of the Marxist-Leninist states, also offers considerable resistance to futures studies. Although Soviet spokespersons acknowledge the global needs described in the literature, in the main they reject the idea of limits to growth. This may be due in part to the Marxist belief that global problems have their origin in the structure of social and economic relationships, particularly those surrounding the means of production and distribution.[24] William Ophuls states the Soviet problem succinctly when he writes that

> the Marxist utopia depends for its achievement on the abolition of material scarcity, so that to abandon growth is tantamount to abandoning a utopian promise that has inspired the whole society.[25]

As a matter of fact, the ideological constrictions—the proclivity to stress production from a power and autarky standpoint, regardless of costs and waste (as in Soviet use of low-grade domestic aluminum ores to avoid importation of raw materials)—have not provided a very favorable climate for futures research in the Soviet Union. Soviet planners understand the questions being asked by the futurists of the free market developed economies, but the Soviet scenarios for the future are different.

One would expect to find the same situation in Eastern European Marxist-Leninist states. Agreement and association with Western futures research is generally viewed as revisionistic. Ferkiss writes, "It is noteworthy that the futurists were prominently active in the ill-fated Dubcek regime in Czechoslovakia."[26] The same might be said of the leadership of the present revisionist movement in Poland. At the moment, the policy of the People's Republic of China (PRC) seem to be more in agreement with the findings of the futurists, with its stress on population control, environment, and so on; but this is probably due to the fact that it is still stressing agriculture and the creation of an infrastructure rather than intense industrialization.[27] However, since it has not yet fully industrialized, the PRC could not be expected to accept the idea of limits to growth in its long-range policy views.

Thus the Second and Third Worlds often find themselves allies in responding to international futures studies. In negotiations on matters dealing with international futures, the Soviet Union often, but not always, supports the Third World.

The New World Order and Global Futures Policy

The post-World War II era has witnessed a great change in the manner in which policy is made in the global community. For instance, the League of Nations finally achieved a membership of fifty nations by 1932, and the United Nations began with a membership of fifty-one nations. Both organizations were in the main white, occidental institutions controlled by developed countries. The bulk of the LDCs were Latin American states, which for the most part followed the European institutional patterns. However, with the demise of colonialism a huge number of newly independent developing countries joined the United Nations and participated in global policy formation. The LDCs now make up an overwhelming majority in the UN. The style of these newly independent LDCs is quite different than that of the older, established powers.

The new order has had less impact on the content and outputs of international policy not purported to be global in nature, but its influence on policies applicable to the entire international community has been profound. The great powers can bypass the LDCs in policy matters not requiring the cooperation of the Third World. Disarmament would be a case in point, where the negotiations of greatest concern to the global community often take place between the major powers. Regional arrangements such as NATO and the European Common Market can also generate policies of global import with minimal participation by Third World actors. The major powers are also often able to negotiate effective policy on a bilateral level, through direct negotiations with LDCs, which would not be possible in the global arena. Although developed countries would have little success in negotiating security measures with the Third World bloc, they are able to negotiate successfully with single entities, such as the United States with Egypt, Kenya, and Somalia or the USSR with Ethiopia, Mozambique, and Angola. If a few major powers adopt policies in some areas, they have a de facto global impact. If the developed powers unilaterally adopt policies affecting the construction and safety regulations of oil tankers, it matters little whether the rest of the world cooperates, as the policies control the vast bulk of world tanker traffic. However, in the area of international futures the policies being negotiated often concern matters that affect the entire globe and cannot be accommodated through regional or bilateral policy outputs. The major powers and the United States in particular have not been conspicuously successful in negotiations with the Third World bloc on matters concerning international futures policy and global policy in general. The negotiating style, global perspective, and differing diplomatic capabilities of the LDCs have proven to be a serious obstacle to the implementation of global futures policy.

Differing Diplomatic Capabilities

The newly independent countries were not experienced in foreign policy making, since their colonial status did not give them training in this area. As a matter of fact, the Rockefeller Foundation sent kits to many such countries because they lacked the foreign affairs libraries necessary for foreign policy planning. Many LDCs have extremely small foreign office staffs, which have neither the trained personnel nor the facilities to carry out intensive research on the complicated technical problems to be negotiated. At the United Nations, an LDC representative often covers a number of committees and UN agencies. Some LDCs send only one delegate to an international conference. Swaziland hired a Sri Lankan to prepare its position papers for the Third United Nations Conference on the Law of the Sea, because the country did not have a negotiator trained in this area. Such situations often restrict the ability of Third World countries to generate policy postures on global issues.

Third World negotiators also often have greater leeway in deciding which policy posture they will assume than is the case with most diplomats representing developed countries. Many Third World delegates attend international conferences relatively uninstructed, unless the issue being negotiated reflects their nation's vital interests. Some delegates may not even have very close ties with the power structure of the country they represent. For instance, it is not uncommon in Africa for a government to give political opponents diplomatic posts as a means of removing them from local power politics. John Akar, Sierra Leone's former delegate to the United Nations, is a case in point. He was a political threat at home, so he was given a UN post. Many representatives of the LDCs are also rather inexperienced in the art of negotiation and accommodation. Many come from one-party states, or military dictatorships, where negotiation and accommodation is not the prevalent style within their domestic political systems. The new states are almost devoid of pressure groups to assist in interest articulation and aggregation. Nor do they have the sophisticated public opinion surveys, so prevalent in the Western world, to tell governments what their people desire. If policy has been formed and instructions given to the delegate for a forthcoming negotiation, such policy is made within a relatively small circle of the executive.

The foreign policy operations of the Third World stand out in sharp contrast to those of the United States, with its vast input of human and material resources. The different approach to U.S. foreign policy formulation was exemplified by Ambassador Jean Wilkowski's call for advice and participation in the preparation of position papers for the 1979 United Nations Conference on Science and Technology for Development. In a speech at a September 1977 meeting of the American Association for the Advancement of Science, she noted that the State Department did not have a monopoly on such activities and said:

> The broad nature of our preparations requires us to reach out to a very large number of specialized departments, agencies and offices—health, education, commerce, labor and natural resources, also to Congress (both Members and staff)—to help us coordinate a realistic U.S. foreign policy for this U.N. Conference. . . . [Also] we expect a substantial contribution from non-governmental entities, both in preparation of a U.S. national paper, and in conceiving and testing out policy recommendations. . . . In our preparations . . . we are currently seized with examining draft proposals on alternative ways for organizing and activating a set of ad hoc study groups with private and public sector representation.[28]

This sort of foreign policy formation, involving large numbers of participants, can have an enormous impact on conference negotiations. For example, at the last World Administrative Radio Conference in 1979, there was some concern that the LDCs would attempt to claim a greatly increased portion of the global radio spectrum. Various interest groups, governmental agencies, and American academics busied themselves generating voluminous amounts of data and numerous position papers. The conference was attended by 1500 delegates from 145 countries,[29] but the United States delegation was composed of 115 members!

Entirely aside from the differences in opinion and national interests, imagine the reaction of a single delegate from a small LDC who arrives with relatively few data and faces a delegation of such size with a vast array of data and technical skills. The delegates of the developed nations in such situations may be extremely skilled in the subject matter being negotiated, but cultural differences and world realities may place them at a greater distance from their Third World colleagues than that between their respective capitals. This is a serious obstacle for technicians of the developed world who attempt to negotiate international futures policies.

Differences in Negotiating Styles

The differences in negotiating styles between the developed nations and the LDCs may be even greater than the disparities among their diplomatic capabilities. The developed nations have not been a very tight negotiating bloc in formulating global policy. Not only are there differences between the free market economies and the Communist bloc, but the free market economies have not acted in concert on a number of important issues. Witness the lack of agreement among the free market economy countries on a proper response to the OPEC threat to their energy supplies. However, despite these differences, the developed economies have indicated a willingness to negotiate with other countries on global policy matters and arrive at specific accommodations that stand out in sharp contradiction to their announced perceptions, ideological stands, and long-term policy goals. In contrast, the LDCs have formed a tight bloc at international conferences negotiating global policy and have repeatedly shown an unwillingness to arrive at policy accommodations on specific matters, even though such accommodations might offer immediate benefits to their respective systems. This lack of accommodation is often used by the Third World countries as a tool to advance their own long-term global policy objectives in the international forum.

Although the developing countries were not initially a tightly knit bloc, they had become so by 1964, when they held the first United Nations Conference on Trade and Development (UNCTAD) and organized the African, Asian, and Latin American countries into the Group of 77, which eventually grew to a membership of 110 nations. They easily controlled a majority in the General Assembly and at international conferences. They concentrated on vote-getting and bloc diplomacy rather than negotiation or accommodation. Since they had the necessary vote to adopt a General Assembly resolution, they would often do so, even though such a measure did not have the support of the developed world. This was a rather hollow victory when such a resolution could not be implemented without assistance of the DCs. This gave rise to the so-called North-South confrontation.

The Group of 77 backed the petroleum-producing countries in their decision to raise petroleum prices in 1973, and their imagination was fired by the ability of OPEC to extract high prices from the DCs. At the Sixth Special Session of the General Assembly in 1974, the LDCs put forth the Declaration on the Establishment of the New International Economic Order (NIEO) in the form of a General Assembly resolution.[30] This document contained the major aims of the LDCs in their attempt to gain global equity. These aims have been introduced and supported by LDCs in every subsequent international conference. It is their scenario for the future. The Declaration advocated the nationalization of natural resources being exploited by foreign companies, without compensation, if deemed necessary for the exercise of national sovereignty. It called for the regulation and supervision of transnational corporations. It favored the tying of prices of LDC exports to the prices of imports from the DCs, and advocated the promotion of raw materials associations of LDCs patterned after OPEC. Full compensation to peoples under colonial rule and apartheid was demanded for the depletion of their natural resources.

The plan was fairly simple. During the previous decade the economic gap between the LDCs and DCs had widened. The LDCs perceived the problem to be a lack of capital and insufficient development aid. They would now attempt to combat economic domination by the DCs and would gain funds for development by extracting higher prices for commodities and raw materials. The dire predictions of future studies on the depletion of natural resources had helped create a climate of public opinion in the developed world that might make the LDCs' task easier.

Thus far, the DCs have not accepted the principles of the NIEO, but the LDCs have repeated their demands at all levels of the United Nations and at international conferences, whether or not the subject matter being negotiated is germane. The developed nations and the United States in particular do not seem to be too adept in responding to the persistent rhetoric and tight-knit coalition of the Third World bloc in global policy negotiations. Although the developed nations have formulated stronger postures on specific issues than most of the LDCs, the latter often have followed the general lead of a few activist countries, such as Algeria, Tanzania, India, and Cuba, which advance strong positions on international futures issues. Once the Third World bloc has taken such a stand, its cohesiveness and numbers prove to be most effective in limiting the policy initiatives of the developed powers.

Selected International Conferences on Global Futures Issues

An examination of selected conferences indicates the ability of the Third World to oppose the policies of the developed world effectively. The problems discussed above are illustrated in the global policy outputs, or lack thereof, in numerous conferences concerned with international futures. Although the Third World countries have been rather successful in countering policies espoused by the developed world, they have not been very successful in offering viable alternative policies on international futures. The policy outputs resultant from such conferences, rather than being negotiated accommodations effecting sound global futures policies, often are policy documents that reflect only a lack of global consensus on the issues concerned.

Perhaps the first realization of the new focus in LDC negotiations came from a series of conferences on world problems which had been popularized by the Club of Rome reports and other futures studies. These were not issues that were high on the agenda of Group of 77. These negotiations are worthy of examination, not only because they treat issues critical to global well-being, but also because they indicate the difficulty of handling global issues through the present international structure. The scope of this chapter will not permit an examination of all such international conferences, but I will concentrate on five that were concerned with international futures.

The Stockholm Conference on International Environment

Environment provided the first major issue to indicate the seriousness of the confrontation between the North and the South. The issue concerned the whole global community. Developed nations were facing enormous difficulties of pollution from hazardous industrial wastes. Problems of water and air pollution had become critical. Population pressures and poor farming methods had badly depleted agricultural lands in many LDCs. The deserts were spreading at an alarming rate. The terraced fields of the Andes had been badly eroded. India, Bangladesh, and many other LDCs were experiencing floods and erosion due to deforestation. Futures studies indicated that a global environmental crisis was imminent. Concerned academics from the developed countries produced voluminous literature on world environmental problems. Public reaction to the environmental threat was enormous in the Western world and in Japan. Powerful interest groups emerged, which brought pressure on their respective governments to rectify the situation.

Athough the LDC leaders were aware of the problems, they did not experience the pressure of public opinion and interest groups that was experienced by leaders in the developed countries. One writer noted that even if 80 percent of the current pollution problems were eliminated, economic and demographic growth would re-create present conditions within thirty-five years.[31] Thus, a clean environment would require enormous expenditures. As a result, economic development might simply carry too high a price tag for many LDCs. The LDCs were well aware of the danger that pollution controls might slow down their economic development. In examining the problem of environmental controls and the LDCs, the MIT study group concluded:

> In no respect . . . is the contrast of interest, priorities and capabilities between the rich states and the poor more stark than in

dealings involving environmental pollution. All the ingredients are present for a classically unproductive dialogue of the deaf.[32]

Developing nations clearly indicated their stand on the matter. The question of a conference on international environmental controls was brought before the United Nations in 1968. The Turkish and Philippine delegates insisted that the issue should be tied to the promotion of economic development.[33] It soon became obvious that the LDCs would utilize the desire of the developed countries to attain environmental controls as a means of extracting concessions on development.

On December 7, 1970, the General Assembly adopted a resolution declaring that

> environmental policies should be considered in the context of economic and social development, taking into account the special needs of development in developing countries.[34]

A resolution adopted by the Second Committee of the General Assembly in 1971 perhaps best summarized the views of many developing countries. It read, in part:

> . . . pollution of world-wide impact is being caused primarily by some highly developed countries, as a consequence of their own high level of improperly planned and inadequately coordinated industrial activities, and that, therefore, the main responsibility for financing corrective measures falls on those countries.[35]

When the United Nations Conference on Human Environment met in Stockholm during June 1972, it was dominated by the LDCs, which made up 82 of the 116 nations in attendance. Prime Minister Indira Ghandi, of India, represented the posture of the LDCs at the conference when she asked:

> How can we speak to those who live in the villages and in slums about keeping the oceans, the rivers and the air clean when their own lives are contaminated at the source?[36]

The Report of the United Conference on the Human Environment, which was the result of the Stockholm meeting, is a document heavily oriented toward the views of the developing nations. The fourth paragraph of the preamble reaffirms that most environmental problems of developing countries are caused by underdevelopment, whereas the environmental problems of the developed countries are related to industrialization and technological development. Principle I of the declaration obviously was included to satisfy the Third World. It condemns colonialism, racism, and the policies of apartheid. The author certainly agrees with the condemnation of these principles, but questions how germane these problems were to the topic under discussion. Although the developing countries did support the inclusion of some of the environmental controls desired by the advanced technological societies, they made it perfectly clear that such support would neither hamper their economic development nor cost them anything. Indeed, it was obvious that they viewed the environmental bandwagon as a good vehicle to attain more technological and financial assistance for their own development.

The declaration affirms that economic and social development are essential to a favorable living standard and environment. There are a number of ways under the Principles that the developed countries are expected to give their financial support to the Third World. The former are reminded that environmental deficiencies can only be remedied by transferring large amounts of financial and technical assistance to the developing countries. Developed countries are also told that stable prices for primary commodities and raw materials are essential if developing countries are to carry out proper environmental management. Environmental policies are also to enhance and not adversely affect the present or future development of developing countries. The declaration states that appropriate steps should be taken by nations and international organizations to reach an agreement on meeting the possible national and international consequences resulting from the application of environmental measures. The document also notes that costs which might accrue to the developing countries as a result of incorporating environmental safeguards into their development planning should be taken into account so that additional assistance can be received.

After the Principles set forth what the developing nations do not want—environmental controls that will detract from or divert money from economic or social development—they include in the Recommendations of the Stockholm Conference a rather long list of items that they do want. The developing nations want priority areas for UN-sponsored research and development assistance in water and sewage systems related to tropical climate, programs for rural development, tropical forest management, tropical marine studies, and water resources management. The developing countries would also like assistance in elementary education with an emphasis on hygiene and in developing methods for health improvement, housing, sanitation, and soil erosion that could utilize local labor and materials. They are also concerned over the inroads synthetics have made on markets for tropical agricultural products such as cotton, rubber, and hemp, and request payment of adequate prices for the agricultural produce of developing countries. The United Nations is requested to undertake studies to determine the cost of natural products versus synthetic products for the same use.[37]

Although the General Assembly did, as a result of the conference, adopt the Human Environmental Program in December 1972, with a governing council of fifty-eight nations headquartered in Nairobi,[38] it was obvious that the LDCs did not see environment as a high-priority issue. It is rather difficult to view the environmental situations in the Sahel, the Andes, India, and Bangladesh as caused by highly developed countries as a consequence of "improperly planned and inadequately coordinated industrial activities." The rather cavalier manner in which the developing countries responded to the serious matter of environmental problems greatly damaged their credibility in the developed world. They had attracted serious attention to the problems of the Third World, but exhibited a shocking callousness on matters critical to the future of the global community.

The World Population Conference at Budapest

The second major problem predicted by futures studies was that if the present demographic trends continued, the world—

particularly the LDCs—would be so overpopulated that the globe would face mass starvation. *The Limits to Growth* predicted that world population would grow to about seven billion by the twenty-first century and that in sixty years there would be four persons in the world for every person living at the time the report was written.[39] The second report of the Club of Rome, *Mankind at the Turning Point*,[40] confirmed these findings and predicted enormous population increases in the Third World.

The United Nations World Population Conference met in Budapest during August 1974 and was attended by 135 nations. From the outset it was obvious that the LDCs would tie the demographic issue to developmental goals. An Indian delegate declared that world food shortages were not being caused by overpopulation but by overconsumption on the part of the richer countries.[41] The Indian minister of health noted, "Development is the best contraceptive."[42] It is indeed true that economic development is correlated with a lowering of the rate of population growth. For instance, in industrialized countries natural growth rates are below 1 percent per annum. That of South Asia is 2.6 percent, Africa's about 2.7 percent, and South America's is approximately 2.9 percent, which means that their populations will double in 27, 26, and 24 years, respectively.[43] However, economic development is a long-term proposition that does not offer an immediate solution to the demographic problems of the LDCs.

The conference did adopt the World Population Plan of Action, which made recommendations for holding down population growth, but it was recognized that "the formulation and implementation of population policies is the sovereign right of each nation."[44] The plan recognized that "the principle aim of social, economic and cultural development of which population goals and policies are integral parts is to improve levels of living and the quality of life of the people."[45] It also declared that true development cannot occur under "colonial domination, foreign occupation, wars of aggression, racial discrimination, apartheid," or other forms of neocolonialism.[46] The developed nations were also reminded of the need for an equitable distribution of world resources under paragraph 19, which reads, in part:

> Recognizing that per capita use of world resources is much higher in the more developed than in the developing countries. The developed countries are urged to adopt appropriate policies in population, consumption and investment, bearing in mind the need for fundamental improvement in international equity.[47]

The plan noted that since economic and social development are central in solving population problems, "national efforts of developing countries to accelerate economic growth should be assisted by the entire international community."[48] In short, the plan gives the impression that many LDCs were more interested in talking about increasing foreign aid rather than the population growth rates which were endangering global stability.

The World Food Conference at Rome

The alarming rate of population growth in the LDCs had not only caused a deterioration in standards of living, but had created serious food shortages. It was estimated in 1975 that the population of the world would double within thirty-five years and that the population of the LDCs would increase from 2.8 to 6.4 billion.[49] Thirty-two of the LDCs had acute food shortages. The Secretary General of the United Nations has estimated that one-half billion inhabitants of LDCs live on the edge of starvation.[50] The Secretary General's estimates may have been exaggerated,[51] but world food reserves had been fluctuating at an alarming rate since 1966.[52] For instance, in 1954 the U.S. wheat carry-over stocks had been 93.3 million tons, which dropped to 47 million tons in 1966.[53] The massive Soviet grain purchases in 1972-1973 further lowered reserves. Rising energy prices, when coupled with shortages, caused the price of wheat to increase 3.5 times and that of corn to increase 2.5 times between 1972 and 1974.[54] The shortages and increased prices worsened the food problems of many LDCs, which simply could not afford to purchase sufficient quantities. Public concern has also been aroused in the Western world by the Club of Rome reports, such as *The Limits to Growth* and *Mankind at the Turning Point*, which carried dire predictions of world food shortages.

In November 1974, the World Food Conference was held at Rome under the auspices of the United Nations. At that conference, Secretary of State Kissinger called attention to the serious shortages and noted that disaster would strike if the world did not act boldly. He continued:

> The political challenge is straightforward. Will the nations of the world cooperate to confront a crisis which is both self-evident and global in nature? Or will each nation or region or bloc see its special advantage as a weapon instead of as a contribution? Will we pool our strengths and progress together or test our strengths and sink together?[55]

Although the LDCs engaged in polemics much less than had been the case at Bucharest, they did tie the matter to development. Resolution 1 reads, in part:

> Recognizing the past trends in food production and productivity in the majority of developing countries have been unsatisfactory, for reasons among others, of inadequate socio-economic structures, insufficient investment funds, paucity of trained manpower, and unfavorable trade relations.[56]

The conference did call on LDCs to give higher priority to agricultural development, to carry out agrarian reforms, and to increase agricultural production. The conference also recommended the establishment of grain reserves to meet the world food emergencies and called on the General Assembly to create a World Food Council.[57] However, large numbers of LDCs are still neglecting agriculture and placing major emphasis on urban, industrial development. A survey conducted in March 1975 by the U.S. Department of Agriculture identified forty-six LDCs that had policies discouraging agricultural production. Government policies in some of the countries under study had actually affected agriculture so adversely that they had caused grain-exporting countries to become grain importers.[58]

The United Nations Conference on Human Settlements

One could assume that the lack of success in the three previous conferences might have been due to the fact that they were concerned with international futures policy matters that did not appeal to the Third World. However, this conference supposedly held a great appeal for the LCDs. At the Stockholm Conference the Third World countries had evidenced considerable interest in human settlements. Therefore, the United Nations Conference on Human Settlements was held in Vancouver from May 31 to June 11, 1976. The Declaration of Principles emerging from this conference was perhaps worse than those of some of the previous conferences. The Declaration was riddled with statements on the New International Economic Order, racial discrimination, permanent sovereignty over natural resources, the need for further developmental aid, and "the duty of all people and Governments to join the struggle against any form of colonialism, foreign aggression and occupation, domination, apartheid and all forms of racism."[59]

The developed countries objected strongly to many of these statements and the U.S. representatives insisted on a roll-call vote on the Declaration. It was finally adopted by a vote of 89 to 15, with 10 abstentions. The Soviet Union and its European satellites[60] were the only developed countries to vote for the Declaration. Professor Qadeer, writing six months later, said thinking about the Conference was "like arriving at an empty station after the departure of the train; there is nothing to see and only a distant echo to hear."[61]

The Third United Nations Conference on the Law of the Sea

The conferences discussed above were in many respects a disappointment to the developed countries of the Western Hemisphere. The subjects treated were very important from the standpoint of international futures, but they did not result in very effective global policies. The LDCs simply were not interested and used the conferences as an occasion to push other issues in which they were interested. Environment was viewed a problem of the developed countries. Food and population were indeed problems of the Third World, but perhaps it was unrealistic to expect the LDCs who had not arrived at viable national policies on these issues suddenly to support the formulation of sound international policies. Perhaps many LDCs had hoped that the Conference on Human Settlements would result in increased aid from the developed countries. The developed countries did not really engage in tough negotiations, since food, population, and habitat were more of a problem for the Third World than the DCs. It would have been nice to have a more effective global policy on environment, but the DCs could handle the matter through domestic legislation and through treaty arrangements with other DCs. However, the Third United Nations Conference on the Law of the Sea (UNCLOS III) has proven to be an entirely different matter. *The Limits of Growth* predicted that known global reserves of many important industrial minerals (which did not include seabed nodules) would soon be exhausted at the current rate of use. According to the projections, reserves of cobalt, nickel, copper, and manganese would be exhausted in 110, 150, 36, and 97 years, respectively.[62] The discovery of mineral-rich nodules on the floor of the seabed promised to alleviate these shortages, as the nodules were rich in cobalt, nickel, copper, manganese, and other minerals. The supply is supposedly virtually inexhaustible, since the oceans contain about 1.5 trillion tons of nodules, which renew themselves at the rate of 10 million tons per annum. At present rates of use, this would supply global needs for thousands of years.[63] Thus, the LDCs, the Soviet Bloc, and the DCs all had a stake in the outcome of the conference. This time the LDCs were intensely interested in negotiating substantive issues.

It was appropriate that the motivation for UNCLOS III came from the tiny island state of Malta. In 1967, the Malta delegate to the General Assembly declared that the seabed and ocean floor were the common heritage of humankind and should be used for the benefit of humankind as a whole, with needy nations receiving special treatment.[64] In 1968, a General Assembly resolution created a Committee on the Ocean Floor Beyond the Limits of National Jurisdiction and declared the Assembly was

> convinced that such exploitation should be carried out for the benefit of mankind as a whole, irrespective of the geographical location of states, taking into account the needs of the developing countries.[65]

A 1969 resolution noted that the Convention on the Continental Shelf of 1958 did not adequately define the area of the continental shelf and requested the Secretary General to convene a conference to review the regime of the high seas, the territorial sea, the contiguous zone, and the continental shelf.[66] In 1970, a General Assembly resolution declared the ocean floor beyond the limits of national jurisdiction to be the common heritage of humankind and not subject to expropriation by any state. All activities in that area were to be governed by an international regime.[67] The first organizational session of UNCLOS III was held in New York in 1973. Numerous negotiating sessions have been held since that time. The 1980 session almost arrived at a completed text for the new law of the sea and it had been expected that the work would be completed in 1981. However, the Reagan administration announced its dissatisfaction with the text in 1981, raising some doubt as to whether the new treaty would be finalized.[68]

The LDCs followed past patterns. They first passed a number of resolutions in the General Assembly with easy majorities and then moved to the conference stage. However, this time the LDCs could not ignore the developed world by simply passing a majority vote as in previous conferences. At Caracas the United States, the USSR, and the EEC nations insisted that decisions must be by consensus during the negotiations, rather than by majority vote. This explains the greater degree of compromise reached on many issues in the UNCLOS III conferences, which stands out in sharp contrast to previous conferences. Obviously, if the major powers were to refuse to sign such a treaty, a majority vote would be of little use against the power and technology of the developed countries.

A full treatment of the UNCLOS III negotiations is beyond the scope of this chapter. Obviously, from the standpoint of international futures, the main struggle centered on control of the mineral resources of the seabed. From the outset forces were divided on a North-South basis. UNCTAD politics and ideology, including the New International Economic Order principles, were applied to ocean law by the LDCs. This is evident in such areas as LDC domination in control of matters concerning deep seabed mining, the limitations on the production of nodules to maintain price stability, and the provisions on the transfer of technology.

However, the Group of 77 did not present as solid a bloc as had been the case in previous conferences. Groups with opposing interests emerged, such as the landlocked and geographically disadvantaged LDCs in opposition to the coastal LDCs, the archipelagic countries, and those LDCs who were land producers of minerals contained in the seabed nodules.[69] Thus, compromises occurred not only on a North-South basis, but within the Group of 77. As a matter of fact, small and medium LDC powers played a prime role in UNCLOS III negotiations. The African bloc was the most solid. However, Africa also had fourteen landlocked countries that caucused with other landlocked and geographically disadvantaged countries to attain concessions on use of the exclusive economic zone (EEZ) and guaranteed transit rights to the sea.

Some of the concessions were obtained by remarkably small groups of LDCs. Not all demands made by the LDCs have been advantageous to the Third World. This may be partially due to a lack of knowledge of the data on seabed resources, but may also have been caused by the willingness of the Group of 77 to follow a few highly active and vocal leaders. A case in point would be the Exclusive Economic Zone (EEZ), which would give coastal states complete control of mineral and living resources within 200 miles of their shores. Latin American countries led by Brazil and Peru wanted a 200-mile territorial sea, since this would include the rich fisheries of the Humbolt Current. Strangely enough, Kenya first introduced the idea of the 200-mile EEZ, which was backed by the OAU.[70] This was rather surprising, since Africa had very narrow continental shelves and a large number of landlocked and geographically disadvantaged countries, but since most countries of the Group of 77 were coastal states, the EEZ appealed to them. This did, however, run contrary to the common heritage principle, as it removed more than 30 percent of the seabed to national control and removed much of the ocean resources from potential international control. The EEZ includes 95 percent of the world's marketable fishing catch and 88 percent of the world's offshore hydrocarbon production potential. The poorest nations in the world will benefit the least from hydrocarbons in the EEZ, as such deposits are more prevalent in the richer countries. The EEZ particularly favors developed coastal countries, for ten countries (including the United States, the USSR, Australia, New Zealand, and Canada) will receive 39 percent of the world's EEZ.[71] Geographic realities also prevent the vast majority of the African countries from achieving the full benefits of a 200-mile EEZ. Africa's fourteen landlocked countries have absolutely nothing to gain, since by the 1958 Geneva Conventions they may at present utilize the high seas up to the territorial waters of the coastal states.[72] There are also sixteen African coastal states that are disadvantaged either by the fact that they are zone-locked (such as the West African States on the Gulf of Guinea), have practically no coast (such as Zaire), or face neighbors across narrow bodies of water (such as the Mediterranean and the Red Sea).

The stand of the Group of 77 on the seabed mining provisions of UNCLOS III has been the source of the greatest friction with the developed countries. The LDCs as a whole have favored a strong seabed authority with a corporate entity, Enterprise, which would directly engage in mining and marketing activities. They feel a strong Enterprise would maximize the profits for developing countries. The LDCs finally agreed that states that are parties to the treaty, or their natural or juridical persons, could also mine in association with the authority. However, it has been made clear in the treaty that the developed states are expected to make their technology available to Enterprise. The LDCs have also insisted on limiting the amount of minerals that can be mined from the seabed in order to maintain the price of land-produced minerals originating from the LDCs.[73] On the other hand, only the developed nations have the technology and capital necessary to carry out seabed mining operations. They do not wish to give up their technology or invest their capital without favorable returns under conditions that are safe for their investments. Until the Reagan administration came into power, it appeared that acceptable compromises had been reached on these matters.

The negotiations on deep seabed mining have demonstrated the susceptibility of the LDCs to radical leadership. Libya and Tanzania were instrumental in applying the principle of the NIEO to the conference negotiations. After the EEZ was adopted, the seabed would have become a rather unimportant issue to many LDCs, since most of the wealth of the sea was in the EEZ. It was, however, Algeria, Tanzania, Mauritania, and sometimes China that continued to push the seabed issue and to advocate the principles of the NIEO.[74] The moderates more or less remained silent, since they did not wish to be considered "pro-imerialists" if they opposed the radical positions.

The LDC stand in favor of limiting the production of nodules in order to maintain high prices for the minerals will place a hardship on most LDCs, since they do not produce such minerals and will be forced to pay a higher price for the finished goods that they must import for development. A total of twenty-six LDCs produce minerals that are contained in the nodules. However, many of the LDCs produce such small amounts of the minerals that such exports would make up a small part of their economies. The African producers and the Philippines would probably be the most hurt, but less than one-fifth of the African countries produce minerals found in the nodules.[75] Thus, the limitation of production does not seem to be too wise.

Conclusions

Attempts to negotiate global policy on international futures subjects have been confronted by enormous problems. A growing diplomatic gap has occurred between the LDCs and the developed countries, due in part to the enormous differences in the diplomatic capabilities and the negotiating styles of the two groups. Many Third World delegates to conferences on international futures lack data, skilled manpower, and instructions from their home governments. In such situations delegates often follow the lead activist countries such as Algeria, Tanzania, India, and Cuba, even though the postures adopted may not necessarily be advantageous to their home countries. The Third World bloc is in the main an extremely cohesive group, whereas the developed countries do not present as united a front.

An examination of selected international futures conferences reveals considerable difficulty in the formulation of international futures policy. The LDC strategy of introducing the principles of the NIEO in all futures negotiations does not appear to have resulted in greatly increased benefits for the economic development of the Third World. LDC stands have at times appeared to be irresponsible and even irrational. The cumbersome international structure has not helped the process, as the one-nation, one-vote practice in international futures negotiations and the UN General Assembly may have given the Third World bloc a feeling of such numerical majority that the need to accommodate and negotiate is weakened. Although the LDCs have the vote, they can not implement their goals without the financial and technical assistance of the developed countries. Thus, the LDCs have been more successful in opposing the policies of the developed world on international futures than they have in espousing viable Third World futures policies. Often international futures conferences have served the LDCs as a forum for the NIEO.

Developed countries, such as the United States, have difficulty in achieving compromises at international futures conferences. The major powers might be well advised to expend more energy through their embassy staffs in LDCs by providing data and discussing issues before international conventions are convened. Large delegations, elaborate position papers, and mountains of data are of little use to the DC delegations if they cannot convince Third World colleagues to support their positions. It seems that resident diplomats of developed powers in Third World countries who understand the political culture and have indigenous contacts would stand a much better chance of effecting compromise than large conference delegations caught in the midst of the highly rhetorical debates of the North-South confrontation. On the whole, one must conclude that neither the UN General Assembly nor international conferences have proven to be very successful institutions for the negotiation of satisfactory global policies in international futures.

NOTES

1. Victor C. Ferkiss, *Futurology: Promise, Performance, Prospects* (Beverly Hills, CA: Sage Publications, 1977), p. 5.

2. Arthur Garcia, "Focusing on the Future," *Exxon USA*, 19, 3 (1980), pp. 12-13.

3. *Ibid.*, p. 6

4. Ferkiss, *Futurology*, p. 6.

5. Donella H. Meadows et al., *The Limits to Growth*, 2nd ed. (New York: New American Library, 1974).

6. Mihajlo Mesarovic and Eduard Pestel, *Mankind at the Turning Point*: *The Second Report of the Club of Rome* (New York: New American Library, 1974).

7. Herman Kahn, William Brown, and Leon Martel, *The Next 200 Years*: *A Scenario for America and the World* (New York: William Marrow, 1976).

8. Council on Environmental Quality and U.S. Department of State, *The Global 2000 Report to the President*: *Entering the Twenty-First Century*, Vol. 1 (Washington, DC: Government Printing Office, 1980).

9. OECD, *Facing the Future* (Washington, DC: Public and Information Center, 1979).

10. W. H. Clives Simmonds, "The Nature of Futures Problems," in Harold A. Linstone and W. H. Clives Simmonds, eds., *Futures Research*: *New Directions* (Reading, MA: Addison-Wesley, 1977), p. 15.

11. Meadows, *Limits to Growth*, pp. 197-198.

12. Mick McLean, "Getting the Problem Right: A Role for Structural Modeling," in Linstone and Simmonds, *Futures Research*, p. 151.

13. Anthony J. Dolman, ed., *Reshaping the International Order*: *A Report to the Club of Rome* (New York: Dutton, 1976).

14. Tarcuato di Tella, "Populism and Reform in Latin America," in C. Veliz, ed., *Obstacles to Change in Latin America* (London: Oxford University Press, 1965), pp. 47-50.

15. Mahbub ul Haq, "The Inequities of the Old Economic Order," in Charles K. Wilber, ed., *The Political Economy of Development and Underdevelopment*, 2nd ed. (New York: Random House, 1979), p. 186.

16. *Ibid.*, p. 187.

17. Willis W. Harman, "On Normative Forecasting," in Wayne L. Boucher, ed., *The Study of the Future: An Agenda for Research* (Washington, DC: Government Printing Office, 1977), p. 77.

18. Comptroller General of the United States, U.S. General Accounting Office, *Disincentives to Agricultural Production in Developing Countries* (Washington, DC: Government Printing Office, 1975).

19. William Orphuls, *Ecology and the Politics of Scarcity* (San Francisco: W. H. Freeman, 1977), p. 209.

20. Kahn et al., *The Next 200 Years*, p. 149.

21. Jay W. Forrester, "Educational Implications of Responses to Systems Dynamics Models," in C. West Churchman and Richard O. Mason, eds., *World Modeling: A Dialogue*, Vol. 2 (New York: American Elsevier, 1976), p. 28. For example, the *Limits to Growth* model omits prices.

22. Harold A. Linstone, "Confessions of a Forecaster," in Linstone and Simmonds, *Futures Research*, p. 151.

23. *The Global 2000 Report*, Vol. 2, p. 16.

24. For a general account of futures in the Soviet Union, see W. L. Boucher, "Forecasting When the Future Is Known," in Boucher, ch. 12.

25. Orphuls, *Ecology*, p. 204.

26. Ferkiss, *Futurology*, pp. 31-32.

27. Orphuls, *Ecology*, pp. 207ff.

28. Jean Wilkowski, "A Call for Advice and Participation: 1979 UNCSTD," *International Studies: Notes of the International Studies Association*, 4, 4 (1977), pp. 14-15. Dr. Robert Jordan, in discussing the role of international scientific and professional associations in UNCSTD, notes that the *1974 Yearbook of International Non-Governmental Organizations* lists 901 international scientific and professional associations. Robert S. Jordan, "International Scientific and Professional Associations and Their Role in the U.N. Conference on Technology and Development," *ibid.*, p. 8.

29. See A. M. Rutowski, "The 1979 World Administrative Conference," unpublished paper. Mr. Rutowski was member of the Federal Communications Commissions's WARC Steering Committee. See also, "Why the Sky Didn't Fall at WARC," *Broadcasting* (December 19, 1979), p. 441.

30. General Assembly Resolution 3201, 6th Spec. Sess., General Assembly, *Official Records, Suppl. 1*, UN Doc. A/9559.

31. Edward J. Woodhouse "Reenvisioning the Future of the Third World: An Ecological Perspective of Development," *World Politics*, 25, 1 (1972), pp. 8-13.

32. MIT Report of the Study of Critical Environmental Problems, *Man's Report on the Global Environment* (Cambridge: MIT Press, 1970), pp. 135-136, 259.

33. United Nations, Economic and Social Council, *Official Records*, 45th Sess., 8 July-2 August 1968, pp. 103-107.

34. UN Doc. A/Res. 2657 (XXV).

35. United Nations, General Assembly, *Official Records*, Annexes, Agenda Item 47, p. 2.

36. Edward P. Morgan, "Stockholm: The Clean (but Impossible) Dream," *Foreign Policy*, 8, 8 (1972), pp. 149-152.

37. See United Nations, General Assembly, *Report of the United Nations Conference on Human Environment Held at Stockholm, 5-12 June 1972*, UN Doc. A/Conf. 4814, 5, July 1972.

38. See "UNEP Reaches First Milestone," *World Environment Newsletter* (June 19, 1973), pp. 33-34.

39. *Ibid.*, pp. 41-45.

40. *Ibid.*, p. 79.

41. "Food and Population," *Resources*, No. 48 (January 9, 2975), p. 20.

42. United Nations Association, "Population Waiting for Development," *The Interdependent*, 3, 6 (1976), pp. 1, 3.

43. National Commission for the Observance of World Population, *Report to the President* (Washington, DC: Government Printing Office, 1975), p. 4.

44. "United Nations World Population Conference Held at Bucharest," *The Department of State Bulletin*, 71, 1840 (1974), p. 14.

45. *Ibid.*, p. 14.

46. *Ibid.*, pp. 14-15.

47. *Ibid.*, p. 16.

48. *Ibid.*, p. 16.

49. "The Question of the U.S. Role in the Allocation of Scarce Resources: Pro and Con," *Congressional Digest*, 54 (1975), p. 195.

50. "Agency for International Development," *War on Hunger*, 9, 9 (1975), p. 195.

51. Kahn, et al., *The Next 200 Years*, pp. 108-109.

52. See Lester Brown, "The Next Crisis? Food," *Foreign Policy*, 13, 13 (1973-1974), pp. 3-33; Philip H. Abelson, ed., *Food: Politics, Economics, Nutrition, Research* (Washington, DC: American Association for the Advancement of Science, 1975), p. 52.

52. *U.S. Code Congressional and Administrative News*, 3 (1966), p. 44.

55. "World Food Conference: Text of Resolutions," *Department of State Bulletin*, 71, 1851 (1974), pp. 821-822.

56. *Ibid.*, p. 831.

57. *Ibid.*, pp. 832ff.

58. Comptroller General of the United States, *Disincentives to Agricultural Production*, pp. 3, 97-103.

59. United Nations, *Report of Habitat: United Nations Conference on Human Settlements*, Vancouver, 31 May-11 June 1976 (1976), p. 203.

60. *Ibid.*, p. 148.

61. MoHammed A. Qadeer, "The Futility of World Conferences," *International Development Review*, 19, 1 (1977), p. 11.

62. *Ibid.*, pp. 64-67.

63. John L. Mero, "Potential Value of the Ocean Floor Manganese Deposits," in David R. Horn, ed., *Ferromanganese Deposits on the Ocean Floor* (Washington, DC: National Science Foundation, 1972), pp. 195-196; John T. Nicholas, "Recovery of Deep Ocean Nodules: A New Approach," *ibid.*, p. 142.

64. United Nations, *1967 Yearbook* (1967), pp. 42-43, 48-49.

65. United Nations, *1968 Yearbook* (1968), pp. 80-81.

66. General Assembly, Resolution 2574, *Official Records*, 24th Sess., Supp. 30 (A/7360).

67. General Assembly, Resolutions 2749, *ibid.*, 25th Sess., Supp. 28 (A/8028).

68. *New York Times* (August 6, 1981), p. A3.

69. See Robert Clute, "The International Rights of African Land-Locked Countries," *Journal of African Studies*, 6, 3 (1979), pp. 165ff.

70. See S. Oda, *International Law of the Resources of the Sea* (Rockville, MD: Sijthoff & Noordoff, 1979), p. 34.

71. See Lewis M. Alexander, "The Extended Economic Zone and U.S. Ocean Interests," *Columbia Journal of World Business*, 10, 1 (1975), pp. 35-36; UN Doc. A/AC. 138/87, 1973.

72. 450 UNTS 82.

73. See *Informal Composite Negotiating Text of the United Nations Third Conference on the Law of the Sea*, UN Doc. A/Conf. 62/WP. 10 Rev. 2.

74. Edward Miles, "The Structure and Effect of the Decision Process in the Seabed Committee and the Third United Nations Conference on the Law of the Sea," *International Organization*, 31, 2 (1977), pp. 159-234.

75. See Robert Clute, "The African Perspective on the Law of the Sea," in *Collected Papers from the Current Issues on the Law of the Sea* (Allentown, PA: Muhlenberg College Press, 1980), p. 17.

6

Macromotives and Microbehavior

A Prescriptive Analysis

WILLIAM O. CHITTICK

In his book, *The Independence of Nations*, David Fromkin restates the fundamental dilemma of international politics: "the fact of political fragmentation and the dream of political unity."[1] This dilemma has become more acute in the twentieth century, particularly the last thirty years, because a proliferation of international actors has accompanied the growth of interdependence among them. At the very time that science and technology have bolstered both our worst fears and our greatest hopes for the achievement of world peace, the number and character of cleavages among the peoples of the world seem most perplexing.

There is no doubt that modern science and technology have contributed to our sense of global community. The astronomer, Carl Sagan, has stirred our imaginations by placing human beings "on a tiny and fragile world lost in immensity and eternity, drifting in a great cosmic ocean dotted here and there with a hundred billion galaxies and a billion trillion stars."[2] Although the human species as we now know it has inhabited the earth for several million years, it is only in the last few years—within the lifetime of those now living—that we have been able to support a society organized on a global basis. Prior to this time, humankind has been an abstraction. Now, for the first time, it is capable of sustaining what Susanne Langer refers to as a "worldwide civilization."[3]

According to Langer, civilization is "the pattern of the practical implementation of life," and thanks to science humankind has now achieved "the practical means and technical ability" to sustain human society on a global basis.[4] The emergence of this new global civilization is reflected in the ease with which people, goods, ideas, and information now flow from one corner of the earth to another. It is also evident in the development of new forms of commerce and industrial organization. It manifests itself in the internationalization of the world economy, in the global diffusion of ideas and fashions, and in the intensity of multicultural exchange around the world.

Ironically, the progress in science and technology that is largely responsible for these developments is also threatening to destroy human civilization. A political scientist, Andrew Scott, believes that this global system incorporates a number of subsystems that, with varying degrees of success, help to satisfy the requisites of the larger system.[5] But each of these subsystems has requisites that, if not satisfied, produce crises or problems with which the system must deal. The dangers of nuclear war, resource depletion, environmental pollution, and population explosion can all be traced to the scientific revolution. There is an urgent need for man to control the new technology. Although all of these dangers require our urgent attention, none of them is beyond the capability of human beings to solve if only we can get our act together.

Unfortunately, an even more fundamental problem for humankind arises from the fact that there is no unity of purpose and action among human beings. As Susanne Langer says, there is no "global culture" to give meaning to contemporary global civilization. According to Langer, culture, as distinct from civilization, is "a symbolic expression of developed habitual ways of feeling."[6] Thus, culture is "the symbolic aspect of behavior" that gives meaning to our lives. Langer believes that we are experiencing "one of the great crises in human history—the final emergence of world society from the long ages of self-sufficient cultural groups."[7] She concludes that

> we are in a socially anomalous state between a world populated by societies with tribal religions and interests, and a world populated by a society with global interests but no symbols to express them, no religion to support the individual in this vast new theater of life.[8]

Another philosopher, Ralph Perry, recognizes that "world unity" in this second or moral sense requires human beings both to live the good life in the context of global society and to accept some negative structure of a wider authority.[9] Yet, there has been no discernible movement in the direction of world government. The advocates of functionalism, regional integration, international organization, and international law have all had to recognize the power of nationalism and statism in today's world. Despite the rational arguments for dealing with a host of global problems at the global level, states and nations continue to hold the primary political and cultural allegiances of human beings. What can and should be done?

A logical place to begin is with the acceptance of the dilemma in which we find ourselves. The one thing that stands out in the thought of Langer, Perry, and others is the change in the scale of human problems. It is becoming increasingly manifest that humankind has a common destiny, that human action can determine that destiny, and that such action is both urgent and desirable. It is equally obvious that global policies must largely be dealt with by individuals and groups working within a fragmented political and social system. The question then becomes how individuals working at the state or local level can pursue global policies.

The objective of global policy studies is to move these actors from a narrow preoccupation with individuals to a more inclusive concern for humankind. Neil Armstrong captured the essence of global policy studies when he took that "one small step for man; one giant step for mankind."[10]

In this chapter we shall discuss this step-level change from individuals to humankind in terms of micro- and macromotives and behavior. Micromotives refer here to the parochial intentions of individuals, groups, and institutions. These motivations are limited in both time and space to the security, well-being, and rights of particular men and women. Similarly, microbehavior refers to the actions individuals, groups, and institutions take. These actions may be inspired by narrower interests or by broader, humanistic concerns.

By contrast, macromotives refer to those impulses that focus on the needs and desires of the human species as a whole. In this case we are thinking of the survival of the human species, the well-being of all humankind, and basic human rights for all peoples, regardless of time and place.[11] These macro concerns are not just the sum of the motives of all of the constituent entities; they are impulses that arise primarily from a concern for the collectivity and not the individual.

Accordingly, macrobehavior refers to the actions of a central or universal authority. Macrobehavior assumes that the individuals, groups, or institutions that compose the whole are capable of acting as if they were directed by one will. As used here, macrobehavior implies the existence of a controlling authority that can act for the collective; it is not just the aggregate of individual actions.

In the absence of a global culture or world government, it is understandable that we tend to think largely in terms of micromotives and microbehavior. When macromotives and especially macrobehavior are discussed, they tend to be defined as derivatives of micromotives and microbehaviors. For example, Thomas Schelling has written an intriguing little book entitled *Micromotives and Macrobehavior*,[12] but he defines macrobehavior in terms of the aggregate outcome of individual actions inspired by micromotives, such as the crowding of individuals into the rear of an auditorium. Schelling's approach is well calculated to explain why we get ourselves into some amusing and not-so-amusing situations, and it is useful in describing the origins of many global ills. However, I do not find it particularly helpful in prescribing solutions.

If global policy requires thinking in terms of humanity as a whole, that is, macromotives, then how do we induce individuals and groups to pursue such policies in the absence of institutions capable of macrobehavior? In this chapter I shall argue that individuals and groups, working through universal institutions at the local level, such as universities, can systematically affect the wider world. By inverting Schelling's emphasis on micromotives and macrobehavior, I hope to shed some light on how individuals can contribute to the solution of global crises. This emphasis on macromotives and microbehavior is reflected in the theme of the First Global Conference of the World Future Society: "Thinking Globally; Acting Locally."[13]

The form of analysis in this chapter is prescriptive. I plan to illustrate the kinds of motives and actions and the types of actors that can contribute to the solution of global problems. The chapter is divided into four sections. The first and second sections explore the meaning of macromotives and microbehavior respectively. The third section examines mediating structures that provide essential linkages between global and local perspectives. The fourth and final section gives special attention to the role of universities in solving global problems.

Macromotives

By the end of this century, the human population may reach six billion. If so, the number of people who inhabit the earth will have quadrupled in the last 100 years. What implications does this spectacular increase in population have for the security, well-being, and rights of members of the human species? The answer is not clear. To a large extent this population increase has resulted from the eradication of disease and improvements in the health of people throughout the world. But these numbers also remind us of the crowded, poverty-stricken life a majority of these people live on a planet that is rapidly depleting its resource base.

Although we cannot foretell the future of humankind, astronomers do offer a cosmic perspective on our recent growth. If we view the earth we live on and the time we have lived on it in relation to the cosmos, then the future of the human race is a legitimate concern, irrespective of our preferred interpretation of population growth. The fact remains that our destiny in this cosmos depends on our ability to live together in peace, tranquility, and human dignity.

The macrovalue or macromotive of security refers to the survival of the human species. The physical survival of humankind depends on the availability of good food, air, and water on a continuing basis. War and revolution, climatic changes, resource depletion, radiation, and a host of other phenomena could endanger the survival of the human species. A single catastrophic event or a fundamental change in the biosphere could eliminate all or most of the human population in a short time. For this reason, the security of humankind is a macromotive of the first order of importance.

To a large extent, our ability to cope effectively with continuing threats to our security depends on the quality of life, that is, the well-being of humankind. I would measure human welfare in terms of the stores of human capital in education, health, religion, and technical and social skills. Although individuals may possess these attributes, what is important in a macro sense is their distribution in the community. Since individuals cannot entirely separate themselves from the community in which they live, it is the common store of these values that best measures the quality of life.

At the same time, the growth of human capital depends on the freedom of individuals to contribute as best they can to the general welfare. These rights have been formally identified for the present in the Universal Declaration of Human Rights. Although human rights and dignity are attributes of individuals, they can also be ascribed to the community as a whole, since no individual is secure in these rights unless he or she shares them with all others. Human rights are a macrovalue because they enable us to develop an active, participatory community that is greater than the sum of individual contributions.

Having identified the macromotives of human security, welfare, and rights, it is important to underscore how these values differ from micromotives. At first blush it appears that the difference between micro- and macromotives reflects the difference between self-regarding and other-regarding motives.

However, macromotives are not simply altruistic, for I assume that individuals cannot really separate themselves from the community in which they live. Since individuals have a self-interest in their community as well as in themselves, macromotives encompass a broader definition of individual interests.

In an age in which there is a global transportation system, a worldwide communications network, international financial institutions, and an elementary collective security system, it should be easy for people to identify their macro interests. However, human beings have developed a mode of thought that gives priority to the narrow, selfish interests of individuals, groups, and institutions over their broader public interests. The conflict between private and public interests is illustrated by Jean Jacque Rousseau in his tale of the deer hunters and the hare.[14] According to Rousseau, a small group of hungry men were closing in on a deer they had surrounded. However, the deer escaped because one of the men left his post in order to snare a hare that crossed his path. The individual who spoiled the hunt did so because he had discovered an immediate way to satisfy his hunger, and we are led to believe that the other men, if they had been in his position, would have acted the same way. Of course, the whole hunting party, including the errant man, would have been better off had they been able to catch the deer.

This tale has a familiar ring to us because there are numerous instances in the world in which the interests of humanity as a whole are sacrificed in the name of national or even more parochial interests. For example, Robert Johansen claims that the human interests that the United States and other governments profess in their declaratory policy on arms control, foreign assistance, self-determination, and marine pollution are frequently undermined in practice.[15] All too often, he argues, these declaratory policies are used to legitimize the effort to gain national advantages in the arms race, international trade, the internal politics of other countries, and the exploration of natural resources. Although this condemnation may be too severe, few scholars or practitioners would deny that there is a wide gap between professed goals and actual behavior.

Why is it so difficult for us to implement policies designed to serve the human interest—specifically, to organize a durable peace in a nuclear world, to reduce the pressures of expanding populations upon limited resources, and to stop continuing threats to elemental human rights? Part of the problem may be that individuals have to learn how to live in a global society that is undergoing very rapid change. In this sense the emergence of "one world of contact and interdependence" has made it even more difficult to develop "one world in the moral sense."[16] People need time to absorb the explosive changes that challenge contemporary global society. Clearly, our inability to forecast events has contributed to our failure to adapt ourselves to a world in the throes of change.

Yet, the problem must reside less in the fact of change than in the character of that change. For one thing there is no one change to which we must all adjust simultaneously; there is a plethora of changes. Moreover, the pace of change is different in different parts of the world. Some regions have had much more time than others to respond to these pressures. The acceleration in the pace of global change may mean that the time will eventually come when there is greater uniformity in the human condition, but at this time the global system is highly variegated.

Identifying macrovalues is also complicated by the fact that not only do human beings in different parts of the world confront quite different situations, but they also have very different governments and cultures. It is important to remember that the world is divided into some 170 sovereign states, a somewhat larger number of governments claiming to make decisions for the people in those states, and thousands of national groups, each seeking their own government of their own state. For some purposes it is meaningful to group allied or like-minded states and nations, but the differences between them are very persistent.

Thomas Hughes has argued that, now more than ever before, national and international leadership requires the management of contradictions.[17] These contradictions arise in part from the fact that even the direction of change among allied states appears to be different. Thus, at the very time that the United States and Britain seem to be experiencing strong conservative trends domestically, France, Germany, and other allied states are experiencing strong liberal movements.[18]

To the extent that the domestic conditions of countries differ from one another, so also do their international situations. Every state is richer or poorer, larger or smaller, more or less democratic or authoritarian than other states in general and its neighbors in particular. These differences influence the interactions and relationships among states and governments and even the various cultures they represent.

These political and cultural differences take on added significance when we consider what it may take in order to promote comparable behavior in different societies. For example, a well-known cross-national study on the influence of local leadership on problem-solving in society found that very different values are often associated with active communities.[19] The authors state that "differences are very great between countries in the values of leaders, in the patterns of community activeness, and in the mix of factors that account for public vitality of the people."[20]

These cultural differences among the world's peoples seriously complicate the realization of general human interests. For one thing, they suggest that in order to evoke the same response in different cultures, it is necessary to employ different signals and methods. They also suggest that individuals in different cultures do not share the same meaning for general values, such as peace and security. Indeed, Kinihide Mushakoji argues convincingly that rather than positing global values, such as peace, we need to determine what these terms mean to individuals and groups in different locales.[21] As Mushakoji contends, "globalism . . . must be based on a variety of endogenous mythologies so as to be easily accepted by all of the local communities of the world."[22] Since values differ at the "grass-root" level and from there to the global level, "no level can be ignored and all should be inter-related."[23]

The emergence of a global civilization makes it both necessary and desirable for us to develop a world culture. The task of developing such a culture is far more complex than most people realize. Some argue that international communications, intercultural exchanges, and even global crises bring us closer to the realization of a global culture; others contend that cultural differences prevent human beings from sharing even these apparently similar experiences.[24] In any event, it should be clear that the development of a global culture will have to exist side by side with the cultural diversity of humankind. Thus, macromotives (or thinking globally) place a premium on our ability to minimize the conflicts of understanding as well as the conflicts of interest that arise among different peoples.[25]

Microbehavior

Contemporary global civilization faces a growing number of crises, any one of which could be catastrophic. A crescendo of inchoate and antithetical problems has produced a global state of uncertainty and confusion that begs for effective action. The need for a global authority has never been more compelling. But there is no common authority—whether a ruler, a set of rules, or a central bureaucracy—that can make and implement a comprehensive program of global action.

Moreover, in the absence of a common culture or morality, it is increasingly doubtful whether a leviathan could govern the world for any appreciable period of time. What remains is the possibility of encouraging microbehavior that can deal with some of our macro problems at the micro level while establishing the foundations for a future world authority and culture. What kinds of microbehavior can serve the macromotives of global security, well-being, and human rights?

As we have already seen, the macrovalue of security is threatened both by events, such as the outbreak of nuclear war or the collapse of the international monetary system, and by continuing processes, such as changes in the world's climate or the depletion of its unrenewable resources. In the face of threats of violence, the dominant response of most states has been to build up internal military forces and external allies. The resulting arms race has seemingly left the world both more capable of self-destruction and less capable of arms control and disarmament.

Are there alternative strategies that might make humankind more secure in a more constructive manner? Two such strategies suggest themselves. The first involves less dependence on large-scale theater units and weapons for deterrence. This strategy is based on the belief that a state can best deter an attack by preparing for the popular military defense of its territory. For example, there is considerable fear in Europe that the Soviets could reach the Rhine river and achieve their primary objectives before NATO could respond effectively with large-scale conventional forces and before the United States could make up its mind to use strategic nuclear weapons.[26] If the U.S. deterrent lacks credibility precisely because NATO countries are not capable of defending against a blitzkrieg attack, then one answer may be found at the level of small-unit action. This action has been referred to as "popular deterrence" because it involves the territorial defense of a homeland by small units composed of local reserve personnel armed with one- or two-person antitank weapons.[27] Although such units could hardly prevent the advance of a major force, they could make the attacker pay such a high price for aggression that he would be deterred.

The second strategy involves a civilian-based defense system. According to Gene Sharp, such a system involves "the use of prepared civilian struggle—nonviolent action—to preserve a society's sovereignty and freedom. Such nonviolent noncooperation, Sharp contends, can deter attack by denying an aggressor its objectives of control, domination and exploitation."[28] The advantage of this second strategy is that a society would not have to engage in a very costly arms race, which is itself a primary threat to global security and which makes little or no contribution to global welfare.

The propensity of states to rely on central decision-making to meet threats to their security is part of the problem as well as part of the solution. For example, the worldwide search for petroleum resources to meet the long-term demand for gasoline, fertilizer, heating oil, natural gas, and other petroleum products has been a priority for both developed and developing societies. Many governments in these societies have tried to develop new energy supplies. However, these large-scale efforts to improve the supply of energy have not kept pace with the efforts of individuals, families, and other small groups to cut energy consumption. As Amory Lovins et al. explain, "In a crisis the normal reflex is to abandon competition among many solutions in favor of a single dramatic nonsolution. But . . . the centrally managed programs are being far outpaced by millions of individual actions in the market."[29] In this case the microbehavior of many individuals—actions, such as using more public transportation, buying fewer automobiles and driving them shorter distances, employing more insulation in the home, and turning the thermostat down—which requires changes in individual lifestyles, may be more effective in coping with the problem than are the actions of national governments.

While popular control over consumption may provide temporary relief from the danger of overdependence on a single commodity, the well-being of humankind requires a more fundamental readjustment in the relationship between technology and resources. If the earth's physical and human resources are going to withstand the shocks of rapid scientific discovery and technological development, some control must be exercised over the direction of this growth. Some provision must be made so that this technology is adapted or implemented at lower levels of society, so that there is a local balance between the supply and demand for resources over the long term. Only in this way can states and peoples expect to maintain their "resource legacy."[30]

However, the well-being of the human species requires not only that individuals in every locale live in harmony with their environment but also that their local culture adapt itself successfully to the changes brought about by modernization. There is a legitimate concern throughout the globe with the apparent disruption of traditional cultures due to the pressures of modernization.

This problem is reflected in the rising incidence of abandoned children, infanticide, abandoned parents, increased insanity, prostitution, and other indicators of social stress in Africa and other developing regions.[31] In this context tribal groups have come under significant criticism because their leaders often try to resist new ways. They are often blamed for divisions in society. However, Pierre Pradervand argues that one of the few resources Africans have to fight the breakup of their culture is solidarity, whether tribal, communal, or family.[32] He argues that Africa will be strengthened, not weakened, by this sense of solidarity at the local level. This suggests that individual efforts to maintain family and community ties may actually foster a global culture in the sense that individuals need to experience community values at one level in order to understand them at another level.

Similarly, the protection of human rights is as much a matter for local as global concern. It is inconceivable to me that a human rights policy could be effectively implemented at the global level alone. The protection of the most elementary human rights must have the active support of individuals and groups at the local level if it is to be viable public policy. Public opinion at the local level must support human rights if these rights are going to be generally respected.

Public opinion is widely recognized to exercise a positive restraint on local leaders. And where that local restraint is insufficient, the power of opinion from a broader public may be useful. This is the power that local chapters of Amnesty International routinely call upon to deal with the most serious infractions of basic human rights in today's world. Although it is not always sufficient to redress an injustice already committed, it is widely believed to be an essential element in efforts to prevent other such abuses from occurring.

In each of these instances, microbehavior is seen as a solution to a macroproblem. Microbehavior involves grass-roots support within a community. It is sufficiently flexible so that it can take into account a range of local and individual differences and still deal with the problem. If we return to the energy problem for a moment, it is always difficult to prescribe the correct behavior for 230 million people in one country or 4.5 billion people on the earth as a whole. It may be better to inform them of the problem and let them decide what makes the most sense for them to do about the problem. As a popular commercial for a utility puts it, the best answer may involve "doing my own thing," whether that happens to be driving less, driving more slowly, dimming the lights, insulating our homes, or all of the above.

In this as in so many areas, there is much to be said for a market economy as opposed to central control. That does not mean that central planning and coordination are not useful or even essential, but it does suggest that few problems of universal importance can be addressed effectively without the active involvement and participation of individuals throughout the world. From this perspective, the question of human survival, well-being, and rights becomes a matter of equipping individuals in local communities with the capacity for acting in their own global interest.

Some will object that such a prescription is idealistic because individuals—however well intentioned they might be or might become—are largely ignorant of what is required. It is unnecessary for us to present here the evidence that most individuals at the local level now lack the knowledge necessary to play a constructive role in global affairs. Even those individuals who are part of the so-called attentive public lack information on many issues of world affairs. Moreover, local sources of information usually lack the capacity for making the essential linkages between local and global affairs.

The fact that local people and events are now part of the problem rather than part of the solution is evidence that this is where much of our attention should be focused. If local people would address some of the problems that manifest themselves at the global level, perhaps these problems would not be so difficult to solve. For example, what good is it to emphasize how complex international issues are when even the experts cannot solve them exclusively at the national level? If local people realized how significantly their perceptions and behavior contributed to global problems, perhaps they could contribute to the identification and solution of them.

Another objection to a local approach to some of these issues is that there is not sufficient time to mobilize all these individuals to address the problem. When we are faced with possible events that could be catastrophic and continuous processes that are encroaching upon seemingly finite limits at geometric rates, it is understandable why so many people despair of dealing with some of the fundamental problems, such as public ignorance and indifference. Few of these people reflect on the capacity of ordinary individuals to grasp the meaning of events and act appropriately when events or diplomats clarify the problem. In most cases it is not the lack of time that precludes public understanding and participation. Person-to-person communication can also occur at geometric rates. Rather, it is the desire to retain central control over decisions.

In presenting these alternative strategies at the local level, we do not wish to imply that there is no need for wider authorities. Indeed, part of our argument is that wider authorities can only be effective if there is a broad base of understanding and support for their activities. Such a base implies a system or network of communications which has both a vertical and a horizontal dimension. In this next section we shall look at some of the mediating structures through which individuals at various levels may learn to coordinate their actions more effectively.

Mediating Structures

One of the shocks of modernization has been the proliferation of actors—both governmental and nongovernmental—who can influence global policy. This profusion of actors is most apparent in the pluralistic societies of the developed world, where new structures have emerged to mediate between the needs of diverse elements in the global system and its many subsystems. The emergence of these nonstate actors has lagged behind in less developed countries and in communist states, with the result that these authoritarian regimes are more prone to make serious errors.

In this regard the Polish situation is most instructive. Central planning under party leadership has led Poland to the brink of economic collapse. The Catholic church, which has generally served to mediate between individual needs and party demands in that society, is incapable of dealing with the economic crisis. A new union, Solidarity, arose as a mechanism for mediating between these conflicting needs. However, the emergence of this new structure has created a revolutionary situation within the country, the outcome of which no one can safely predict.

As the global system develops, we can expect new actors with varied objectives and functions to emerge. These new and existing governmental and nongovernmental organizations will play a vital role in mediating between the many diverse interests of humankind. On the whole, they will contribute to world order by providing two essential processes of communications. One of these processes involves vertical communications between individuals and groups operating at both the local and global levels. This type of communications is important because people everywhere must have a concrete sense both of the way in which the global community has an impact on the quality of their lives and of the way in which local habits and customs affect the quality of human existence on the planet as a whole.

The other process involves horizontal communications among various local communities. This transnational linkage is essential if groups and individuals are going to understand differences in values and perspectives among them. It is the only way that human beings can begin to share the same experience. Most important, this type of communications will reaffirm that macromotives are not something that can, a priori, be imposed from above but must emerge from the amalgamation of local values in relation to similar global experience.

Although the governments of states are the main structural feature of the existing international system, they are dependent upon institutions at both a higher and a lower level for assistance in mediating between the needs of many diverse individuals and the demands of a dynamic global society. In this section we shall explore the role both government and nongovernment organizations can play at three general levels of society: (1) the regional, international, or global level; (2) the nation-state level; and (3) the substate or local level.

The distinction between government and nongovernment organization is important even though the number and function of such organizations will vary significantly from one state to another. Generally speaking, government structures provide the dominant framework for global civilization. There are some 170 sovereign states whose governments exercise varying degrees of authority over a wide range of values for the populations residing in them. The governments of these states may share lesser powers with governments at both the local and international levels. Since the governments of states have exclusive jurisdiction over the peoples in their territories, they must ordinarily deal with the citizens of other states through other governments.

By contrast, the more numerous nongovernmental organizations only exercise limited authority over those who belong to them. Membership or affiliation with these organizations may be voluntary or involuntary; they are usually based on shared values and distinguished from one another on a functional basis. These organizations may focus mainly on business, agriculture, education, culture, religion, athletics, and other concerns.[33] Many of these groups are transnational, and they often have more flexibility than governments in dealing with individuals and groups in other countries.

Because most authority resides with the governments of states, the leaders of international governmental organizations (IGOs) have less power than their sphere of action might imply. Nevertheless, international governmental organizations, such as the United Nations and its specialized agencies, the Organization of American States, the British Commonwealth, and the Organization of Petroleum Exporting Countries, play an important role in coordinating and extending joint efforts on behalf of their member states. Many of these organizations have developed a cadre of international public servants who can perform services that none of the individual states can perform for themselves. IGOs are particularly useful in expressing intergovernmental consensus and in defining the areas of conflict among peoples and states. However, the actions of these organizations are carefully circumscribed, particularly in the realm of political and security affairs.

In contrast, international nongovernmental organizations (INGOs), such as the International Red Cross, the World Council of Churches, the Atlantic Institute for International Studies, and various multinational corporations, represent individuals and groups who share more specific interests. These organizations are often important actors on the international scene in their own right. They also monitor the activities of governmental actors in their areas of interest and play an important behind-the-scene role in the actions of government organizations. These institutions are especially important in building a consensus on emerging global issues. Although INGOs generally are engaged in facilitating voluntary cooperation rather than passing resolutions, they can sometimes be as effective as IGOs, "and on occasion even more effective."[34]

Government organizations at the state level are the primary institutions for mediating between international and local needs in global society. "The national security big six," the ministries or departments of state, defense, justice, treasury, commerce, and agriculture, are usually responsible for dealing with a wide range of problems that have both global and local repercussions.[35] They play an essential role in negotiating and otherwise coping with "the process of adjustment to change that is an increasingly demanding one in the modern complex and rapidly altering world society."[36] However, they are often less effective than one would hope, either because they are restrained by the "national security straightjacket" or because they have been immobilized by "incrementalism."[37]

In the United States alone there are also tens of thousands of nongovernmental organizations (NGOs) at the state level, such as the American Legion, the U.S. Chamber of Commerce, the Arms Control Association, and the American Jewish Committee. Although there are some organizations at this level that have a primary interest in global issues, such as the Council on Foreign Relations and the Overseas Development Corporation, most state-level NGOs have only a secondary interest in international affairs, e.g., the AFL-CIO, the National Association of Manufacturers, and Kiwanis International.[38] Since most of these NGOs engage in transnational activities, their leaders develop specialized sources of international information that often rival government sources. However, only a few of these organizations, such as the League of Women Voters, have developed regular procedures for tapping the international views of their members. Indeed, a growing number of NGOs have no membership at all; they simply broadcast the views of their leadership to an audience.[39] Nevertheless, many of these organizations serve a variety of important functions, including interest representation, idea generation and dissemination, and overseas action programs.[40]

Local governmental organizations (LGOs), such as the commercial or cultural offices of city, county, or provincial governments, have generally been quite restricted in their overt participation in global affairs. They are usually required to work through "the national security big six" if they want to have an input on international issues. However, the growth of local and regional consulates and offices in sea- and airports throughout the world, as well as the growth of sister states and sister cities overseas, suggests that these LGOs are by no means unimportant, particularly in economic, commercial, and cultural relations.

Local nongovernmental organizations (LNGOs), such as world affairs councils, and the local chapters of the United Nations Association, the Association of University Women, and various church groups, reflect the whole panoply of human interest in world affairs. Since global policies are usually a secondary rather than a primary interest of these organizations, their leaders often rely upon their national counterparts for ideas and resources for international programming.[41] Nevertheless, there is evidence that some local organizations "are directly involved in international processes, thus bypassing their national offices."[42]

Individuals participate in organizations at all levels, but the role of local groups, such as the family, the neighborhood, the church, and the university, is particularly important because these groups stand "between the individual in his private life and the large institutions of public life."[43] Since these mediating groups have both a private and a public face, they play an essential role in linking individuals to the wider political community. They help individuals translate global challenges into actions in their daily lives; they provide larger institutions with funds, ideas, and manpower.

This brief survey of mediating structures at various levels in global society cannot do justice to the range and diversity of such institutions. In the next section we shall focus our attention on the role of just one of these mediating institutions: the university. Universities are one of the local institutions that can play an increasingly important role both in shaping a global culture and in identifying lifestyles and behaviors that are most consistent with the survival and improvement of the human species.

The Role of Universities

There are universities in virtually every country in the world. Some of them are over a thousand years old.[44] Universities are educational institutions whose primary purpose is to maintain "cultural continuity in successive generations of individuals."[45] This is no easy task in a global society experiencing rapid if not revolutionary change. Serving this function is not just a matter of being a storehouse of knowledge; it increasingly means that those in the university must explore and develop new ways for people to cope with the human condition. In every good university, there is tension between the old ways and the new.

Although universities are becoming more involved than ever before in continuing or adult education, the main focus of universities has historically been the youth or, more accurately, young adults. Society as a whole probably benefits the most if universities can provide formal training in values and skills that will serve the needs of the rising generation. In an era of revolutionary change in technology, there is a special need to provide young people with the most up-to-date knowledge and skills.

Training the new generation increasingly involves international education. Although every university possesses some obvious parochial features, universities by their very nature have a more global reach. The term "university" means "totality" or "pertaining to the universe." Universities are often filled with individual specialists who are wrapped up in some particular phenomenon, but universities as institutions seek universal knowledge based on the totality of human experience. This means that a university is not just concerned with the political or the economic person, but with the whole person.

It also means that universities cannot afford to focus exclusively on knowledge of those subjects that are close at hand. If universities hope to provide the new generation with a sense of where they are going as well as a sense of whence they came, it is essential for them to view society in its broader context. As international affairs become more domesticated, universities must prepare people to deal with the wider world.

Because universities seek knowledge without temporal and spacial bounds, they attract people from other cultures. In this sense universities are often cosmopolitan centers for cross-cultural experiences. In the contemporary period, most universities not only attract persons from throughout the immediate area but also from across the globe. For example, it is estimated that "nearly half the students in the world studying outside their own country are here [the United States]. The current number, approximately 300,000, is likely to grow to half a million by the end of this decade."[46] Thus, universities often constitute natural experiments in international living from which American as well as foreign students should learn a great deal.

In addition, most universities, especially in a developed world, have become centers for scientific inquiry. The object of science is to provide explanations that are acceptable to all. This search for universal knowledge implies that science is self-correcting as well as cumulative. In the process of building universally acceptable explanations, science must discard partial or false explanations in favor of broader, more verifiable ones. Thus, science involves humankind in a common search for truth that does not recognize or accept particular doctrines or fashions. This search for truth may be less precise but is no less persistent in the humanities than in the sciences.

The efforts of students and teachers alike to seek universal understanding involves both vertical and horizontal communications. The search for universal knowledge leads to a more inclusive frame of reference that encompasses all experience. This conditions us to think in terms of the whole human species. Universities form a network of institutions that look both up and across for the most authoritative knowledge statements and also across and down for possible exceptions to these statements.

As research institutions, universities are not equipped to make decisions for society, but they are heavily engaged in problem-solving. Universities cannot always help decision makers with current issues. However, they can bracket the limited time perspectives of most practitioners both by researching the historical record for lessons of the past and by anticipating some of the strategic changes that global society must confront in the future. Universities can also do much more than they have in the past in studying local-global linkages. This research and problem-solving potential of universities is reflected in the plans of the Founding Committee for a United Nations University, which envisions

> a global decentralized network of centers and programs of research and training focused on the aspiration, the needs and problems of contemporary society . . . problems concerning all mankind, that is to say such problems as human survival, development and human welfare.[47]

Finally, the search for knowledge has given universities a certain detachment from the communities in which they exist. More often than not, universities are accorded a special status in their communities and regarded as neutral ground. To the extent that the university is insulated from local politics, it may be able to play an essential role both in studying local-global linkages and in engaging local groups with conflicting interests in a constructive dialogue with each other.

As service centers, universities have become much more involved in outreach activities that have an international dimension. Some universities have become centers for problem-solving to which people all over the world can appeal for help. They have become centers for information on global affairs for all those within their reach. They can become instruments for mediating conflicts of interest and conflicts of understanding among peoples.

In short, universities are key institutions in the search for global culture. Their devotion both to understanding the totality of human experience and to expanding scientific knowledge is vital for strengthening macromotives. Their capacity for teaching, research, and service in a local, intercultural environment is important for encouraging appropriate microbehavior. They should be in the forefront of our efforts to reconcile future dreams and present realities about the wider world we all share.

NOTES

1. David Fromkin, *The Independence of Nations* (New York: Praeger, 1981), p. 121.
2. Carl Sagan, *Cosmos* (New York: Random House, 1980), p. 318.
3. Susanne K. Langer, *Philosophical Sketches* (Baltimore: Johns Hopkins University Press, 1962), pp. 105-106.
4. *Ibid.*, p. 100.
5. Andrew M. Scott, "Threat and the Global System," paper presented at the annual convention of the International Studies Association—South, University of Florida, Gainesville, October 30, 1981, p. 3.
6. Langer, *Philosophical Sketches*, p. 98.
7. *Ibid.*, p. 104.
8. *Ibid.*, p. 104.
9. Ralph Burton Perry, *One World in the Making* (New York: Current Books, 1945), pp. 43-46.
10. Neil Armstrong, Apollo Mission, 1969.
11. These three macrovalues are the ones chosen for special emphasis by the World Order Models Project. See Gerald Mische and Patricia Mische, *Toward a Human World Order* (New York: Paulist Press, 1977), p. 270.
12. Thomas C. Schelling, *Micromotives and Macrobehavior* (New York: Norton, 1978).
13. *New York Times*, July 23, 1980.
14. Robert C. Johansen, *The National Interest and the Human Interest* (Princeton,

NJ: Princeton University Press, 1980), p. 18.

15. *Ibid.*, chs. 2-5, pp. 38-363.

16. Perry, *One World*, pp. 13-14.

17. Thomas L. Hughes, "Carter and the Management of Contradictions," *Foreign Policy*, 31 (1978), pp. 34-55.

18. Thomas L. Hughes, Address to the Alumni Seminar, University of Georgia, 1981.

19. International Studies of Values in Politics, *Values and the Active Community* (New York: Free Press, 1971).

20. *Ibid.*, p. 32.

21. Kinihide Mushakoji, "Peace Research as an International Learning Process: A New Meta-Paradigm," *International Studies Quarterly*, 22 (1978), pp. 173-194.

22. *Ibid.*, p. 190.

23. *Ibid.*, p. 183.

24. See Edmund S. Glenn, Robert H. Johnson, Paul R. Kimmel, and Bryant Wedge "A Cognitive Interaction Model to Analyze Culture Conflict in International Relations," *Journal of Conflict Resolution*, 14 (1970), pp. 35-48; Miriam Steiner, "Conflicts of Understanding in a World of Diversity," paper presented at the annual convention of the International Studies Association—South, University of Florida, Gainesville, October 30, 1981.

25. *Ibid.*

26. Robert Close, *Europe Without Defense*? (New York: Pergamon Press, 1979).

27. *Ibid.*, pp. 216-220.

28. *Macroscope*, newsletter of the Transnational Academic Program of the Institute for World Order, New York, No. 10 (1981), p. 1.

29. Amory Lovins, L. Hunter Lovins, and Leonard Ross, "Nuclear Power and Nuclear Bombs," *Foreign Affairs* 58, 5 (1980), p. 1164.

30. The research effort and experience of those involved in the National Reconstruction Committee, Guatemala, is particularly instructive here. Presentation of Luis Alberto Ferraté Felice at the Symposium on Food and Development, Center for Global Policy Studies, University of Georgia, Athens, October 17, 1981.

31. P. Pradervard, "Africa—The Fragile Giant?" *Christian Science Monitor* (December 3, 1980), pp. 14-15.

32. *Ibid.*,

33. See "National Organizations of the U.S.," *Encyclopedia of Associations*, (Detroit: Gale Research, 1981).

34. Harold K. Jacobson, *Networks of Interdependence* (New York: Alfred Knopf, 1979), p. 418.

35. Mische, pp. 101-03.

36. John W. Burton, "International Relations or World Society?" in *The Study of World Society: A London Perspective*. An occasional paper of the International Studies Association, 1974, p. 17.

37. Mische and Mische, *Toward a Human World Order*, p. 141.

38. William O. Chittick, "The Group Perspective in Foreign Policy: A Report on U.S. World Affairs Organizations," unpublished report prepared for the Department of State, 1977.

39. *Ibid.*, p. 53.

40. *Ibid.*, pp. 63-66.

41. Chadwick F. Alger, " 'Foreign' Policies of U.S. Publics, " *International Studies*

Quarterly, 21, 2 (1977), pp. 307-308.

42. Paul E. Masters, Jr., and R. E. Vogel, "International Linkages: The Role of Local Churches in World Affairs Education," *International Studies Notes* 7, 3/4 (1981), pp. 7-12.

43. Peter L. Berger and Robert J. Neuhaus, *To Empower People* (Washington, DC: American Enterprise Institute for Public Policy, 1977), p. 2.

44. See *International Handbook of Universities* (London: Macmillan, 1981).

45. Perry, *One World*, p. 204.

46. Sven Groennings, "Foreign Policy and the American University: Converging Interests," *International Studies Notes*, 7, 3/4 (1981), pp. 1-5.

47. Quoted in Paul J. Braisted, *Toward a New Humanism* (New Haven, CT: Hazen Foundation, 1975), p. 61.

About the Authors

GARY K. BERTSCH is Professor of Political Science at the University of Georgia. He earned his B.A. at Idaho State University and received his Ph.D. from the University of Oregon. In 1969-1970 he was an IREX exchange scholar at the University of Zagreb in Yugoslavia. He held research appointments at the Institute for East Central Europe at Columbia University, the Kennan Institute for Advanced Russian Studies at the Woodrow Wilson International Center for Scholars, and the Air Command and Staff College at the U.S. Air Force's Air University. His principal research interests are in the areas of comparative politics, communist systems, and East-West relations. Among his numerous publications are *Comparing Political Systems: Power and Policy in Three Worlds, Values and Community in Multi-National Yugoslavia*, and *Power and Policy in Communist Systems.*

WILLIAM O. CHITTICK is Director of the Center for Global Policy Studies and Associate Professor of Political Science at the University of Georgia. He was born and raised in South Dakota, where he earned his B.S. at South Dakota State University. He received his Ph.D. at The Johns Hopkins University. His principal research and teaching interests are democracy and foreign policy, and he is particularly interested in the role of individual citizens and local publics in global policymaking. Among his many publications are *State Department, Press, and Pressure Groups* and *The Analysis of Foreign Policy Outputs.*

ROBERT E. CLUTE is Professor of Political Science and Graduate Coordinator at the University of Georgia. He earned his B.A. from the University of Alabama and received his Ph.D. from Duke University. His major research and teaching interests are social change and political development, African politics, and international law. He is a former Fulbright Scholar to Sierra Leone and an American specialist in Africa with the Cultural Affairs Division of the U.S. Department of State. He is author of *The International Legal Status of Austria* and *The International Law Standard and Commonwealth Developments*, and has contributed to numerous professional journals.

PHILIP J. MEEKS is Assistant Professor of Political Science at the University of Georgia. He was born and raised in Indiana, earning his B.A. from the University of Notre Dame. He received his Ph.D. in government from the University of Texas at Austin. His principal research interests are European economic policymaking and international economic relations. Among his publications are "Political Responses of Advanced Countries to Crises in World Political Economy," *Crisis in World Political Economy*, "Crisis of Public Policy and the Postindustrial State," *Studies in Political Science*, and "Ecological Analysis of Presidential Voting in France," *L'évolution de la Présidence en France et aux Etats Unis.*

HAN S. PARK is Associate Professor of Political Science and Director of M.A./Ph.D. programs in the Department of Political Science at the University of Georgia. He was born in China and raised in Korea, where he earned his bachelor's degree at the Seoul National University. He received his Ph.D. from the University of Minnesota. His principal research and teaching interests are political development, East Asian affairs, human rights, and comparative politics, and he has produced numerous scholarly publications in such journals as *Human Rights Quarterly*, *Asian Forum*, and *International Journal of Modern Sociology*.

DEAN RUSK is the Sibley Professor of International Law at the University of Georgia's School of Law. He was born in Georgia and received his bachelor's degree from Davidson College in North Carolina. He was a Rhodes Scholar at St. John's in Oxford and studied law at the University of California, Berkeley. He was Associate Professor and Dean of the Faculty at Mills College, served in the U.S. Army for six years, and was Assistant Secretary of State for United Nations Affairs and for Far Eastern Affairs with the Department of State. From 1952 through 1960, he was president of The Rockefeller Foundation, and from 1961 to 1969 he served as Secretary of State in the U.S. Department of State. Professor Rusk has held the Sibley Professorship at the University of Georgia since 1970.

E. MIRIAM STEINER is Assistant Professor of Political Science at the University of Georgia. She earned her B.A. from the University of Cincinnati and received her Ph.D. from the University of Pittsburgh. Her principal research interests focus on the interplay between worldviews and decision-making. She has published articles in *International Organization*, *International Studies Quarterly*, *Alternatives*, and other scholarly journals.